Sustainable Business

Sustainable Business: Key issues is the first comprehensive introductory-level textbook to address the interface between environmental challenges and business solutions and to provide an overview of the basic concepts of sustainability, sustainable business, and business ethics. The book introduces students to the background and key issues of sustainability and suggests ways in which these concepts can be applied in business practice. Though the book takes a business perspective, it is interdisciplinary in its nature and draws on knowledge from socio-economic, political, and environmental studies, thereby providing a practical and critical understanding of sustainability in the changing paradigm of global business. It goes beyond the conventional theories of sustainability and addresses critical issues concerned with population, consumption, and economic growth. It discusses realistic ways forward, in particular the Circular Economy and Cradle to Cradle frameworks.

The book is both a theoretical and a practical study guide for undergraduate and postgraduate international students of broad areas of sustainability, teaching ways to recognize opportunities for innovation and entrepreneurship at the intersection of environmental, economic, ethical, and social systems. It takes a strategic approach in applying the power of business methods and policy to address issues of global importance such as climate change, poverty, ecosystem degradation, and human rights.

This textbook is essential reading for students of business, management, and sustainability courses. It is written in an engaging and accessible style, with each chapter including case studies, discussion questions, end of chapter summaries, and suggestions for further reading.

Helen Kopnina is based at The Hague University of Applied Science, the Netherlands, as a coordinator of the Sustainable Business program and researcher of environmental education. Her books include *Environmental Anthropology Today* (Routledge 2011) and *Environmental Anthropology: Future Directions* (Routledge 2013).

John Blewitt is Co-Director of the MSc Social Responsibility and Sustainability at Aston Business School, Aston University, UK. His books include *The Ecology of Learning* (Earthscan-Routledge 2006), *Searching for Resilience in Sustainable Development* (Earthscan-Routledge 2013), the four volume major work, *Sustainable Development* (Routledge 2013), and *Understanding Sustainable Development* (second edition: Earthscan-Routledge 2014).

Key Issues in Environment and Sustainability

This series provides comprehensive, original and accessible texts on the core topics in environment and sustainability. The texts take an interdisciplinary and international approach to the key issues in this field.

Low Carbon Development: Key issues
Edited by Frauke Urban and Johan Nordensvärd

Sustainable Business: Key issues
Helen Kopnina and John Blewitt

"*Sustainable Business* is a solid introductory volume that allows students not only to get familiar with the issues of (un)sustainability in corporate contexts, but also to learn to recognize global obstacles to sustainability, as well as equipping students to find viable solutions from the business perspective. The importance of the Cradle to Cradle and Circular Economy frameworks is outlined as particularly relevant to strategic management of sustainability."

—Frans Meijers, The Hague University
of Applied Sciences, the Netherlands

"This book represents a welcome addition to the burgeoning literature on sustainability and business by offering a refreshingly different perspective from many mainline works in the field. The authors couple an insightful critique of current conventional viewpoints on sustainability with a conceptual menu of reasoned alternatives to move our global economic system closer to true sustainability."

—Peter N. Nemetz, University of British Columbia, Canada

"This book is a much needed accessible text that addresses the most challenging issues of our age in a business context. In taking an interdisciplinary approach and tackling such a range of subjects and contemporary issues, the book not only provides both students and business professionals with an understanding of what sustainable business really means, but also outlines practical application of strategies to inspire action."

—Carole Parkes, Aston University, UK and Chair of UK & Ireland
Chapter of the UN backed Principles of Responsible
Management Education (PRME)

"This book is bound to stimulate the reader's interest in the complex relationship between business and sustainability. With its comprehensive approach, covering a broad range and variety of issues, a critical discussion of traditional approaches and an offer of alternative views, it is certain not only to increase the reader's awareness of the business role in sustainability but also to engage them in thinking about effective solutions for sustainable business practices."

—Damir Urem, The Hague University of
Applied Sciences, the Netherlands

Sustainable Business

Key issues

Helen Kopnina and John Blewitt

Routledge
Taylor & Francis Group

LONDON AND NEW YORK

First published 2015
by Routledge
2 Park Square, Milton Park, Abingdon, Oxon OX14 4RN

and by Routledge
711 Third Avenue, New York, NY 10017

Routledge is an imprint of the Taylor & Francis Group, an informa business

British Library Cataloguing in Publication Data
A catalogue record for this book is available from the British Library

Library of Congress Cataloging in Publication Data
Kopnina, Helen.
Sustainable business : key issues / Helen Kopnina and John Blewitt.
    pages cm
  Includes bibliographical references and index.
  1. Social responsibility of business. 2. Sustainable development.
  3.Business ethics. I. Blewitt, John, 1957- II. Title.
  HD60.K655 2015
  658.4´083--dc23   2014010583

ISBN: 978-0-415-73950-4 (hbk)
ISBN: 978-0-415-73952-8 (pbk)
ISBN: 978-1-315-81658-6 (ebk)

Typeset in Sabon
by HWA Text and Data Management, London

Helen Kopnina dedicates this book to her father, Nikolai B. Kopnin (1946–2013), credited with discovering Kopnin spectral flow force and my inspiration forever.
http://en.wikipedia.org/wiki/Nikolai_B._Kopnin

Contents

PART IV
Solutions   **201**

Figures

Tables

Boxes

Preface

Sometimes we can define something by the absence of its opposite. For example, we can define health by the absence of disease. What is the opposite from sustainability? Is 'unsustainability' something we need to discard and is sustainability something that we really need? We can argue that people do not know what they need, in the practical sense, until they no longer have it, and sometimes not even then. Surely needing something is not merely a matter of conceiving that one needs something. Did we not have a need for a magnetic field shielding us from cosmic rays, before we discovered that the Earth's magnetic field bestows that benefit upon us? Did medieval farmers' basic understanding of the benefits of fertilization mean that nitrogen was not the key mineral for increasing production until science advanced to a certain point to understand what nitrogen is and the role it plays in plant growth? Did the inventor of the first wheel know how dramatically his invention would change the world and lead to the enormous demand for and dependence on fossil fuels that we know today? Our need for sustainability surely depends on an infinite number of elements that most of us take for granted, such as the fresh air we breathe, potable water for drinking and doing the myriad tasks we do on a daily basis from showering, to washing and preparing food, laundry, or the bread that we put on our table. We only realize that something is wrong when the air becomes polluted or we cannot afford the bread.

Sustainability involves many fields of study and truly understanding sustainability requires a broad understanding of those disciplines – e.g. biology, ecology, economics, political science, and ethics. Understanding our behaviour and motivations requires the social sciences (such as sociology, anthropology, and psychology) as well as ethics. Quantifying the challenges related to sustainability and being able to track progress (or lack of progress) requires knowledge of the natural sciences (such as biology and meteorology). Building solutions require technical insight into complex systems (such as engineering, planning, environmental economics, public policy, business and ecosystem management).

This volume therefore taps into various disciplines with the aim of creating not only a holistic overview that more accurately reflects the kaleidoscopic nature of sustainability within the context of business, but also combines insights from different disciplines in order to suggest concrete, practical and viable solutions to environmental and social problems we are facing. This book allows you to get a taste of these disciplines and to learn what you can do in your own career to address the challenges of reconciling business with environmental sustainability. The following chapters aim to give a brief overview of the roles that business, globalization, consumerism and environmentalism play in today's world, with particular focus on sustainability.

This book is unique in that it combines an overview of the context in which sustainability management takes place with corporate-level perspectives, offering both comprehensive theory and empirically rich case studies. The inclusion of key economic concepts such as the tragedy of the commons as well as critical insights into ethical consumption or sustainable development with current corporate sustainability practice sets this project apart from existing volumes. This book is intended both as an introductory theoretical guide and as a practical manual, with the aim of first introducing you fully to the complex challenges and paradoxes of sustainability, and then guiding you toward incorporating that understanding into your respective field so that you can focus your targets and metrics for what makes a successful business on more than profit. That in turn has the potential to dramatically change what our common future will be.

Using this book

Within the text, you will encounter Definitions and Illustration boxes.

- Definitions provide concise descriptions of the terms
- Illustration boxes provide illustrations to these definitions.
- At the end of each chapter, you will encounter key terms, discussion questions, end of chapter summaries, further reading, and case studies.
- Key terms are used to highlight useful concepts from the chapters
- Discussion questions are placed both at the end of the chapters and sometimes following the illustration boxes
- End of chapter summary outlines some of the key subjects discussed in the chapter
- Further reading per chapter will only list some central texts. A complete bibliography can be found at the end of this volume
- Case studies provide concise illustrations to theoretical discussions in the chapters.

Acknowledgements

HK would like to express special thanks to Thomas Reid who gave invaluable comments and suggested critical edits to the first chapters of this manuscript. The patience and support of her family at the time of writing this book deserves her deep gratitude.

JB would like to thank his wife Lorna who has to put up with him when he is holed up in the office in front the computer.

Figure credits

Abbreviations

AACSB	Association to Advance Collegiate Schools of Business
BAT	British American Tobacco
BOP	Bottom of the pyramid
BREEAM	Building Research Establishment Environmental Assessment Methodology
CBD	Convention on Biological Diversity
CDM	Clean Development Mechanism
CDP	Carbon Disclosure Project
CEO	Chief executive officer
CFC	Chlorofluorocarbon
CHC	Chlorinated hydrocarbon
CH_4	Methane
CITES	Convention on International Trade in Endangered Species of Wild Fauna and Flora
COP	Conference of the Parties
CO_2	Carbon dioxide, one of the greenhouse gases
CPD	Continuing professional development
CSR	Corporate social responsibility
CTIF	CITES Technology and Innovation Fund
C2C	Cradle to Cradle
DESD	Decade of Education for Sustainable Development
DfE	Design for the Environment
DfR	Design for Recycling
DfREM	Design for Disassembly and Design for Remanufacturing
DJSI	Dow Jones Sustainability Indices
DSP	Dominant Social Paradigm
EA	Environmental assessment
EEA	European Environment Agency
EFA	Education for All
EIA	Environmental impact assessment
EICC	Electronics Industry Citizenship Coalition
EKC	Environmental Kuznets Curve
ELF	Earth Liberation Front

EMAS	Eco-Management and Audit Scheme
EMS	Environmental Management System
ENGO	Environmental non-governmental organization
EOL	End-of-life [management]
EPA	United States Environmental Protection Agency
EPR	Extended Producer Responsibility
ERSI	Extraordinarily realistic self-image
ESD	Education for sustainable development
ESKTN	Environmental Sustainability Knowledge Transfer Network
FDI	Foreign direct investment
FLA	Fair Labor Association
FSSD	Framework for Strategic Sustainable Development
FTC	Federal Trade Commission
GAAP	Generally accepted accounting principles
GAP	Global Action Plan
GDP	Gross domestic product
GHG	Greenhouse gas
GISR	Global Initiative for Sustainability Ratings
GM	Genetically modified (abbreviation also stands for General Motors)
GMO	Genetically modified organism
GNP	Gross national product
GRI	Global Reporting Initiative
HFC	Hydrofluorocarbon (refrigerant gas)
HIPPO	Habitat destruction, invasive species, pollution, population increase and overharvesting
HRD	Human resource development
HRM	Human resource management
ICPD	International Conference on Population and Development
ICT	Information and communication technology
IIRC	International Integrated Reporting Committee
ILO	International Labour Organization
IMF	International Monetary Fund
IPCC	Intergovernmental Panel on Climate Change
IRF	Integrated Reporting Framework
ISDF	International Sustainable Development Foundation
ISO	International Organization for Standardization
ISS	International Space Station
IUCN	International Union for the Conservation of Nature
JI	Joint Implementation
JRC	Joint Research Centre
KM	Knowledge management
L&D	Learning and development
LCA	Life Cycle Assessment
LCD	Life Cycle Design

LCM	Life Cycle Management
LEED	Leadership in Energy and Environmental Design
MBA	Master of Business Administration
MDG	Millennium Development Goal
MEA	Millennium Ecosystem Assessment
MNC	Multinational corporations
NBS	National Building Specification
NEP	New Ecological Paradigm
NGO	Non-governmental organization
NPI	Net positive impact
N_2O	Nitrous oxide
OECD	Organisation for Economic Co-operation and Development
PFC	Perflurocarbon
PR	Public relations
PRME	Principles for Responsible Management Education
PSS	Product service shift
PV	Photovoltaic
PVC	Polyvinyl chloride
R&D	Research and development
RAN	Rainforest Action Network
REDD	Reducing Carbon Emissions from Deforestation and Forest Degradation
RIBA	Royal Institute for British Architects
ROI	Return on investment
SDG	Sustainable development goal
SDSN	Sustainable Development Solutions Network
SETAC	Society of Environmental Toxicology and Chemistry
SF_6	Sulfur hexafluoride
SLF	Sustainable Livelihoods Framework
SME	Small and medium enterprise
SUV	Sport utility vehicle
TEEB	The Economics of Ecosystems and Biodiversity
TNC	Transnational corporation
TNS	The Natural Step
UCIL	Union Carbide India Limited
UN	United Nations
UNCCD	United Nations Convention to Combat Desertification
UNCED	United Nations Conference on Environment and Development
UNDP	United Nations Development Programme
UNEP	United Nations Environment Programme
UNESCO	United Nations Educational, Scientific and Cultural Organization
UNFCCC	United Nations Framework Convention on Climate Change
UNFPA	United Nations Population Fund
UNGC	United Nations Global Compact

UNICEF	United Nations Children's Fund
UK	United Kingdom
US	United States
USSR	Union of Soviet Socialist Republics
VOC	Volatile organic compound
WBCSD	World Business Council for Sustainable Development
WEF	World Economic Forum
WHO	World Health Organization
WTO	World Trade Organization
WWF	World Wide Fund for Nature (World Wildlife Fund)
ZERI	Zero Emissions Research & Initiatives

Part I

Concepts, tools, and initiatives

1 Introduction

Key concepts in sustainability and business

What is this book about?

If you are someone who opened this book because you are curious about what sustainability is and are wondering how to be more 'sustainable', you have probably already taken the important first step of recognizing that some of what is going on around you is not sustainable. You might be also aware of the fact that at the same time that you are picking up that fair trade coffee brand from the supermarket shelf, or putting a piece of used paper in the recycling bin, the person next to you might be picking up a generic brand of coffee (because it is cheaper) or throwing his or her piece of paper in the rubbish (because it is closer). Perhaps you have read an article about fair trade products and question how much extra income your purchase really generates for the coffee farmer in Guatemala – would it be enough to feed his or her entire family? Perhaps you have heard that recycling is a form of downcycling, and was wondering how much recycled paper will actually be produced from your contribution? Perhaps you just felt good thinking that you are doing a good deed. After all, sustainability starts with good intentions.

If only there weren't people telling you how to do things, if only all these obligations were not forced upon you, you might actually figure out what is really important to you. Maybe what really matters to you are the cool gadgets, nice clothes or trips that money can buy. Maybe what you want has nothing to do with sustainability. For now, let us at least hope that you will pass the course, and perhaps even find an interesting tidbit or two in this volume that you can take with you wherever your yet-to-be-defined path will lead.

If you are someone who wants to get a good job and sees opportunity in innovation, perhaps your interest in this volume is sparked by the promise that sustainability is about the future and about becoming a successful businessman or businesswoman doing something that is relevant in today's globalized world. Maybe there is an idea in this book that will help you figure out how to adapt waste products for use in other products or systems. You might not be sure how to evaluate what constitutes success, but willing to learn. Perhaps this whole 'sustainability' thing will be your golden ticket to self-actualization and living a fulfilling life as a global citizen leading change. Who knows?

Perhaps you are an environmentalist who wants to know how your cause relates to the often-used sustainability buzzword. What does sustainability have to do with the spotted owl you are trying to protect from the continually expanding urban development that threatens your local forest? Perhaps this book will help you to acquire the vocabulary necessary to more effectively compel people to understand how special that spotted owl is and the important role it plays in the wider ecosystem that makes all life possible.

Perhaps you are a community leader in a small town who wants to organize popular support to force a nearby factory to reduce harmful emissions or effluent to the adjacent lake or river. Or perhaps you also hope that this book might give you practical tips on how to speak to your own community members and key authority figures so that they will not only listen but be compelled to effective action.

There you have, in a nutshell, a few of those issues we shall discuss in this book.

Brief definition of sustainability

We are facing many daunting problems that have not been seen before in human history. These problems range from climate change to biodiversity loss, from health threats to social injustice and global poverty. Current estimates put more than a billion people below the poverty line. Human population growth and increased consumption, conversion of pristine areas to agricultural land, climate change, as well as pollution all have a devastating effect on nature and natural resources (IUCN 2013). We recognize that these issues might not be solvable using the same approach, yet they are interconnected through the concept of sustainability.

Before we address these issues in relation to business and consider how each of us, teachers, students, business people, politicians and activists can contribute to a better future, we first need to ask: what is sustainability?

> **Sustainability** is the capacity to support, maintain or endure; it can indicate both a goal and a process. Sustainability can be maintained at a certain rate or level, as in sustainable economic growth. It can also be upheld or defended, as in sustainable definitions of good corporate practice.

In ecological studies sustainability describes how biological systems remain diverse, robust, and productive over time, a necessary precondition for the well-being of humans and other species. Sustainability has come to be strongly linked with the environment and a better way to structure our societies, companies, and our daily lives in order to protect the long-term future of our planet and the ability of future generations to exist and thrive (Figure 1.1).

Figure 1.1 Child in the woods (source: Helen Kopnina)

We can distinguish between different types of sustainability. Social sustainability is often conceived in terms of sustaining the well-being of people. Environmental sustainability often refers to sustaining nature or natural resources. The two are intricately interlinked, due to the fact that human welfare depends on the sustainability of the environment.

In business, there are different terms that people use to refer to or relate to sustainability: 'industrial ecology', 'corporate social responsibility' (CSR), 'business ecology', 'Cradle to Cradle', 'green capitalism', 'eco-efficiency', 'social and environmental responsibility', the 'triple bottom line' ('People, Profit, Planet'), and many others. As governments moved away from command-and-control regulatory approaches in favour of a more market-based approach, multinational corporations (MNCs) or transnational corporations (TNCs) have become key players in world commerce. Recognizing that some corporations constitute economies that are significantly larger than the gross domestic products (GDPs) of a number of countries, the economic power and importance of global corporations in shaping global policy cannot be ignored. In fact, they have and continue to reshape how countries, corporations, and individuals interact.

Evolution of sustainability

The concept of sustainability, as we know it today, first emerged in conjunction with the birth of the environmental movement in the 1960s in response to growing concerns over increasingly visible environmental and health issues resulting from poor resource management and insufficient control of hazardous chemicals and waste products from the significant economic growth in the decades following World War II. As a point of reference, the Organisation for Economic Co-operation and Development (OECD) was created in 1960 to promote the highest levels of sustainable economic growth in member countries and drive the global economy toward the twin goals of increased employment and higher standards of living.

The Club of Rome, an influential think-tank that brings together the world's leading scientists and politicians, has produced the Limits to Growth report (Meadows et al. 1972). The report demonstrated that an economy built on the continuous expansion of material consumption is fundamentally not sustainable. Based on the emerging evidence that demonstrates the uncanny correlation between escalating rates of economic growth and environmental degradation, international governments, corporations, and citizens were called upon to address global population growth and increasing consumption. Following this report, the United Nations Conference on the Human Environment held in Stockholm in 1972 highlighted that civilization is exhausting the resources upon which its continued existence depends. Unprecedented economic growth and technological progress were linked to severe environmental consequences. Global awareness of environmental issues increased dramatically in the wake of the conference, as did international environmental law-making and corporate involvement in decision making. Sustainability became an outgrowth of an increased awareness of our connection to the environment and the negative impacts of our actions.

Another important international conference was the so-called Earth Summit in Rio de Janeiro in 1992. In the run-up to the Earth Summit, MNCs presented themselves as part of the solution, rather than the problem. A group of forty-eight industrial sponsors brought a business perspective to this high-profile political gathering. The World Business Council for Sustainable Development (WBCSD) was invited to compile recommendations on industry and sustainable development and MNCs were seen to have made an evolutionary leap. MNCs were no longer entities to be managed by governments, but 'had mutated into "valued partners" and "stakeholders" formulating global policy on their own terms' (Ainger 2002: 21). Both governments and MNCs were to share the task of positing the legal and political underpinnings of sustainable development. The Earth Summit set a precedent and established a framework for conventions that were to focus on climate change and biodiversity, identifying basic aims, principles, norms, institutions, and procedures for action. These conventions will be discussed in greater detail in Chapter 2.

Climate change is one of the largest challenges we face as a species and as a planet. Climate patterns as well as certain by-products of human activities such as point-source air pollution and carbon emissions impact local and global weather and climate patterns. The primary international body for monitoring and promoting action to address climate change is the Intergovernmental Panel on Climate Change (IPCC). Established in 1988, the IPCC gathers scientific information, assesses environmental and socio-economic impacts, and devises a response strategy for climate change and serves to provide input for policymakers. Recent IPCC reports states that greenhouse gas (GHG) concentrations have increased due to human activity; and that global average temperatures have risen significantly over the past decades as a result.

While public and governmental interests started to increase in the 1980s, the main driver of change in corporate strategy was the adoption of the Kyoto Protocol in 1997. This event spurred the development of new regulations and increased pressure from non-governmental organizations (NGOs) urging companies to take appropriate steps to address GHG emissions. However, since the signing of Kyoto Protocol global GHG have gone up by around 30 per cent (Chapter 2). Due to the inherently global nature of the problem and its causes, climate change serves as an interesting case study to examine what we can(not) do as a global society.

While international agencies and financial institutions such as the United Nations (UN) and the World Bank still advocate for a 'balanced' approach to harmonizing social and economic and ecological interests, the rate of resource depletion and species extinctions has accelerated. According to the International Union for the Conservation of Nature (IUCN), and the United Nations Environment Programme (UNEP), the effects of industrialization have been disastrous for the non-humans on this planet.

However, the focus is shifting away from the environment and towards material well-being. The key social challenges identified in the UN Millennium Development Goals (MDGs) are the eradication of extreme poverty, halting the spread of HIV/AIDS and providing universal primary education. As will be discussed in Chapter 5, in conjunction with concerns over climate and the environment, population and development conferences have focused international attention on the demographic and humanitarian aspects of sustainability. The International Conference on Population and Development (ICPD) held in Cairo in 1994 concentrated on the challenge of reducing mortality and fertility rates around the world. The ICPD Plan of Action included a focus on sexual and reproductive health services, education, and gender equality. The combination of health services targeting infant mortality with improvements in medical science and available technologies has led to unprecedented population growth. Family planning and increased education for women has had a demonstrable positive effect on reducing fertility rates, which in turn has had a positive effect on reducing population pressures, as well as ensuring a higher survival rate of newborn children and improved opportunities and quality of life.

This book will link corporate responsibility and sustainability. We shall speak of business in a broader sense, including institutions and organizations that can be characterized by their 'business-like activities'.

A business can be described as a commercial enterprise, company or firm involved in the trade of products and services to customers for profit. Businesses are predominant in capitalist economies and are usually privately owned; in socialist economies businesses are more frequently state-owned. Businesses may also be operated as not-for-profit enterprises.

There is a clear distinction of purpose between profit, non-profit, and social enterprises. While commercial businesses are normally concerned with maximizing profits, or otherwise ensuring the highest possible sales turnover, be it in products or services, NGOs may be more concerned with furthering their wider social agendas. The term NGO came into use in 1945 in response to the need to differentiate in the UN Charter between participation rights for specialized intergovernmental agencies and those for private international organizations.

It is important to outline here which objectives these broadly defined 'businesses' serve in relation to sustainability.

Why do business sustainably?

Business activities came to be viewed with suspicion due to their profit-oriented policies. While it was feared that MNCs would always put profit first and hold no allegiance to any particular place, community or environment, businesses started moving towards greater environmental and social accountability. Milton Friedman has proposed, for example, that the business of business is business and the social and sustainability stuff is for governments, charities, and NGOs. One of the factors that contributed to corporations turning toward sustainability was mounting pressures from NGOs and changes in consumer preferences (Elliot 2013). Time has shown that one of the most powerful tools for ensuring greater transparency and accountability among businesses has been public access to information. Being sustainable can be thus good public relations (PR) for business.

Cynical readers might suggest that businesses want to convince the public that they are conscientious and, besides wanting to make profit, are seeking to fulfil their obligations to people and the environment. In making business activity sustainable, businesses give credibility to their actions, and, in a way, attest that their operations can be trusted by suppliers and customers as well as setting an example for their competitors. In this view, the maxim 'business is business' implies that since a company's aims are purely commercial, sustainability will be accepted in as far as there are external pressures for doing so.

In this regard, we can think of sustainability as 'hype' that businesses have learned to use to their benefit, (e.g. green-washing, which is a term used to describe an individual or business promoting something as green – either their business as a whole or an initiative, product or activity while actually continuing to operate in socially and environmentally damaging ways). Examples of green-washing companies are Coke, chastised for using hydrofluorocarbon (HFC) refrigerant gases; Pepsi, criticized for dumping plastic waste; and Unilever, singled out for its ties to palm oil companies, which are a major contributor to tropical deforestation.

Increased awareness has encouraged and empowered civil society to play a more active role in the regulatory process, motivated MNCs to engage in CSR, as well as increase transparency by including relevant details in their public reporting on their operations. The UN Sustainable Development Solutions Network (SDSN) explains that innovation, management skills, and corporate financial resource will be a major provider of solutions to most of the sustainability challenges that we face.

Organizations such as the International Organization for Standardization (ISO), the world's largest developer of voluntary International Standards founded in 1947, cover almost all aspects of technology and business operations such as ISO 14001 for environmental management systems, EMS 9000 for quality management, and 50001 for energy management systems. Similarly, the Global Reporting Initiative (GRI) was set up to provide all companies and organizations with a comprehensive sustainability-reporting framework that is now widely used around the world. Some of these reporting schemes and certifications will be discussed in greater detail in Chapters 7 and 8.

Many companies, partially in response to resource constraints in their own industry, and partially in response to pressures from public and environmental groups, have embraced green investment. In some cases, the companies have actually served as pioneers of change, despite the confusion and indifference of the public and political procrastination, according to Forum for the Future's Founder and Director Jonathon Porritt. Despite the failures of international political summits to address such pressing environmental issues as climate change and the loss of biodiversity, and the economic downturn in many Western countries, a poll published by Ernst and Young (2013) shows that a large proportion of MNCs want to increase their investments in sustainability measures.

Also, being sustainable makes obvious commercial sense, with improved energy efficiency and waste management strategies enabling companies to save billions on their bills. As will be discussed in Chapter 2, according to the Carbon Disclosure Project (CDP), an organization that collects information on the GHG emissions from over 500 large companies, the majority of

educing investments made so far will pay for themselves in
riod, perhaps even 1 or 2 years. Thus, businesses that want to
istain' themselves by sustaining their workforce (for example, by
od working conditions) or being more efficient in their use of
(for example, by saving electricity) are likely to have employees
that stay and save money.

In a resource-constrained world, companies can create new opportunities for making a profit by developing products that reuse or recycle valuable materials or enable consumers to use less. Unilever, for example, started selling products in Asia specially designed for the resource-constrained future. Products include detergents that clean well at low temperatures and use relatively little water. As will be discussed in Chapter 11, companies following the Cradle to Cradle and the circular economy frameworks, propose to completely eliminate waste and actually add value. Sustainable business can be good business, as many MNCs have demonstrated.

Some businesses choose to be sustainable in order to prevent government intervention or policies that might restrict their operations. They use sustainability measures to forestall legislation or to avoid persecution and litigation (e.g. polluting industries or factories with poor working conditions). Fearing external restrictions, many businesses prefer to be pioneers of reform; innovators, rather than dragging their feet until being shamed into compliance either by public boycotts of their products or by being forced by governmental regulation. On the other hand, businesses sometimes welcome legislation that levels the playing field by preventing their competitors from less cost-intensive but more unsustainable practices that were at least perceived as necessary to maintain competitiveness.

Those who are less disenchanted with human nature would find the above-mentioned reasons inadequate to explain the goodwill that many businesses show in 'cleaning up their act'. If the above reasons suggest that it is more important for corporate leaders to achieve business success, more optimistic readers would point out that these ulterior motives detract from the true motivation of sustainable business. Simply put: it is the right thing to do. This belief suggests that if all the external incentives were removed, businesses would still choose to be sustainable.

Ensuring greater business transparency, accountability, and public access to information that encourages and empowers civil society to join the regulatory process, MNCs increasingly engaged in CSR activities. CSR can involve incurring short-term costs that do not provide an immediate financial benefit to the company, but instead promote positive social and environmental change.

Sustainability can thus mean anything from businesses that are working to minimize or eliminate negative environmental impacts thereby becoming environmentally positive as opposed to a business that is merely able to sustain itself over time. In this book we want to talk about 'environmental sustainability' rather than just being a successful business in traditional business terms.

Crucial for the understanding of sustainable business is the concept of sustainable development.

Sustainable development and the triple bottom line

The idea of sustainable development, or development that meets the needs of present generations without compromising the ability of future generations to meet their own needs, has become widespread. The pursuit of sustainable development is often stated as the key policy goal of many international organizations including the UN, the World Bank, the International Monetary Fund (IMF) and the World Trade Organization (WTO). Since the 1980s, sustainability has been defined as the integration of the environmental, economic, and social dimensions of responsible management of natural resources. In business, these objectives came to be known as triple P – People, Planet, Profit. A great impetus to the interconnecting triple objectives was the publication of the report of the UN World Commission on Environment and Development, the Brundtland Report, published under the title *Our Common Future* (WCED 1987).

> **The Brundtland Report** refers to sustainable development as development that meets the needs of the present without compromising the ability of future generations to meet their own needs. Sustainable development is targeted at finding strategies to promote economic and social development in ways that avoid environmental degradation, over-exploitation, and pollution, often known in business as the triple bottom line.

Agenda 21, a key set of plans aimed at achieving global sustainable development in the twenty-first century was adopted by the United Nations Conference on Environment and Development (UNCED) as a programme of action on sustainable development for all sectors of government and society in each country. Agenda 21 suggests that a balance must be found between the needs of the environment and those of humankind, placing an emphasis on environmental management, economic and social development, moving away from blaming environmental problems solely on human mismanagement, and seeing technological innovation as one of the key factors in finding viable solutions.

Rather than perceiving social and environmental problems to be solely the result of the consequences of industrial expansion, sustainable development often places an emphasis on poverty reduction. Living in poverty can restrict the options people have for resource management because they have to use environmental assets unsustainably due to short-term necessities (e.g. destroying limited remaining forested areas to clear land for agriculture). Differences in income can be seen as an important factor in explaining 'unsustainable development', and preventing what is often described as ecological modernization. In ecological modernization theory (Mol and Sonnenfeld 2000), discussed in Chapters 5 and 9, it is believed that enlightened self-interest, economy, and ecology can be favourably combined and productive use of natural resources can be a source of future growth and development. Thus, poverty is seen as both a major cause and effect of global environmental problems and addressing inequality is presented as a long-standing concern of sustainable development.

Similar to the ecological modernization theory is the so-called Environmental Kuznets Curve (EKC) hypothesis. In EKC it is believed that during early industrialization, economies use material resources more intensively until a threshold is reached after which structural changes in the economy lead to a progressively less intensive use of materials. It is believed that higher income levels and economic growth will lead to environmental improvement or at least reduced environmental degradation.

A similar curve was expected for developments in agriculture after the Green Revolution. As will be discussed in Chapter 3, the Green Revolution refers to research, development, and technological initiatives that increased agricultural production worldwide, particularly in the developing world. Beginning most markedly in the late 1950s, gains in agricultural output helped the global food supply keep pace with continued population growth. Some observers suggested that these changes, together with development of medical technologies, have enabled the global population to grow while simultaneously increasing the efficiency of land use.

As we will discuss in Chapter 5, both ecological modernization and EKC are highly disputed due to the fact that the lifestyles of today's citizens of wealthy Western countries are by no means sustainable. The rhetoric of ecological modernization tends to downplay the essentially insatiable appetites of an increasingly global consumer class. Critical observers have noted that, practically speaking, expanding the 'economic pie' to include the most dispossessed will inevitably require even more natural resources to be consumed and the unsustainability of the situation to worsen.

Social and economic sustainability

Social sustainability is often conceived as well-being and includes meeting a human's physical, emotional, and social needs. Well-being can also be measured by considering the various objective and subjective components and can be seen as context-specific, and sensitive to cultural diversity and societal autonomy. There is also a universally shared definition related to basic human needs, such as food and shelter. Well-being can have many dimensions, such as physical and emotional, including health or the subjective perception of happiness.

> **Social sustainability** refers to issues concerned with social equality, poverty, and problems associated with justice. Equity considerations are primary in order to have the resources to reduce poverty and increase well-being in developing countries.

The European Environment Agency (EEA) defines sustainability as

> a concept and strategy enabling sufficient delinking of the "use of nature" from economic activity needed to meet human needs to allow it to remain within carrying capacities; and to permit equitable access and use of the environment by current and future generations.

> **Economic sustainability** is linked to well-being in relation to financial indicators such as GDP and is characterized by underlying economic approaches to the range of social issues attempting to capture the values embedded in human and natural capital.

In the crudest sense of the term, economic sustainability is about sustaining the current economic system, which is characterized by the continued growth of the global market based on neo-liberal capitalism. This will be further discussed in Chapter 4. Economic sustainability also often refers to doing more with less, by becoming increasingly efficient as a result of gradual market changes and technological advances. Some experts also refer to employing eco-efficiency and eco-effectiveness measures. Additionally, economic sustainability can be seen as a combination of five different capitals: natural, social, human, financial, and manufactured. In the Sustainable Livelihoods Framework (SLF), social challenges, such as poverty, can be addressed through accessing a range of these livelihood capitals in different contexts, something that businesses are well positioned to do as they have access to all these resources.

Economists have often focused on viewing the economy and the environment as a single interlinked system with a unified valuation system. Increasingly, environment and nature have come to be seen as a valued 'resource', or 'service'. As will be discussed in Chapter 2, this system is often linked to the commodification process, putting a price on anything from natural resources (such as minerals or even entire ecosystems) to values (such as freedom or rights). It is now common in economic valuations to include climate change economics or biodiversity into monetary considerations. The Stern Review on the Economics of Climate Change (2006) for example, by the prominent economist Nicholas Stern, put a price on climate change by discussing the effect of global warming on the world economy.

Similarly in the case of biodiversity, The Economics of Ecosystems and Biodiversity (TEEB), a global initiative focused on drawing attention to the economic benefits of biodiversity, has as its objective to highlight the growing cost of biodiversity loss and ecosystem degradation. Many banks have changed their pattern of investment to both profit from as well as pioneer 'sustainable investment', something we shall discuss in Chapter 11. Through investment, regulative policies, or public initiatives, international communities are anticipating a major shift in their economies, effecting both environment and society, and these shifts will have a profound effect on business. However, it is not always clear what businesses should do – or can do – to be sustainable. This is in part due to the fact that the central assumptions of sustainable development are often disputed.

The Rio treaties, the Plan of Action on Population and Development and the MDGs can be called our millennium promises for sustainable development. All the MDGs refer to better and more equitable outcomes in areas such as health, gender equity, housing, and sanitation that affect poorer groups, particularly in developing countries. Yet, as the well-known economist Jeffrey Sacks (2008) once remarked, these millennium promises might also do little more than join history's cruel dustbin of failed aspirations (p. 13).

It takes political and corporate leadership and civil society's involvement to guarantee that the millennium promises are adequately addressed and positive changes are not reversed. For example, international attention and funding for reproductive and family planning services have recently declined. The Johannesburg World Summit on Sustainable Development (in 2002) has discussed demographic issues but mostly from the point of view of promoting health and policies to increase economic prosperity rather than addressing continued high fertility rates, particularly in some developing countries. Instead, funding focused on increasing fertility has continued, counteracting progress made on slowing population growth (Wijkman and Rockström 2012). If sustainability challenges are to be taken seriously, corporate responsibility should return to mitigating the negative effects of the growing population, as the *Our Common Future* report has suggested.

Critical approaches to sustainable development

Some social and environmental problems can potentially be solved by the same strategies. For example, access to better education for girls can lead to better social positions for women and lower birth rates. Innovation in power generation from renewable sources can lead to a better quality of life for people resulting from cleaner air and other improved environmental factors. Sustainable development, which will be discussed in Chapter 5, attempts to combine both social and environmental aims.

Other types of problems cannot be solved by the same formula. Michael Blowfield (2013:50), the author of *Business and Sustainability,* reflects that including poverty does not appear to be logical when addressing sustainability challenges. Logically, population growth associated with elevating poverty

Figure 1.2 An ethical issue? (source: Engelbert Fellinger)

actually deepens sustainability challenges. In the context of business and sustainability, Blowfield reflects, the question is not whether poverty is a moral issue, but to what degree a failure to address poverty will exacerbate other sustainability challenges (Figure 1.2).

While the conventional wisdom of combining social, economic, and ecological interests is widely advocated, this book takes a more critical approach. Critics have noted that the term 'sustainable development' is an oxymoron, as the two terms 'sustainable' and 'development' have contradictory meanings. Per definition, as physicist Albert Bartlett has noted, growth of population and consumption on a planet of finite resources simply cannot be sustained indefinitely, however inventive we are. One could see political leaders using the term 'sustainable' to describe their goals as they worked hard to create more jobs, to increase population, and to increase rates of consumption of energy and resources. Bartlett (1998) wryly commented:

> A spherical earth is finite and hence is forever unappealing to the devotees of perpetual growth. In contrast, a flat earth can accommodate growth forever, because a flat earth can be infinite in the two horizontal dimensions and also in the vertical downward direction. The infinite horizontal dimensions forever remove any fear of crowding as population grows, and the infinite downward dimension assures humans of an

unlimited supply of all of the mineral raw materials that will be needed by a human population that continues to grow forever. The flat earth removes all the need for worry about limits.

Concern for future generations of humans tends to exclude consideration of non-human species. Mainstream sustainability thinking is concerned with the rights of disadvantaged human groups entangled with notions of economic development. This process involves the exportation of unsustainable economic practices to all corners of the globe. While these may provide immediate benefits for human populations, they have had enormous negative impacts on non-human species, which in turn cause long-term negative impacts on the health of the ecosystem to which all species, including humans, belong.

According to sociologist Eileen Crist (2012) while 'raising the standard of living' may be shorthand for the worthy aim of ending severe deprivation, the expression is also a euphemism for the global dissemination of consumer culture. This raises ethical questions regarding ecological justice or justice between species, and animal rights (Figure 1.3) in relation to feeding a growing human population.

Increasing numbers of people in the consumer class will only exacerbate the problem, calling for ever more intensified uses of land and waterways for habitation, agriculture, and farming; for the continued extraction, exploitation, and harnessing of the natural world. It is implied that 'feeding the world' will inevitably be achieved through the ongoing displacement and extermination of plants and animals that human food production and transportation entail (Crist, 2012: 142).

At present, sustainability solutions aimed at improving human health and poverty reduction do not necessarily address long-term needs connected with population and consumption growth (Chapter 3). Better medical technologies lead to larger populations, in part from faster growth but equally from fewer deaths due to longer lifespans. Furthermore, successful economic development often leads to higher rates of consumption. Based on this line of reasoning, urgent action could be required, including population control and zero-growth in the global economy, as will be further discussed in Chapter 9.

As noted in a recent report to the Club of Rome (Wijkman and Rockström 2012:82), while some people claim that the size of the world population has no impact on sustainability because of the low resource consumption and small carbon footprints of the poor, this argument is only valid in the short-term perspective. In the long term, as most of us recognize, all people on this planet have a right to decent living conditions. But that raises important questions: how do we define what constitutes decent living conditions? Does the rest of the world need to be brought up to the same level as Western consumers? If that is the case, we will need several more planet Earths to accommodate the current global population, let alone if population growth

Figure 1.3 Animal rights (source: Engelbert Fellinger)

is to continue. Or do we need to find an acceptable middle ground where both the most developed and the developing populations can converge?

This is one of the reasons why this book is different from many other books on sustainability which often advocate for a more conventional approach to solving environmental problems – which, as we now witness, has not proved effective. Causes of both social and environmental problems will be discussed in greater detail in Chapters 2 and 3, while the paradoxes of the sustainable development framework will be discussed in Chapter 9. Part IV (Solutions) will discuss ways forward in the quest to advance sustainability in spite of these paradoxes and challenges.

Environmental sustainability

Much of the literature on environmental (un)sustainability shows that one of the biggest threats to the environment at the moment is industrial development. Recent literature on sustainable solutions to world problems points to the fact that sustainable development solutions have failed to recognize and address environmental threats like climate change, pollution, deforestation, and species loss. The crisis will be exacerbated by the combination of climate change, ecosystem decline, and resource scarcity, in particular crude oil and water.

Since the Industrial Revolution (discussed in Chapter 3), there has been a massive acceleration in the rate of species extinction. Within the next 40–50 years, the coral reefs, upon which about one quarter of the oceans' species depend, will have disappeared. If this trend continues, it means that in the coming decades, about 25 per cent of the mammals on this planet will be extinct, and over 40 per cent of its amphibians will also have gone. According to a Millennium Ecosystem Assessment (MEA) report, humankind has increased the rate of extinction by about 1000 times the fossil record rate.

> Over the past 50 years, humans have changed ecosystems more rapidly and extensively than in any comparable period of time in human history, largely to meet rapidly growing demands for food, fresh water, timber, fiber and fuel. This has resulted in a substantial and largely irreversible loss in the diversity of life on Earth. In addition, approximately 60% of the ecosystem services it examined are being degraded or used unsustainably, including fresh water, capture fisheries, air and water purification, and the regulation of regional and local climate, natural hazards, and pests.
>
> (UNEP 2013)

Ironically, if the objectives of social and environmental sustainability are to be achieved without a decoupling of concerns about human well-being from economic factors, environmental sustainability might be all but impossible to achieve.

Eco-efficiency and eco-effectiveness

Sustainability is often discussed in terms of eco-efficiency. One example would be improving the performance of a car engine to use less fuel or replacing petrochemicals and other non-renewable resources with renewable alternatives. Another good example would be policies that increase efficiency while also increasing human welfare, such as decentralized power generation from small solar *photovoltaic* (PV) systems that provide electricity to isolated communities that have never before been connected to the grid. Eco-efficiency seeks to address the unintended negative consequences of production and consumption by reducing negative social and environmental impacts.

> **Eco-efficiency** refers to the idea of doing more with less. Compared to early industrial products, modern alternatives are able to generate more value by being produced on a much larger scale with less impact and using less material.

The OECD definition of sustainability in relation to eco-efficiency is 'the efficiency with which ecological resources are used to meet human needs' and represents it as a ratio of output divided by the input. The output includes the value of products and services produced by a firm, sector, or economy as a whole. The input typically refers to the sum of environmental pressures generated by the firm, the sector, or the economy.

The WBCSD defines eco-efficiency as being

> the delivery of competitively-priced goods and services that satisfy human needs and bring quality of life, while progressively reducing ecological impacts and resource intensity throughout the life-cycle to a level at least in line with the Earth's estimated carrying capacity.

Eco-efficiency can also be seen as a quantitative management tool that enables the consideration of life cycle environmental impacts of a product system alongside its product system value to a stakeholder.

Eco-efficiency proponents tend to view industrial development and business not as an environmental problem but as part of the solution to protect and improve the environment. The advantages of eco-efficiency to most business operations are widely recognized: valuable materials are saved and retained by the manufacturer, including human and natural resources. In business terms, it is now widely recognized that eco-efficient production is a major opportunity to enhance a company's competitive position in the market.

Critics have noted, however, that eco-efficiency enables production processes that, despite good intentions, still result in massive amounts of waste in the endless spiral of production and consumption. In this view, eco-efficiency only works to slow the process of destruction and perpetuate the bad system, allowing products such as fossil fuels or non-biodegradable plastic to last longer than they otherwise would. Making a system that pollutes and generates waste more efficiently will only prolong an essentially unsustainable system. If population growth and increase in global consumption are largely responsible for environmental degradation, eco-efficiency results only in tinkering at the margins of the problem without addressing its root causes.

While eco-efficiency and technological innovations can allow more people to have a smaller impact on the planet, capitalism requires constant growth. The rebound effect (or Jevons paradox) suggests that eco-efficiency ultimately leads to more consumption. As we shall discuss in Chapter 9, rebound effect refers to the consumer response to the introduction of new eco-efficient technologies. These tend to offset the beneficial effects by perpetuating or actually increasing consumption of these products. Also, many new technologies, such as carbon capture and storage to mitigate climate change, or solar radiation management systems, will not solve the long-term problem of non-renewable energy, but just help to sweep it under a rug.

Eco-effectiveness addresses the major shortcomings of eco-efficiency approaches, such as their inability to address the necessity for fundamental change in the way products and waste are currently produced.

> **Eco-effectiveness** advocates for the production of goods and services by focusing on the development of products and industrial systems that maintain or enhance the quality and productivity of materials rather than depleting them.

The role of eco-effectiveness as a characteristic of resilient and productive systems and a business opportunity for achieving true sustainability will be further discussed in Chapter 11.

The circular economy and Cradle to Cradle

As we shall discuss in Chapter 11, proponents of the circular economy propose the closed loop production system where nothing gets wasted. Highlighting the role of diversity as a characteristic of resilient and productive systems, the circular economy supports an endless cycle of material regeneration that mimics nature's 'no waste' nutrient cycles. The application of this idea at an economic level has risen to prominence since the World Economic Forum support for the circular economy and has been propelled forward by the Ellen MacArthur Foundation.

Box 1.1 World Economic Forum Report

If everyone lived like an average North American, we would need four planets to sustain our needs, according to the World Wide Fund for Nature (WWF) Living Planet Report 2012.

There is a paradox here. On the one hand, globalization in recent decades has helped to lift hundreds of millions out of poverty. But on the other hand, the ever increasing extraction of resources and economic activity has placed increasingly unsustainable pressures on the environment upon which we all depend.

A recent World Economic Forum Report noted this paradox, stating that in recent years an estimated 450 million people had been lifted out of poverty. But in the same period, about 21 million hectares of forest had been lost, 9.1 billion tons of municipal solid waste was generated and some 50 billion tons of fossil fuels were consumed…So, how can responsible businesses compete for this prize in the decades to come without damaging the planet and putting greater pressure on scarce resources?

With interest in the circular economy gaining ground, we may see more and more companies exploring this option.

Source: http://forumblog.org/2013/01/the-case-for-the-circular-economy/

The **circular economy model** uses the functioning of ecosystems as an exemplar for industrial processes, emphasizing a shift towards ecologically sound products and renewable energy

The idea of the circular economy was adopted by the American architect William McDonough and the German chemist Michael Braungart. They have claimed that most of the eco-efficient strategies we now use, including reducing and recycling, still tend to support the cradle-to-grave trajectory of the product, only making the 'death' of the product in landfills or incinerators one step removed. For example, recycling practised today is mostly downcycling, where materials are reused to make products of lower quality using energy and chemicals to give the material(s) a new (and lesser) life. Another example is burning garbage to produce energy – once burned, the product 'dies', while valuable materials get lost in a short-lived energy boost.

Cradle to Cradle (C2C) considers not just minimizing the damage, but proposes how contemporary waste and depletion of resources can be avoided by adhering to a cyclical 'waste=food' principle.

This principle is well illustrated by the metaphor of the cherry tree that produces 'waste' (berries, leaves, etc.) that actually serves as food for other species or that add to the soil. Industry, on the other hand, follows a one-way, linear, cradle-to-grave manufacturing line in which products are created and eventually discarded. Unlike waste products from natural systems, the waste from human industry is not 'food' but often poison. Thus, the end products are very different: a pile of cherry blossoms and a heap of toxic waste in a landfill.

The C2C framework proposes that biodegradable materials (biological nutrients) and non-compostable materials (technical nutrients) should be used for agricultural fertilization or reused without the loss of quality and energy for a different product. The added long-term advantage of eco-effective systems is that no useless and potentially dangerous waste is generated as might still be the case in eco-efficient systems. Thus, proponents of both the circular economy and C2C approach propose eco-effectiveness, which supports an endless cycle of materials that mimics nature's 'no waste' nutrient cycles.

This implies that industry faces a new range of opportunities and challenges – in product design, material and supplier choice, and producer responsibility for the production and waste stage.

ks business, ethics and sustainability?

: business and environment?

basic, the environment helps to sustain businesses by providing _____als. In a more profound way, humans cannot do without the environment and businesses for obvious reasons cannot do without both. Failing to consider the environment in business operations disregards the very foundations upon which human industry is based.

What links business and society?

Business has in fact become part of society (Figure 1.4), and CSR has grown in prominence, as we shall discuss in greater detail in Chapter 7. The link between business and social responsibility is not always a straightforward one.

What links business and ethics?

Sustainability is often connected to ethics, as both imply that one should act within governmental law (adhering to regulations and policies that control business) and conventional law (adhering to the prevailing standards accepted by society). Business people aspiring to be ethical or act sustainably may be expected to adhere to the same standards of behaviour in business as they would in their private lives. Just as one does not leave rubbish in the middle of one's house or force one's children to do heavy work, so are business people expected to fulfil their responsibilities in their business activities and beyond. However, sustainability and ethics in business are not the same as running a household – in fact they involve global dimensions that render conscientious behaviour all the more important (Chapter 7).

Every day, executives confront practical ethical and business issues – both within their companies and in their dealings with suppliers, clients, competitors, government agencies concerned with corporate regulations, and the general public. Consider the following questions:

- How do we balance what is right with what is profitable?
- How do we choose whether it is 'right' to invest in poor nations?
- Considering that the wealthiest nations historically have profited from industrialization, should poor nations have the right to rapid economic growth even if that leads to increased GHG emissions that exacerbate climate change?
- Considering that the poor suffer disproportionately the consequences of climate change and considering that the rich nations have historically been responsible for higher levels of GHGs, is it fair for the rich nations to pay for developing nations to follow the same flawed path toward industrialization?

Figure 1.4 What links business and society? (source: Engelbert Fellinger)

- Should population growth be treated as an ethical question?
- Is poverty reduction a moral imperative?
- Should concern for animal rights be considered on a par with human rights?
- What could or should businesses do to address all of these questions?

There are many organizations that deal with ethics in business, such as the Global Council on Business Conduct, the Society for Business Ethics, and the Ethical Consumer. Normally, in business we speak of normative ethics, where we distinguish between prescriptive and descriptive ethics. Prescriptive ethics prescribe norms and standards and typically urge moral improvements. Descriptive ethics describe what business people think is right and wrong and typically involve the study of ethical views held, their origin and subjective justification, attempting to clarify and analyse ethical beliefs rather than change them. In this book, we shall lean toward descriptive ethics, although sometimes we shall openly state our own beliefs on what we think is right or wrong.

do business ethically and sustainably

...isions on how to act in business will come naturally. As resources ...come scarce they become more expensive, serving as a direct driver for conservation strategies in manufacturing. As such, efficient production, including longevity and cycling, is a rational strategy for manufacturers. Some other decisions, while well intentioned, might miss the mark as sustainability is far from straightforward. Once you realize that sustainability itself involves many paradoxes, the 'right' course of action for business becomes a bit hazy.

You might realize that what seemed so obviously 'good' (for example, textiles made of organic cotton) may not be environmentally sound (organic cotton may use much more water and land than genetically modified or GM cotton). A similar case can be made for the biofuels favoured by European countries on the premise that they reduce GHG emissions. Critics have argued that biofuel crops actually increase emissions and cause biodiversity loss, as well as create competition for agricultural land that would otherwise be used for edible crop production (Phalan 2013). Where does that leave energy suppliers, policymakers, and corporations concerned with research into sustainable energy?

In this book we will attempt to alert you to many different ways in which business and sustainability can be mutually beneficial. However, many decisions will depend on your own critical faculty, on your ability to see challenges as well as possibilities, and to use your own head and heart to distinguish between what is sustainable, what is less sustainable, and what is not sustainable at all.

You need to maintain a healthy scepticism, constantly questioning and reconsidering concepts, products and technologies that appear to be green and fair on the surface. Your ability to discern and navigate these contradictions and to keep yourself well informed of the global context and technical aspects of different sustainability choices is crucial. Last but not least, you should retain your imagination, goodwill, and ability to work towards combining business and sustainability in the most inspired, illuminating, and innovative ways. This is what we hope this book will help you do.

Chapter organization

Following this Introduction, Chapter 2 introduces environmental challenges. It starts by questioning what we mean by 'the environment' and distinguishes between environmental values and environmental impacts. This chapter discusses global and national organizations concerned with the environment. The second part of the chapter focuses on environmental problems such as climate change and biodiversity loss, as well as environmental disasters. In relating environmental issues to business practices, this chapter discusses limits of growth and natural resources and the ethical implications thereof.

Chapter 3 focuses on social and economic challenges, particularly poverty and its causes. Socio-economic causes of unsustainability are explored. Particularly pertinent to the case of business sustainability is the critical exploration of the power of corporate elites. This chapter will also address a number of the causes of unsustainability, including human, political, and structural causes. The chapter also briefly addresses the consequences of the Industrial Revolution, placing special emphasis on developments in the fields of medical and agricultural technology. This chapter addresses some politically loaded topics such as the relationship between economic development and neo-colonialism.

In continuing the discussion of the leading factors in unsustainability, Chapter 4 will concentrate on the context of globalization, inquiring about the various uses of the term 'globalization' and discussing trends in increasingly globalized societies, such as the 'risk society'. This chapter will focus on the relationship between the globalization of the market economy and neo-liberal capitalism. Globalization of consumption is discussed in relation to opportunities for sustainable consumption with reference to consumer choice editing. Global organizations concerned with sustainability and the universal spread of sustainability concerns are highlighted. The greening of global supply chains is discussed in the context of neo-liberal democracy and cultural hegemony. The chapter will also address globalization of education.

Sustainable development, both as ideology and practice, are discussed in Chapter 5. As sustainable development is closely linked to business, theories of development and innovation such as post-material value theory, EKC, and ecological modernization theory are discussed. Conferences and international agreements regarding sustainable development are linked to business, with special reference to the work of the WBCSD. This chapter poses some difficult questions, such as: Who is responsible for poverty in the Global South? The chapter concludes with discussion of education for sustainable development or ESD.

Chapter 6 takes as its starting point a discussion of competitive advantage and its relationship to sustainable business practice. A key factor in both is effective knowledge management which leads on to a discussion of how innovations can be nurtured through encouraging creativity and how all stakeholders in an enterprise are in effect important to a business's success and prosperity. In this context organizational communication, green marketing, responsible advertising, and sustainable brand development become important factors in envisioning and realizing a sustainable business.

Chapter 7 takes these arguments forward in a discussion of sustainability and business ethics. Once perceived as an oxymoron, business ethics is now a key driver in many change management practices. CSR and corporate sustainability are now viewed by many companies not as a nice add-on or a latter day example of philanthropy or charity but integral to what a good business is all about. In this context, a discussion of labour rights and human rights more widely, fair trade, animal welfare, pollution control, and environmental remediation indicate that the business of business is far broader than a concern with a single bottom line. Most important and indeed crucial to this is good corporate governance, and the chapter ends with some questions board members need to ask of their company.

Chapter 8 explores how businesses can adapt and change through the use of various tools, frameworks, and guides. To a large extent environmental regulation, legislation, and national and international agreements establish the parameters in which a business should legitimately and legally operate. However, many companies now wish to go beyond compliance and look to a range of environmental management and audit schemes as a way of structuring and progressing necessary change. Sustainable supply chain management, life cycle analysis, accreditation, and eco-labelling schemes together with some inspirational guides such as The Natural Step are all part of the picture. Companies also need to report and demonstrate that they are changing sustainably. Transparency in reporting, investment, and changes to accountancy procedures are of vital importance too.

Chapter 9 outlines a number of challenges to traditional views of sustainability. We put forward the argument that sustainability cannot be met by simply tinkering with the current economic system, but will require major changes in the way members of political and corporate elites and the general public perceive and address environmental and social issues. The changing global business environment requires understanding of the paradoxes of sustainability and necessary choices between growth and conservation. This chapter disputes mainstream theories of sustainability, including the triple bottom line and challenges the myths of eco-efficiency and sustainable consumption. The second part of the chapter outlines a number of ethical challenges concerned with intergenerational justice and biospheric egalitarianism. The role of corporate and political decision makers is stressed as the key to resolution of those challenges.

Chapter 10 focuses on knowledge, learning, and skills and the part human resource management can play in rendering business more environmentally sustainable and socially responsible. Doing new things and doing things differently requires education in a variety of forms and learning occurs in informal as well as formal institutional settings. The UN Principles of Responsible Management Education are becoming increasingly important in changing the curriculum in university business schools where the future leaders of business and sustainability are being nurtured. Without leadership the global economy cannot be greened, work become more meaningful and rewarding, or new green jobs and occupations created. This chapter concludes with a discussion of the importance of sharing and cooperation – a counterpoint and counterweight to a sometimes overly emphatic emphasis on the benefits of competition in the business literature and trade press.

Chapter 11 addresses the structural and social solutions to the challenges of overpopulation, industrial production, and consumption. New forms and mechanisms of consumption, including consumer choice editing and sharing economy are outlined. Strategic choices in terms of direct and indirect impacts as well as private and public actions are stressed. Tackling oil dependency and climate scepticism are highlighted as necessary ways forward. Concrete business solutions are proposed through a number of frameworks that are significantly different from the conventional ones criticized in Chapter 9. These solutions involve the understanding and application of business ecology, and specific focus on the C2C and the circular economy frameworks.

This book concludes with an outlook on the future of business and our beautiful planet (Figure 1.5).

Key terms

Brundtland Report; business ethics; business sustainability; the circular economy; Cradle to Cradle; eco-effectiveness; eco-efficiency; economic sustainability; environmental sustainability; limits to growth; social sustainability; sustainable development; the triple bottom line.

Figure 1.5 Our beautiful planet (photo by ©André Kuipers http://www.flickr.com/photos/astro_andre/ with permission of WWF Karin Gerritsen).

Discussion questions

1   What are the major stakeholders (international organizations, corporate and civil society members) involved with sustainability?
2   What do you think are the greatest challenges to sustainability?
3   What are the main differences between the limits to growth and sustainable development frameworks?

End of chapter summary

This chapter described what sustainability is, explaining both conventional uses of the term, such as sustainable development or triple bottom line, as well as alternative approaches, such as C2C and circular economy. This chapter has traced the evolution of sustainability, both as a concept and as a practice, as well as introduced the main stakeholders involved in the sustainability enterprise, with particular focus on business.

2   Environmental challenges

What is meant by 'environment'?

As far back as ancient Greece and Rome, humankind has made a continual effort to situate itself within nature or nature within itself according to our dynamic and evolving understanding of ourselves and our environment. Humans have influenced their environment since ancient times. Renaissance scholars saw that deforestation, irrigation, and grazing altered the land and affected local habitats and ecosystems. However, human impact has never been as far-reaching as in the years since the Industrial Revolution, or the Anthropocene. This informal geologic term was coined by ecologist Eugene Stoermer and has been popularized by the Noble Prize winner chemist Paul Crutzen. The Anthropocene encompasses the age of human activities that have had significant global impact on ecosystems and climate.

> **Anthropocene** describes a new era comprising recent centuries where human behaviour has had an increased influence and impact on the Earth's atmosphere seen as so significant as to constitute a new geological epoch.

Before we discuss the Anthropocene from a business point of view, we need to address the question of what is meant by environment. We can start by defining certain environments by comparing and contrasting one from the other: biophysical or natural, built or modified, social, and business environment.

> **Biophysical or natural environment** refers to the surroundings of an organism, and includes the factors that have an influence on its survival, development, and evolution.

The biophysical or natural environment includes complex climatic factors that act upon an organism(s) and determine its form, survival, and how it adapts to its environment over time. The natural environment includes 'ecosystem' and all living organisms, and emphasizes interrelated systems, such as habitats, and relationships between these systems. Natural environments can include humans but can also refer to the world outside human existence.

The built or modified environment typically refers to man-made structures or spaces that provide the setting for human activity – from gardens to car parks, from furniture and houses to entire cities. Businesses often refer to the effects of their operations (e.g. air quality) on modified environments such as cities. In many languages the word 'environment' can also be associated with social, cultural, or business contexts (we have all heard of 'business environment'), milieu or social structure.

When we talk of business environment, we can distinguish between internal and external factors that influence a business's situation. The business environment can include clients, suppliers, competitors, and owners; social institutions such as laws, government activities, and markets; and technological and economic trends.

The reason why these distinctions are important for business practitioners in the quest for environmental sustainability is that it makes it clearer what is actually being 'sustained'. Business practices that consider the environment attempt to restore, mitigate, or compensate for damages caused by its operations on the natural environment. Large companies' reports often include environmental assessments (EAs), EA follow-up and voluntary corporate responsibility reports.

Environmental impacts

Some businesses proclaim that they strive to protect the environment without specifying what kind of specific environmental benefit this action provides in context. It could be that new trees are planted where the company's old factory once stood in order to 'return' the habitat back to certain local species (thus serving the natural or biophysical environment), or the trees could be planted in places where pristine forest once stood and is actually intended to provide raw materials for the same business (thus serving as built/modified environment for making paper, or producing biofuel), generating income and stimulating a 'good business environment' (being beneficial to the company and its stakeholders). If a distinction is made between different types of environment it could be the case that one type of environment is being destroyed, while another type is being created.

Impacts to existing wetlands, which are usually protected areas, are often mitigated as part of a development project. A common solution to mitigate the destruction of existing wetland areas is to construct a certain area of wetland in another location near the existing one. Yet, it has been well established that a constructed wetland will only have a fraction of the biodiversity of the original wetland.

Environmental impacts can be direct or indirect (Stern 2000). Some activities, such as clear cutting a forest or disposing of household waste, directly cause changes to the environment. Other activities indirectly change the environment, by shaping the context in which choices are made. While a government can be good at supporting waste recycling schemes, it can be less effective at monitoring investments in companies that produce environmentally damaging goods. Behaviours that affect international development policies and commodity prices on world markets can indirectly have a great environmental impact. Depending on the particular issues and context, businesses will use environmental impact assessments (EIAs) to thoroughly identify and evaluate the possible impacts a proposed project could have on all the environment types named above and 'sensitive receptors' and stakeholders. EIAs and other environmental assessments are holistic exercises and include environmental, social, and economic aspects.

Environmental problems

The Earth Charter asserts that the dominant patterns of production and consumption are causing environmental devastation, the depletion of resources, and a massive extinction of species. Also, the publications of IPCC, UNEP, and MEA link many environmental problems to the processes of industrialization and population growth. Environmental problems range from climate change to the depletion of natural resources, to biodiversity loss, and pollution. Here we will focus only on a few of the problems commonly addressed in business practice.

Climate change

Climate change is a significant and lasting change in the statistical distribution of weather patterns over periods of time. General scientific consensus is that current climate change, and in particular the greenhouse effect, is caused by human activities.

The **greenhouse effect** is a process by which thermal radiation from a planetary surface is absorbed by the atmosphere and is re-radiated in all directions. Since part of this re-radiation is back towards the surface, it results in an elevation of the average surface temperature.

Anthropogenic factors contributing to climate change include the increased emission of GHGs such as carbon dioxide (CO_2), methane (CH_4), nitrous oxide (N_2O), HFCs, perflurocarbons (PFCs), and sulfur hexafluoride (SF_6) as a result of fossil fuel combustion, intensified agricultural production (both crop and livestock), ozone depletion, and deforestation. CO_2 can remain in the atmosphere for more than 200 years, giving it a cumulative long-term impact as more and more is added to the atmosphere. Aside from GHGs, other chemicals, such as sulfur dioxide, can cause smog and acid rain.

While public and government interest had already been ignited in the 1980s, the main driver of corporate strategic change was the adoption of the Kyoto Protocol to the United Nations Framework Convention on Climate Change (UNFCCC) in 1997. Policy instruments for meeting emissions targets include regulation, carbon pricing, and subsidies. Governments prefer regulation; economists prefer carbon prices; and businesses prefer subsidies.

Actions taken by developed and developing countries to reduce emissions were to include support for renewable energy, improving energy efficiency, and reducing deforestation. Many developed countries have agreed to legally binding limitations in their GHG emissions in two commitment periods between 2008 and 2012, and between 2013 and 2020. The protocol was amended in 2012 to accommodate the second commitment period, but at the time of writing this book this amendment had not entered into legal force. The protocol included the so-called flexibility mechanisms: Joint Implementation (JI), international emissions trading, and Clean Development Mechanism (CDM).

> **Joint Implementation**: industrialized states share the credit for emission reductions achieved in specific joint projects.

The mechanism's purpose was to achieve emissions reductions in the most cost-effective way by taking into account differences in the marginal abatement cost between countries. JI offered parties a flexible and cost-efficient means of fulfilling part of their Kyoto commitments while the host party benefited from foreign investment and technology transfer. JI can only be used between two countries that both have an obligation to reduce emissions and they have to agree on the distribution of reduction credits.

> **Emissions trading** is exchanging part of national emissions allowances, allowing developed countries to trade their excess allotted emissions allowances, and allowing other countries to consider the purchased allowances in achieving their respective commitments under the Kyoto Protocol.

Countries and in some cases MNCs can trade emissions quotas among themselves and can also receive credits for financing emissions reductions in developing countries. Developed countries may use emissions trading until late 2015 to meet their first-round targets. In contrast to a command and control approach in which the governments prescribe which technology has to be used to reduce emissions, emissions trading gives corporations more flexibility.

Clean Development Mechanism (CDM): emission credits for financing approved climate-friendly projects in developing countries.

The global dimension of the CDM, which covers projects in developing countries, made it attractive for MNCs that were already active in these countries through foreign direct investment (FDI).

Failing goals of reducing emissions

In December 2012, no new treaty came about to replace the expiring Kyoto Protocol and consequently there was no prospect of binding agreements covering the period up to 2020. PricewaterhouseCoopers, a major global consulting firm, asked whether it was too late to achieve the goal of limiting global temperature change to the 2 degrees targeted in the Kyoto Protocol and concluded that such a goal was, indeed, no longer possible. Instead, experts have shifted the focus to dealing with the impacts of more realistic scenarios based on global temperatures that are 4 to 6 degrees hotter. Climate change summits have done little more than '[promise] more talks about talks' (*The Economist* 2012:62).

A report for the World Bank by the Potsdam Institute for Climate Impact Research (2012) suggested that oceans could rise by 0.5–1 metre by 2100, which would devastate coastal cities; three quarters of tropical rainforests could die, creating feedback loops that would only expedite further climate change; crop yields would fall drastically; and droughts would become more common and more severe. The threat of rising sea levels is not a far off danger.

The impacts of climate change have already begun. For example, some areas, such as the Sundarbans in India and Bangladesh, the largest single block of tidal mangrove forest in the world, are already being threatened by rising sea levels, with their villages largely submerged (Figure 2.1).

Corporate response to climate change

In the early 1990s there was a varied reaction on the part of companies, including indifference, ignorance, fear of harm to competitiveness, and a rejection of (scientific) evidence that climate change is taking place. In more recent years, many politicians and corporate leaders have, at times slowly, moved into action to combat climate change, demonstrating a reluctant acceptance of the scientific evidence, improving their processes and products, cooperating with other companies, governments and NGOs to exchange technologies and best practices, and engaging in emissions trading schemes.

In the last decade, company responses have gone beyond government regulations and included voluntary agreements and partnerships; emissions reporting and reduction targets; and even the incorporation of carbon disclosure into standard company reporting. Company-specific factors

Figure 2.1 Sundarbans village (source: Helen Kopnina)

that appear to determine the adoption of proactive climate policies include the company's positioning within the supply chain, the broader economic situation and the company's market positioning, a history of involvement with (technological) alternatives, the degree of (de)centralization, the degree of top management internationalization, the availability of internal climate expertise, the corporate culture, and management perceptions (Pinske and Kolk 2009). Yet, witnessed by failure to control climate change, all these actions have proved inadequate.

Loss of biodiversity

According to the IUCN (2013), over 19,000 species out of the 53,000 assessed to date are threatened with extinction. Within the next 40–50 years, the coral reefs, upon which about one quarter of the ocean's species depend, will have disappeared. It means that about 25 per cent of the mammals (Figure 2.2) and about 41 per cent of the amphibians on this planet will be extinct. The convergence of population growth, expanding agriculture, deforestation, and climate change is likely to create immense challenges for humanity and will certainly worsen the biodiversity crisis.

The UN's third *Global Biodiversity Outlook* report stresses that ocean pollution and deforestation are proceeding at an unprecedented rate, destroying rich habitats upon which many species depend. A report from the World

Figure 2.2 Red panda (source: Helen Kopnina)

Commission on Forests and Sustainable Development suggests that forests (Figure 2.3) have been exploited to the point of crisis and that major changes in global forest management strategies are needed to avoid devastation. However, a lot of 'sustainability' rhetoric masks the fact that vast amounts of what used to be diverse habitats have been converted into productive wood factories (for example, those used by Forest Stewardship Council), in both developed and developing countries. More than half of Finnish forests, for example, have been planted for timber production, and an increasing proportion of forests in Indonesia are used for palm oil plantations for biofuels or crops.

In the words of prominent anthropologist Vandana Shiva (2001:1):

> It is true that cutting down forests or converting natural forests into monocultures of pine and eucalyptus for industrial raw material generates revenues and growth. But this growth is based on robbing the forest of its biodiversity and its capacity to conserve soil and water. This growth is based on robbing forest communities of their sources of food, fodder, fuel, fiber, medicine, and security from floods and drought.

Recent findings compiled in a study by TEEB, indicate that those corporate chiefs who fail to make sustainable management of biodiversity part of their business may find themselves increasingly out of step with

Figure 2.3 Forest (source: Engelbert Fellinger)

the marketplace. Companies with net positive impact (NPI) on biological diversity are designated as winners in a resource-constrained world, with one in four global chief executive officers (CEOs) seeing biodiversity loss as a strategic issue for business growth (UNEP 2013). A NPI commitment to biodiversity ensures that the protection of biodiversity is ultimately a benefit resulting from a company's activities in a particular region. However, such commitment does not assure success (see the TEEB case study at the end of this chapter and the Rio Tinto case study in Chapter 5).

Limits to Growth

Both fossil fuels and biodiversity are finite, and so are 'natural resources'. In the first chapter of this book, we mentioned the *Limits to Growth* report (Meadows et al. 1972), which demonstrated that an economy built on the continuous expansion of consumption as well as population growth is not sustainable in the long term. Traditional views of sustainability often ignore the 'elephant in the room' – population growth – which tends to exacerbate sustainability challenges. If population growth continues (or stabilizes at the current level, according to the demographic transition theory discussed in Chapter 3), something radical needs to happen with the way we currently produce and consume. Yet, it seems impossible to decouple the current system of production and consumption from the underlying political and ideological processes of neo-liberal democracy.

Hall and Day (2009) and Turner (2010) argued that the problems predicted by *Limits to Growth* had not gone away and would only take the world population by surprise if they were ignored. The data shows that both resource use and costs have only risen, and are not effectively mitigated by market forces.

Pollution and the industrial disasters

Since the Industrial Revolution, many great discoveries and transformational inventions have been made. Unfortunately, some of them have backfired. The publication of the Canadian biologist, Rachel Carson's book *Silent Spring* in 1962 was intended to warn the public of the threats posed by chemical pesticides on human health and the environment and, more broadly, the potential dangers of chemicals in general. There are many examples of technology-caused disasters that have occurred since the turn of the twentieth century.

One such example is Love Canal, a chemical waste dump turned residential community in the United States (US) that was one of the first cases that demonstrated a clear and undeniable link between human illness and the dumping of chemicals. Another example is the so-called Toxic Fog in London, United Kingdom (UK), in 1954. A combination of air pollution and extreme weather conditions led to hundreds of lives being lost in less than a year and thousands of cases of respiratory disease. Such disasters have caused heightened public awareness of environmental health risks and the widespread public protests in Western countries in the 1970s.

However, some of the worst episodes of industrial disasters have occurred outside Western countries. One of the worst accidents of the previous century, the Bhopal Disaster in India in 1984, was caused by a gas leak from Union Carbide India Limited (UCIL). The leak killed at least 4,000 local residents instantly and caused health problems in approximately 500,000 people, who are still suffering from chronic disease linked to the gas exposure.

The Chernobyl disaster in1986 was caused by an explosion and fire at a nuclear power plant in Ukraine, then part of the former Union of Soviet Socialist Republics (USSR), that resulted in the release of radioactive particles being spread across much of the western USSR and Europe. An estimated 600,000 Belorussian citizens suffered radiation exposure, and 4,000 suffered cancer deaths, with approximately 100,000 cancers still expected. More recently, the nuclear disaster at the nuclear power plant near Fukushima, Japan, following a severe earthquake and tsunami that devastated parts of Japan in 2011, has caused not only death and illness, but at the time of writing this book, is still estimated to be causing severe pollution in the waters around the plant, affecting fish stocks and safety for hundreds of miles around the affected area. Oil spills in areas ranging from the Gulf of Mexico to Nigeria and the Arctic have become commonplace as well.

What should be even more concerning is not so much the occasional industrial disaster but everyday pollution such as particulate matter emitted by cars, and massive amounts of plastic waste found in the oceans, seas, lakes, rivers, and city parks. The everyday pollution has a much larger impact on a far greater portion of the planet than major disasters. Sadly, it is also more easily and cheaply prevented, but it is up to each of the 6 billion residents on the planet, which represents a much greater challenge to educate and motivate on such a large scale.

Waste

Perhaps one of the greatest challenges to sustainability is the production of waste (Figure 2.4) that ends up either in landfills or incinerators. Unilever (2012) defines corporate waste as any packaging which ends up in a landfill, products left over in their original packaging at the time of disposal, and waste from manufacturing processes. In most cases, only a small proportion of physical throughput ends up as product, the rest goes into the process of making it, packaging, and transportation.

Traditional corporate responses to this challenge have been to minimize the damage by introducing the concept of eco-efficiency. The WBCSD issued a *Changing Course* report that stressed the importance of eco-efficiency for all companies aiming to be competitive, sustainable, and successful in the long term.

However, as will be further discussed in Chapter 11, the circular economy, C2C, and the Blue Economy approaches suggest that being less bad is not good enough. Eco-efficiency may reduce resource consumption and pollution in the short term, but it will not eliminate the root causes of the problem. Rather, the current eco-efficiency framework tackles problems without addressing their source, sustaining a fundamentally flawed system.

Proponents of alternative production models propose redesigning products so that after their useful life has ended they can serve as 'food' for new products (McDonough and Braungart 2002). Within these frameworks lies the promise to create economies that purify air, soil, and water relying on solar and wind power, generating no toxic waste by using safe, healthful materials that replenish the earth or can be perpetually reused, yielding benefits that enhance all life. These alternatives present a great opportunity for sustainable production and elimination of waste (see Table 11.1). At the moment, however, these sustainability solutions do not come close to achieving these objectives.

Figure 2.4 Waste (source: Engelbert Fellinger)

Causes and explanations

Giddens (2009:2) posed seemingly simple questions about sport utility vehicles (SUVs) and climate change:

> Why does anyone, anyone at all, for even a single day longer, continue to drive an SUV? For their drivers have to be aware that they are contributing to a crisis of epic proportions concerning the world's climate? On the face of things, what could be more disturbing than the possibility that they are helping to undermine the very basis of human civilization?

Giddens' questions strike directly at the heart of many of the problems society is facing in modern times. The underlying question goes far beyond the reach of sustainability: Why would anyone do something that is completely counter their own self-interest and well-being? Why do people smoke? Why do people choose not to exercise? Why do people choose to build houses in flood plains only to watch their lives be washed away by a flood that scientists (and politicians for that matter) know will come? There is no good answer, but it is an important human behaviour trait to consider when evaluating the factors that are preventing us from living an environmentally benign existence.

Historical causes

Major forces behind our most serious ecological problems, including global climate change, habitat loss and species extinctions, air and water pollution, food and water scarcity, concern historical developments that led to the present state of the world.

Industrial Revolution

The Industrial Revolution that many historians trace back to eighteenth century England caused major changes in agriculture, manufacturing, mining, and transportation as well as having a profound effect on socio-economic and cultural conditions. A number of interrelated changes were ushered in by the Industrial Revolution, including a rapid intensification in the use of materials and energy, especially fossil fuels, resulting in water and air pollution and soil contamination. The underlying assumption of early industrialists was that natural resources are unlimited and could be exploited for manufacturing products, subsequently bringing wealth to their manufacturers.

As we shall discuss in Chapter 5, some technological inventions have led to cleaner technologies, giving rise to ecological modernization theory. However, despite the availability of renewable energy technology such as PV panels and wind turbines, many countries continue to rely on fossil fuels. They are cheaper and the necessary equipment and infrastructure for extracting, processing, and distributing them is already well developed. Also, as the population and its demands grew, the benefits of efficient production were outstripped, as we shall discuss in Chapter 9.

Tragedy of the commons

One of the most common although disputed explanations for environmental problems is the so-called tragedy of the commons.

> The **tragedy of the commons** is defined as free access to and unrestricted demand for a finite resource that ultimately depletes it. The benefits of exploitation accrue to individuals, while the costs of the exploitation are borne by all those to whom the resource is available. This, in turn, causes demand for the resource to increase.

The rate of depletion of a common resource depends on three factors: the number of users, the intensity of the use, and the relative robustness of the common. The notion of the tragedy of the commons shows how it is possible that 'rational' individual actions can employ 'irrational' collective practices resulting in over-exploitation. While some scholars have disputed the notion of the tragedy of the commons, it is still widely used in relation to socio-economic causes of environmental degradation. Possible solutions to address the tragedy of the commons have been suggested, including privatization (such as the UN's Convention on the Law of the Sea, and Exclusive Economic Zones), and systems of governance to prevent damaging practices.

Political causes

In the neo-liberal climate of most countries, systems of governance need to be both democratic as well as stringent in the implementation of necessary measures. The willingness of political leaders to prioritize family planning policies that address population growth on the one hand and consumer-related policies that address unsustainable consumption on the other hand is of paramount importance.

In the Introduction we have noted the shift from a 'command and control' governmental regime toward corporate self-regulation. It is therefore extremely important that you, as a student of (sustainable) business, realize that the power lies in your hands. Understanding the political factors responsible for (un)sustainable practices is imperative for addressing the deeper challenges of sustainability identified in Chapter 9. One of the most hopeful political as well as corporate mechanisms is consumer choice editing, which denies consumers the chance to buy non-sustainable goods, and will be further discussed in Chapters 4 and 11.

Let us return to the issue of climate change. Ironically, the political paralysis evident at climate change summits illustrates how social justice may be impeding the process of 'global thinking' in search of viable solutions for all, as we shall further discuss in Chapter 9. *The Economist* (2013a) has argued that although global warming began with industrialized countries it must end – if it is to end – through actions in developing ones. Yet, poor nation-states fear that international agreements will limit their efforts to grow their economies and economically powerful nation-states refuse to make substantial reductions of their GHG emissions if developing countries do not make a similar sacrifice (Lidskog and Elander 2009).

The causes of climate change are deeply embedded in the socio-economic fabric of modern society and regulation of GHGs goes right to the heart of domestic policies, such as energy and transport policy. Thus, we live in a paradoxical situation where society increasingly recognizes the seriousness of climate change yet lacks the motivation to take the significant actions to slow, mitigate, or reverse the effects that are going to create major problems for us all (Lidskog and Elander 2009).

Historically, it has been government-imposed regulations and enforcement, inspections and penalties (command and control) that has prompted business and industry to change. Under this approach, governments set standards, such as establishing minimum levels of dissolved oxygen in rivers or maximum concentrations of N_2O in the air, and then set about enforcing these standards through regional and local agencies. However, such regulatory controls also have a number of problems.

To be effective, they require a well-resourced and powerful regulatory infrastructure to 'police' and enforce compliance with the legislation. Attempts to impose tighter regulations in one country have also encouraged industry to relocate to other, less-restrictive countries. Governments have been guilty of what is also known as a 'race to the bottom', decreasing business regulations or taxes in order to keep or attract businesses to their jurisdictions.

Also, due to the fact that the dangers posed by global warming are not tangible, immediate, or readily visible in the course of day-to-day life, many individuals, governments, and companies do not feel the need or urgency to take concrete actions in order to address or prevent the threat of climate change. Instead, the unspoken and potentially unintentional plan is to wait until the problems become too prevalent to ignore any longer and then be stirred to take action, when it will be far too late to prevent the immediate effects of climate change. This back-of-the-mind issue is due to 'future discounting' (Giddens 2009).

In sum, the failure to address climate change so far can be explained by six factors:

1   rich countries have exported some of the dirtier industrial operations to developing countries;
2   not all countries ratified the protocol;
3   some countries have failed to cut their emissions as promised;
4   businesses are not getting the correct signals from their respective governments;
5   fossil fuel-related industries still have sufficient money and power to dictate or override governmental regulations; and
6   developed and developing countries cannot agree on who needs to decouple economic development from environmental degradation by moving away from a fossil-fuel dependent economy.

These failures have a great bearing when considering competitiveness related to companies from different regulatory settings.

Lobbying

Democratic systems are not immune to power and political pressures. Despite overwhelming scientific evidence of anthropogenic climate change, 'climate sceptics' and 'climate deniers', sponsored by certain industrial lobbies that have a stake in maintaining high demand for fossil fuels and a strong interest in preventing the adoption of GHG emissions regulation, continue to dispute and attempt to undermine the science of climate change.

While industrial lobbyists have been lobbying governments since the 1950s, they now have to compete with the demands of mainstream environmental groups. The 'Green 10' (http://www.green10.org/), a group of the largest environmental organizations and networks at the European level, for example, laid down common rules for lobbying from the turn of this millennium.

Commodification of nature

Governments have increasingly shifted the onus of addressing environmental problems onto the private sector by using market-based mechanisms and often employing management vocabulary. Framing 'environment' as a 'common good' and putting a price on 'ecosystem services' or 'natural capital' became increasingly prominent in international political debates. With organizations like TEEB (see the TEEB case study at the end of this chapter), ecological preservation became a commercial matter, with the natural environment amounting to a set of tradable goods.

Mark Tercek, CEO of The Nature Conservancy and a former investment banker, along with science writer Jonathan Adams, argue that nature is not only the foundation of human well-being, but also the smartest commercial investment any business or government can make. Forests, floodplains, and oyster reefs, often seen simply as raw materials or as obstacles to be cleared in the name of progress, are, in fact, as important to our future prosperity as any technology or law or business innovation. The two authors inquire: Who invests in nature, and why? What rates of return can it produce? When is protecting nature a good investment? Arguing that organizations obviously depend on the environment for key resources, they can also reap substantial commercial benefits in the form of risk mitigation, cost reduction, new investment opportunities, and the protection of assets. Once leaders learn how to account for nature in financial terms, they can incorporate that value into the organization's decisions and activities, just as routinely as they consider cost and revenue (Tercek and Adams 2013).

Yet, the economic capture approach could be considered to be inadequate because it does not capture the expanse, nuances, and intricacies of many of the ecosystem services and emotional attachments to nature. Some scholars argue that 'all' biodiversity is needed in order to address human needs for clean water, clean air, and waste decomposition, due to the fact that complex ecological systems are required to provide all those services. Others argue that preservation of 'some' biodiversity would be sufficient to satisfy human needs. According to Unmuessig (2013), this is not to say that market-based mechanisms cannot contribute to environmental protection and restoration. They can (and they have), but only if they are part of a more comprehensive framework that accounts for the natural environment's true – and unquantifiable – value.

Figure 2.5 Leftovers (source: Engelbert Fellinger)

Ethical considerations

It is questionable whether an economic approach to nature is sufficient to protect the 'left over' species (Figure 2.5) not used for consumption, medical experimentation, companionship, or entertainment. To ensure protection of nature, biodiversity protection and animal rights may need to be integrated into policy, the way other forms of human rights and non-discrimination measures are currently embedded within national legal systems (Kopnina 2014a, 2014b)).

Environmental values

Philosophers, sociologists, and psychologists distinguish between different types of values in relation to the environment. Environmental values can range from anthropocentric (human-centred) to ecocentric or biocentric (ecosystem- or biosphere-centred).

> **Anthropocentrism** is the position that humans are more important or morally superior to most other species or the assessment of reality through an exclusively human perspective.

> **Ecocentrism** is a term used in environmental ethics to denote a nature-centred system of values. An ecocentric approach recognizes the intrinsic value of other species independent of human interests.

Box 2.1 UNEP ecosystems management

Ecosystem management is an approach to natural resource management that focuses on sustaining ecosystems to meet both future ecological and human needs. Ecosystem management is adaptive to changing needs and new information. It promotes a shared vision of a desired future by integrating social, environmental and economic perspectives for the management of geographically defined natural ecological systems. Ecosystems promote human well-being through the various services they provide. The UNEP Ecosystem Management Programme is centred on the functioning and resilience of ecosystems and the services they provide. The programme aims to support countries and regions to:

a   increasingly integrate an ecosystem management approach into development and planning processes;
b   acquire the capacity to use ecosystem management tools; and
c   realign their environmental programmes and financing to tackle the degradation of selected priority ecosystem services.

Source: http://www.unep.org/

Environmental philosopher Arno Naess (1973) has distinguished between 'shallow' and 'deep' ecology. Shallow ecology is anthropocentric and can be subdivided into self-interest and altruism concerns. Self-concerned individuals are worried about how air pollution affects their own lungs; altruistic individuals worry about the health of other people. Altruistic concerns include global health, addressing inequality and social justice, fair distribution of wealth, intergenerational justice, human rights, and the eradication of poverty. Shallow ecology is concerned with environmental risks and benefits, viewing species and habitats as 'resources', as in the case of livestock, fisheries, or fertile land. The intrinsic value of non-human species is rarely recognized and management of resources is limited to the protection of functionally useful areas used for extraction of raw materials, agriculture, urban parks, or ecotourism.

By contrast, deep ecology recognizes that humans are interconnected with nature, that biodiversity has intrinsic value, and that other species have a right to exist independent of human interests. Deep ecologists place humans within and not above the rest of the ecosystem. They value all lives and do not treat biodiversity as a 'resource'. This position is related to the *land ethic*, a philosophy developed by Aldo Leopold (1887–1948) that seeks to guide the actions when humans use or make changes to the land and to the animals and plants upon it. Since most members of an ecosystem have no economic worth, the dominant ethic can ignore or even eliminate these members when they are actually necessary for the health of the biotic community of the land. Dominant ethics (or the absence of ethics) tend to relegate conservation necessary for healthy ecosystems to the government and these tasks are too large to be adequately addressed by such an institution. Thus, true environmental sustainability requires an alternative environmental ethics based on respect for all living beings, as will be discussed in Chapter 7.

This has important implications for the project of economic development, in which plant and animal species are treated as natural resources that can bring wealth to less economically developed areas. According to the prominent anthropologist Veronica Strang (2013):

> There remains a thorny question as to whether anyone, advantaged or disadvantaged, has the right to prioritise their own interests to the extent that those of the non-human are deemed expendable. Discourses on justice for people often imply that the most disadvantaged groups should have special rights to redress long-term imbalances. Clearly there is a case to be made. However, if the result is only a short-term gain at the long-term expense of the non-human, this is in itself not a sustainable process for maintaining either social or environmental equity.

An even stronger position is emphasized in Box 2.2.

The position articulated above is more provocative than the conventional anthropocentric ethics as it embraces sustainability for all species, and far beyond the clever use of natural resources. More common in sustainability is the more moderate combination of anthropocentric and ecocentric concerns, as exemplified in Box 2.3.

Case studies

TEEB

In an interview with Yale Environment 360 editor Roger Cohn, Pavan Sukhdev, who heads international projects for TEEB, cited crucial benefits from nature that are often overlooked, including the capacity of wetlands for trapping and filtering water, the role of forests in preventing erosion and flooding, and the importance of bees in pollinating crops. 'When did the bees last send you an invoice for pollination?' he asks.

e360: How do you realistically get governments and businesses to think this way and to start acting this way? It's one thing to sit here and theoretically talk about it. How do you do that?

SUKHDEV: Well, we found in the TEEB project that there's actually a strong correlation between the persistence of poverty and the dying out of

Box 2.2 Environmental costs

Regarding the Earth as our resource-base embeds the reigning belief that the Earth is our property: humanity's commonwealth. The affiliated presumption is that the Earth can, and even should, be maximally populated by people, as long as the consequent exploitation of resources does not endanger people themselves. Because humans are spellbound by the idea that the Earth is our planetary real estate, cognitive and pragmatic activity is funneled into working with the plasticity of resources...Consider the ways. The resource base can be enlarged: for example, more land under the plough, more groundwater discovered, more oil and mineral reserves found, etc. The services of previously depleted or forsaken resources can be accessed through new or alternative ones: for example, biofuels, tar sands, wind energy, electric cars, artificial meat, hydroponics, etc. Resource-use efficiency can be intensified or revolutionized: for example, by eliminating food waste, dematerialization, recycling industries, etc. Resources can be technologically manipulated to amplify or prolong their productivity: for example, hydrofracking, genetic engineering of crops and animals, fish factory farms, genetically modified bacteria for mineral extraction, etc. And the pricey extraction or conversion of resources might eventually be made affordable: for example, desalinization, solar fuel cells, extraterrestrial mining, etc.

As long as such a 'resource enhancement portfolio' can be developed and implemented, then an increasing and eventually very large stable population might be supportable; maybe such a large population can even be provided with a high-consumption way of life...More serious than modern society's potential ability to technologically fix or muddle through problems of its own making is people's apparent willingness to live in an ecologically devastated world and to tolerate dead zones, endocrine disruptors, domestic animal torture (aka CAFOS [Concentrated Animal Feeding Operations]), and unnatural weather as unavoidable concomitants of modern living...

What is deeply repugnant about such a civilization is not its potential for self-annihilation, but its totalitarian conversion of the natural world into a domain of resources to serve a human supremacist way of life, and the consequent destruction of all the intrinsic wealth of its natural places, beings, and elements. 'Project Human Takeover' has proceeded acre by acre, island by island, region by region, and continent by continent, reaching its current global apogee with the final loss of wild places and the corollary sixth mass extinction underway.

Source: Crist (2012:148).

Box 2.3 The Earth Charter

Humanity is part of a vast, evolving universe. Earth, our home, is alive with a unique community of life. The forces of nature make existence a demanding and uncertain adventure, but Earth has provided the conditions essential to life's evolution. The resilience of the community of life and the well-being of humanity depend upon preserving a healthy biosphere with all its ecological systems, a rich variety of plants and animals, fertile soils, pure waters, and clean air. The global environment with its finite resources is a common concern of all peoples. The protection of Earth's vitality, diversity, and beauty is a sacred trust.

We urgently need a shared vision of basic values to provide an ethical foundation for the emerging world community. Therefore, together in hope we affirm the following interdependent principles for a sustainable way of life as a common standard by which the conduct of all individuals, organizations, businesses, governments, and transnational institutions is to be guided and assessed.

Source: http://www.earthcharterinaction.org/

nature. Typically we find that the people who suffer the most when you lose forest, or you lose wetlands, are actually the poor. I mean, the forest is not theirs, but the poor farmer is the one who suffers from the flood or the drought. If the forest is not there, then it's his goats and cattle who can't go in and forage for leaf litter. If the forest isn't there, it's his wife that has to walk an extra ten miles to get fuel wood for the cooking. So it's usually the poor farmer and the poor pastoralist who are the sufferers of loss of nature.

By various estimates, there's something like a billion to 1.2 billion people around the world who are still dependent on natural ecosystems for their survival. And we did economic projections for Brazil, India, and Indonesia and found that the costs of these ecosystem services are not huge if you compare them with the GDP of developed countries. But if you look at the poorest people, this is, like, 50 to 90 percent of their total livelihood income — all the stuff that comes to them free from nature. That's its real value. So once governments get that logic, then attitudes do change.

e360: What countries are those that have been receptive to what you've been saying in the TEEB reports?

SUKHDEV: Well, the ones who have actually sort of embraced the TEEB project, who actually started local implementations, are Brazil, India, and the rich ones you sort of expect — Norway, Germany, and the Scandinavian countries. And we are finding a very interesting set of developing countries like Georgia, where the president has just written us and the UN a letter saying, 'Can you please assist with a Georgia TEEB study?'... I mean, there are about 20-odd countries where there is an interest in taking this forward and basically working out nature values. And there are some developed countries where work is really pretty advanced, like the UK, for instance. They've done a complete ecosystem assessment.

e360: What about business? Has business been as receptive as government?

SUKHDEV: With business, it's a lot more difficult, because business is driven by profits. It has to be by law. It's about shareholder value. So you have to prove it on one of three counts. Either that they're missing out on risks which they've not recognized — for instance, if BP had thought about the ecological value at-risk concept [before the 2010 Gulf of Mexico oil spill], then they might have come to the view that these pressure-sealing, sound-sealing caps — which close immediately whenever there's a shock or a sound and are worth half a million dollars [apiece] — are actually a good investment. They're an insurance policy against a huge ecological value at risk.

So sometimes companies can get it right because they understand risk. Sometimes they get it right because they see an opportunity, as in there is a carbon market, or an eco-certification market, or an eco-labelling market, or there's a premium being paid on such and such. And sometimes it's that you will have to disclose these impacts eventually anyway [in public and shareholder documents].

e360: Can you give some of the examples besides BP and oil where a type of company or a specific company would have to factor in and disclose something like that?

SUKHDEV: Sure. Let's take a construction company, for instance, which is using logs or wood. Now if it's sourcing them sustainably, that's fine. It's probably worthwhile for them to disclose how little impact that has on ecosystems. But if it's sourcing its logs and wood unsustainably, you need to disclose the total of forest impact.

For example, we did a study of the entire construction sector in China between the years 1950 and 1990 using data from China — correlating the drawing of wood from China's forests and working out what was on the Chinese people in terms of loss of nutrient value, disruption due to floods and droughts, loss of waterway value, and things like that, which are basically a result of deforestation. To give you an example, in 1997, there was a severe drought. The Yellow River went dry for nine months. No water. Villages lost their entire livelihoods. 1998, a year later, the Yangtze floods, and 5,500 people die after a lot of destruction. During the period from 1950 to 1998, there was a huge amount of cost.

So we calculated what the costs would have been if you were a construction company in China — how much would the cost be? — and then we converted that into what would have been the real price of wood in China had you accounted for these costs? And lo and behold, the answer was 250 percent higher.

e360: Wow.

SUKHDEV: Another example is fresh water. Take the impact of the cotton industry in central Asia on fresh water and on the drying up of the Aral Sea, and the economics of that. There are many examples where at a company level, or at a sector level, you can calculate the impacts.

e360: A cynic might say that you actually in a sense devalue nature by putting a price on it because there's no way of calculating the intrinsic value in nature. How do you respond to that?

SUKHDEV: I respect that cynic, because that is a valid point and a genuine concern that's been bothering us literally from the beginning. The people who worked on the TEEB project all agree that the economic invisibility of nature is a problem. But we also all agree that there's a huge risk in blind monetization. And that's not what we're about. So when we talk about valuation, we see it as a human institution. And we know that there are societies, and there should be societies, that just value pristine nature because it's a connection. It's a spiritual connection.

In my country in India, there are sacred groves. Thousands, literally thousands of sacred groves where villages will just simply not touch that piece of forest. They will not allow it to be touched because, you know, it's their spirits and their ancestors and their deities that live there, and they're concerned. Now, what's the value of that sacred grove? Well, it's infinity, because you have to kill them before they let you cut it. So society has valued it, in a sense, at a spiritual level. That's valuation as well, right?

(Cohn, 2012)

Question

Discuss this excerpt from the interview. Do you agree with Sukhdev's position? Why or why not?

Marriott

Marriott hotel group received the highest ranking in the hotel sector from 2008–2012 on the Climate Counts company scorecard. Climate Counts is a nonprofit ratings organization that scores companies annually on their climate strategies and overall commitment to sustainability.

Marriott focuses their attention on five specific areas of environmental responsibility: 1. Energy, water and waste; 2. Supply chains; 3. Green hotels; 4. Engaging guests and associates; 5. Conservation. Marriott elaborates further on concrete environmental goals in its Corporate Responsibility Report:

- Further reduce energy and water consumption 20 percent by 2020;
- Empower our hotel development partners to build green hotels;
- Green our multi-billion dollar supply chain;
- Educate and inspire associates and guests to conserve and preserve; and
- Address environmental challenges through innovative conservation initiatives including rainforest protection and water conservation.

To mitigate the direct and indirect environmental impacts of their business operations, Marriott is investing in a portfolio of innovative conservation initiatives. In 2008, Marriott pledged $2 million in corporate funding to help preserve 1.4 million acres of rainforest in the Juma Reserve in the state of Amazonas, Brazil. Since then, we have raised an additional $170,000 for the Reserve through partners, promotions, and the contributions of our guests and associates. The Juma Reserve is the first Reduced Emissions from Deforestation and Degradation (REDD) initiative validated by the Climate, Community, and Biodiversity Alliance.

Question
Check online whether Marriott's pledge led to positive results.

Key terms

Anthropocene, anthropocentrism, biodiversity, climate change, development, ecocentrism, ecological justice, environmental certification, environmental impact assessment, environmental justice, Industrial Revolution, *Limits to Growth*, net positive impact, pollution, tragedy of the commons.

Discussion questions

1   What are the similarities between the Stern Report and TEEB? What do they value and seek to address?
2   Why do you think climate change is given more attention than biodiversity loss?
3   What are ecocentric people concerned about in regard to 'natural resources'? Do you think their concerns are justified?
4   What do you think are the greatest achievements of the Industrial Revolution? What do you think 'went wrong' after the Industrial Revolution?
5   Imagine an 'ideal future' for yourself and the environment. What would that be?
6   Describe different types of environment. Choose a company that claims to address environmental impacts. What type of environment do they address?

7   Consider Box 2.2. In this view, what is wrong with 'working with the plasticity of resources'?

End of chapter summary

This chapter introduced environmental concepts and challenges, questioning what we mean by the environment and distinguishing between environmental impacts. The chapter has addressed environmental problems such as climate change and loss of biodiversity, as well as industrial disasters. This chapter discussed the limits to growth, and ethical issues connected to preservation of natural resources. Finally, this chapter has discussed strategies of environmental management, including commodification of nature.

Further reading

Carson, R. (1962) *Silent Spring*. Boston, MA: Houghton Mifflin.
Stern, P. (2000) Toward a coherent theory of environmentally significant behavior. *Journal of Social Issues*, 56(3):407–424.
Tercek, M. and Adams, J. (2013) *Nature's Fortune: How Business and Society Thrive by Investing in Nature*. New York: Basic Books.

3 Social and economic challenges

Poverty

Before we address poverty, we need to ask a few essential questions. First, what is poverty? Second, what is the origin of poverty, or when and where did it start? Third, what is the relationship between poverty and sustainability? Answering the first question requires distinguishing between absolute poverty and relative poverty.

> **Absolute poverty** refers to the amount of money necessary to meet basic needs such as food, clothing, and shelter.

Economists and financial institutions such as the World Bank often seek to identify the families whose economic position (defined as command over resources) falls below some minimally acceptable level. As will be discussed in Chapters 7 and 10, low wages are a major indication of poverty. One of the MDGs is to eradicate extreme poverty and hunger, and the United Nations Development Programme (UNDP) seeks to halve, between 1990 and 2015, the proportion of people whose income is less than US$1 a day. By contrast, relative poverty, used by the United Nations Children's Fund (UNICEF) and the OECD, emphasizes the percentage of the population with an income less than some fixed proportion of the median in a given country. The Webster dictionary defines poverty as 'the state of one who lacks a usual or socially acceptable amount of money or material possessions'.

> **Relative poverty** is defined in relation to the economic status of other members of the society: people are poor if they fall below prevailing standards of living in a given societal context.

However, both of these concepts fail to recognize that beside income, individuals have important social and cultural needs. Hunter-gatherer societies, traditional tribes who barter and exchange goods and services or informal activities of the housewife, therefore fall outside the scope of GDP measurement. Also, the cash value of having a network of extended family to help with childcare, or of living in a place with clean water

Box 3.1 Sociological definitions of poverty

Rather than being interested in its measurement, sociologists generally study the reasons for poverty, such as the roles of culture, power, social structure and other factors largely out of the control of the individual. Accordingly, the multidimensional nature of poverty, in particular social aspects such as housing poor, health poor or time poor, needs to be understood in order to create more effective programs for poverty alleviation. Hypotheses that typically play a role in sociological theories of poverty are based on the idea that individuals are influenced by the physical and cultural context in which they live, and it gives importance to gender and household structure.

Today it is widely held that one cannot consider only the economic part of poverty. Poverty is also social, political and cultural. Moreover, it is considered to undermine human rights – economic (the right to work and have an adequate income), social (access to health care and education), political (freedom of thought, expression and association) and cultural (the right to maintain one's cultural identity and be involved in a community's cultural life).

Source: UNESCO

without the need to pay for 'ecosystem services' is not accounted for. By the monetary definition, a family living on their own farm in an idyllic valley in the Himalayas, with plenty of food, clothing, and a beautiful house, may be 'poorer' than a family working in sweatshops and living in a slum in Mumbai (see the What is poverty? case study at the end of this chapter).

Origins of poverty

The second question about the origin of poverty is even trickier. If we imagine our ancestors – in whatever country they have come from – from 'cavemen' origins to agrarian development, and up to the time when money became widely used, we may ask ourselves whether we can speak of our ancestors as poor, at least in terms of absolute poverty. From time immemorial social stratification is part and parcel of any human society. If we assume that a certain percentage of any population will remain poor due to various individual and social factors, the larger the absolute population, the more – in absolute numbers – poor people there will be. This implies that the objective of 'ending poverty' without addressing population growth is no more than an empty slogan.

Poverty and sustainability

The relationship between poverty and sustainability is complex. On the one hand, it is believed that poverty causes environmental degradation. Many parts of the world are caught in a vicious downward spiral where poor people are forced to overuse environmental resources to survive from day to day and the impoverishment of their environment further impoverishes them. According to Jennifer Elliot (2013:94), the author of *An Introduction to Sustainable Development*, the poor are both victims and unwilling agents of environmental degradation. Living in poverty can restrict the options for resource management, pushing the poor to cultivate marginal lands or remove woodlands in order to sustain themselves in the short term, with detrimental effects for their own longer-term livelihoods. The type of poverty known in the contemporary world, and particularly the scale of its spread, is unprecedented in human history. Some believe that economic development can lift people out of poverty; others believe that Western-style development has caused poverty in the first place.

Development

Various terms associated with economic development came about as means of measuring well-being, such as per capita income, GDP, gross national product (GNP), unemployment rate, literacy rate, and many more. Development has often been identified as one of the key goals of sustainability. However, as discussed in Chapter 5, its aims are often disputed.

* As noted by John Bodley (1998), the social advantages of development defined in terms of higher standards of living, greater security, and better health are thought to be positive, universal goods, to be obtained at any price. In practice, however, many traditional societies have become the 'losers' of modernization. People in developing countries feel deprivation not only when the economic goals they have been encouraged to seek fail to materialize, but also when they discover that they are powerless, second-class citizens who are discriminated against and exploited by the dominant elites (Figure 3.1).

Yet, the potential of turning all 7 billion people currently inhabiting our planet into the 'winners' of development can spell the collapse of our planet's carrying capacity. According to Peter Nemetz, the author of *Business and the Sustainability Challenge* (2013:36–38), if the alternative path to economic development cannot be found, raising the standard of the living for developing countries' people will have potentially catastrophic impacts on the global ecosystem. It is questionable whether human equality and prosperity as well as population growth can be achieved with the present rate of natural degradation. The current emphasis on economic growth is simply inherently unsustainable. The communication of the International Development Research Center reflects on these concerns by asserting that many of the development paths followed by the industrialized countries of

Figure 3.1 Do they welcome development? (source: Helen Kopnina)

the North are not viable. Simultaneously, there is a moral imperative for the economies of the South to continue to grow to redress some of the disparities between South and North.

Development and poverty

Some observers believe that eliminating poverty will lead to sustainability, as exemplified in the case of the ecological modernization theory, the EKC hypothesis (Introduction) and post-material values hypothesis. The first two theories postulate that during early industrialization, economies use material resources more intensively, until a threshold is reached after which structural changes in the economy lead to progressively less-intensive materials use. The post-material values hypothesis states that only wealthier societies can 'afford' to care about the environment (Inglehart 1977). Thus, it is believed that prosperity would simultaneously create the means of addressing environmental problems and poverty through global economic development. The problems inherent in these theories will be discussed in Chapter 5 and 9.

 ### Inequality and development

Critics of top-down development projects have noted that foreign aid, and structural adjustment programmes may have caused more harm than good

in exacerbating global inequalities and have largely failed in ad/
ecological crises. Another critique is that the very term 'developn..
largely paternalistic, as it implies that some countries (particularly the sc
called Global North or 'West') are more 'developed' or 'progressive' than
others. This critique stems from the moral rejection of colonialism and
imperialism. Colonialism began when a few European powers (particularly
England, Spain, France, Portugal, and The Netherlands) established colonies
in Mid-America, Asia and Africa between 1400 and the 1970s. Former
colonies established independence from colonial powers after World Wars I
and II, yet the influence of imperialist hegemony may still be present.

Post-colonialism and neo-colonialism

In the post-colonial decades, the social, economic, and cultural domination
praxis of formerly colonized countries shifted.

Post-colonialism signifies the shift in power and trade relations,
characterized by international development programmes and labour
migration. Post-colonialism examines the manner in which emerging
societies grapple with the challenges of self-determination in relation to
Western norms and conventions, such as legal or political systems, left in
place after direct administration by colonial powers ended.

According to the dependency theory, wealthy countries continue to exploit
poor countries through foreign debt and disadvantageous trade. Economist
William Easterly (2006) has brought into doubt whether poverty is helped
by economic development, since development aid places many post-colonial
nations into positions of dependency.

Neo-colonialism refers to an unequal economic and political power
between former colonial powers and former colonies, and continuous
influence of developed over developing countries. Neo-colonialism is
the geopolitical practice of using capitalism, business globalization, and
cultural imperialism to influence a country, in lieu of either direct military
control or indirect political control.

Globalization of democracy and liberal values, including universal access
to education, has not been uncontested. As we shall discuss further in Chapter
4, critical thinkers examine the hidden assumption of cultural superiority
behind development aid projects, and particularly education, which overtly
aim to help children escape to a 'better life', implicitly suggesting that the
'old ways' have no valuable lessons.

Often, criticism of development contains scepticism as to the motives of
the involvement of MNCs in the developing country, with the suspicion that
the good intentions of foreign aid and 'helping the poor' mask continuous
exploitation of the natural resources, and of 'human capital'. Western

hegemony imposes its own version of 'equality', propelled by underlying economic reasoning necessitating the need to 'harmonize global markets' on the one hand, and the need to sate the post-colonial guilt by 'doing good deeds'. At best, as some critics like the well-known philosopher Slavoj Zizek argue, these efforts are the result of ignorance, and at worst, the result of cunning selfishness in the world driven by desire for profit. After all, large population promises endless expansion of the market and cheap labour. Child labour, child prostitution, and child soldiers are a direct effect of unwanted pregnancies and the side effect of development that disrupts systems of social control and traditional forms of family support.

Population growth

One of the positive aspects of economic development is advances in medical and food production technologies, which have enabled many children born today to survive into maturity. Despite unprecedented losses of lives during the two world wars and genocide in countries such as Cambodia and Rwanda that cost millions of people their lives in the previous century, and despite relatively high child mortality rates in poorer counties, the human population has continued rising and reached 7 billion in 2012. After the initial depopulation suffered during colonialism in developing countries, most populations began to experience rapid growth. Consider the numbers in Box 3.2

However, population growth and decline are not evenly spread throughout the world. Between 85 and 90 per cent of growth occurs in developing countries. The average number of children in Niger is 7.5 per woman; in Europe it is 2.1 per woman. By 2050, the human population is projected to reach as high as 10.5 billion, with Uganda growing from 33.8 million to 91.3 million; Niger from 16 million to 58 million; and Afghanistan from 29 million to 73 million.

There are many ways of looking at population growth. One of them was discussed in the eighteenth century by Thomas Malthus (1766–1834).

Box 3.2 Population growth

1800 – 1 billion people
1900 – 2 billion
1930 – 3 billion
1945 – 4 billion
1970 – 6 billion
2050 – 9 billion (US Census) as high as 11 billion (IIASA)

Sources: Census, IIASA

Malthus predicted that human population increases geometrically and, if unchecked, would lead to starvation. Malthus also argued that there are preventative checks such as war and disease. From the time of publication of *An Essay on the Principles of Population* by Thomas Malthus in 1798, a forced return to subsistence-level conditions once population growth had outpaced food production was predicted. Malthus (1826: 61) wrote: 'The power of population is so superior to the power of the earth to produce subsistence for man, that premature death must in some shape or other visit the human race.' The dire predictions of Malthus that included 'the great army of destruction', the 'war of extermination, sickly seasons, epidemics, pestilence, and plague advance in terrific array' as well as 'gigantic inevitable famine', aside from some areas of the world, have not struck yet. A more contemporary book, *The Population Bomb* by Paul Ehrlich (1968), re-ignited heated debates about neo-Malthusian predictions.

However, as critics have pointed out, Malthus has not considered human ingenuity, food production, technological innovation, and medical technology. Malthus, who believed that population was restricted to available resources, could not predict the technological developments that allowed humans to keep pace with population growth. Before the twentieth century, the populations of most developed countries grew slowly enough to be outpaced by gains in productivity, but with the introduction of medical technologies that wiped out many human scourges, and advanced food technologies, the population has plummeted.

Recent publications by the World Bank and many development agencies praised human ingenuity in overthrowing Malthusian doom and gloom scenarios. As Martha Campbell asserts, '"Malthusian" and even "demographic" became derogatory terms describing anybody still concerned about population growth' (2012: 46). In breaking the long silence on population, Wijkman and Rockström (2012) state:

> Some people claim that the size of the world population has no importance for sustainability because of the low-resource and carbon footprints of the poor. While such an argument may be valid in a short-term perspective…it totally misses the point in the longer term. All people born on this planet have the right to decent living conditions.

Thus if all people on this planet were to survive into adulthood and live wealthy lives (as most of us would undoubtedly wish for others), securing natural resources – let along protecting non-human species – might become an insurmountable challenge. The biggest gains from significantly lower birth rates then would be the combination of a better quality of life for both women and children and a greater potential for stabilizing the climate (Wijkman and Rockström 2012: 82–84).

Causes of population growth

Aside from better health and food production technologies, other factors effecting population growth are relative peace; the lack of political initiatives to curb population growth such as one-child policy in China; and a sharp decrease in funding for family planning and contraception in the developing countries. According to UNFPA, the United Nations Population Fund, at least 200 million women want to use safe and effective family planning methods, but are unable to do so because they lack access to information and services or the support of their husbands and communities. The need for voluntary family planning is growing fast, and it is estimated that the 'unmet need' will grow by 40 per cent during the next 15 years. But even though it is an economically sound investment, family planning has been losing ground as an international development priority. Funding is decreasing, and the gap between the need and the available resources is growing. The international community has agreed that reproductive choice is a basic human right. But without access to relevant information and high-quality services, that right cannot be exercised.

As Bodley (1998) notes, authorities attribute this growth to the introduction of new health measures and food production technologies and the termination of intertribal warfare, which lowered morality rates. Additionally, what is more significant for understanding why fertility in some countries has not gone down, most tribal areas have experienced the loss of traditional birth spacing and contraceptive mechanisms. This change was partially influenced by Christian missionaries and 'developers' who promulgated that the traditional way of life was inferior to modern lifestyles. It was also speculated that in some areas cultural beliefs, such as seeing large families as a sign of wealth, is responsible for continuous population growth. The natural and cultural checks on population growth have suddenly been pushed aside by culture change, while consumption levels have risen. In many tribal areas, environmental deterioration due to overuse of resources has set in, and in other areas such deterioration is imminent as resources continue to dwindle relative to the expanding population and increased use (Bodley 1998:149).

Also, cultural and religious practices prevent women in some countries from taking control over their own reproduction. Last but not least the dominant 'endless growth' paradigms of countries like Canada, America, Australia, and even Europe maintain a death grip on any discussion of overpopulation. While birth rates fall, the sheer number of humans causes growth, due to 'population momentum'. Anti-abortion activists, religious leaders, and conservative think tanks and those interested in the expansion of the market have intentionally reduced attention to population growth. Even after the Cairo Population conference and the Earth Summit, there is still not enough financing of family planning programmes on a global level.

Demographic transition theory

The so-called demographic transition theory indicates that the present rate of population growth is likely to stabilize.

> **Demographic transition** is the process by which a country moves from high birth and high death rates to low birth and low death rates.

According to this theory, Stage One of population growth before the Industrial Revolution can be characterized as 'Malthusian', as it is characterized by both high birth and high death rates, producing a low and stable population. The industrial Stage Two involves a decline in death rates and thus the increasing survival of children, leading to the population becoming increasingly youthful. At this stage, an increasing number of children enter into reproduction while maintaining the high fertility rate of their parents.

Stage Three, often referred to as a post-industrial phase, is predicted to occur this century, and moves the population towards stability through a decline in both death and birth rates. The decline in birth rates in developed countries began towards the end of the nineteenth century in northern Europe and is associated with the higher use of contraception, and women's right to reproductive choices. Studies have proven that higher educational attainment is usually negatively correlated with the number of children. This shift is attributed to improvement in socio-economic conditions which change child survival rate and fertility preferences, producing a return to low or stable population rates. Investment in contraception, education, and change in cultural perceptions is a crucial opportunity for sustainability investment.

Technology: from failure to control?

Capitalism, an economic system in which the means of production are mostly privately owned and operated for profit, meant that distribution, income, production, and pricing of goods and services were determined through the operation of a market economy. While Karl Marx argued that conditions of the workers in factories will worsen to a degree to halt capitalism through a proletariat revolution, many industrializing countries have actually witnessed improved productivity through better technologies as well as improvement in working conditions and the emergence of the welfare state. As will be discussed in Chapters 7 and 10, globally there are still plenty of 'bad' jobs and exploitation especially in the countries of the Global South. Technology, as well as increased population, has also led to deskilling, precarious employment, underemployment, and unemployment. The manufacture of cheap products has further led to the increase in the material life standard of the workers. There have been other benefits that have accompanied the rise of capitalism in the wake of the Industrial Revolution. No other system has been capable of widespread wealth generation; technological developments have enabled scientific progress. Further, medical and agricultural technologies have improved, ensuring that some people became wealthier and healthier.

Health: medical technology

One of the greatest inventions of the nineteenth century has been antibiotics, which has rid most parts of the world of diseases that used to wipe out entire populations, such as cholera, plague, and tuberculosis. The treatments for many infectious diseases such as measles became more efficient and their prevalence has radically declined, particularly in the Western world. However, other diseases are still considered to be largely incurable, such as cancer, HIV/AIDS, and malaria, although patients can survive into old age if the correct treatments are used. The prevalence of certain chronic diseases has changed due to better diagnostic and treatment technologies on the one hand and environmental factors (such as pollution or changing lifestyles) on the other hand. According to the World Health Organization (WHO), due to the greying population and the increased welfare of Western society, other diseases, such as Alzheimer's, asthma, cancer, diabetes, and obesity, have increased.

In developing countries, the scale and distribution of diseases as well as the availability of medication and expertise have changed significantly. Lung and skin diseases have increased due to higher pollution levels. Thus, while some diseases became relegated to the poorer parts of the world (such as cholera, tuberculosis, and, for a large part, AIDS), others became designated as the 'rich countries' diseases' (such as obesity). However, the rich country' diseases can also be found elsewhere in the world as welfare spreads and globalization slowly erases developed and developing country distinctions.

There has been a general shift across the world towards the greater use of Western medicine, while the prevalence of indigenous medical knowledge has reduced. Still, medical technologies' access is spread unevenly, and many people in developing countries have limited access to medicines and equipment. Big pharmaceutical companies have been blamed for preventing cheaper drugs from being distributed.

Agriculture: the Green Revolution

The basic components of the Green Revolution include increased crop yields through the use of mechanical irrigation, systematic application of fertilizers and pesticides, the mechanization of agricultural processes, and, more recently, genetic manipulation. The Green Revolution stimulated growth in the agricultural technology that had begun to expand following World War II.

> Green Revolution refers to the programmes of agricultural research funded by international agencies and sponsors that allowed food production to keep pace with population growth.

These technological developments, led by Norman Borlaug, the 'Father of the Green Revolution', involved the development of high-yielding, fast-growing, and disease resistant varieties of cereal grains, expansion of irrigation infrastructure, modernization of management techniques, and the distribution of hybridized seeds, synthetic fertilizers, and pesticides to farmers. This system relied on high energy-intense machinery such as tractors and irrigation pumps, and increased reliance on monocultures. Triggered by Borlaug's work at the International Maize and Wheat Improvement Center in Mexico, the Green Revolution was based on intensive chemical inputs. Borlaug's work led to Mexico's self-sufficiency in wheat production in the 1950s. By 1964 Mexico had become one of the major exporters of wheat in the region. Following this success, Pakistan became self-sufficient by 1968 and India by 1974. The Green Revolution has allowed food production to keep pace with population growth, and Borlaug was credited with saving over a billion people from starvation.

At present, many other agricultural technologies are fully deployed, such as GM crops, which have taken the idea of efficiency in food production to a new level, and created an enormous surplus of production in some areas (Figure 3.2). However, while many Western consumers are familiar with this surplus and the enormous waste created by it, the distribution of food is not spread evenly throughout the world, due to some of the socio-political factors mentioned above.

Nemetz (2013:36–38) has stressed at least two major factors associated with agriculture and its devastating environmental impact: deforestation and irrigation. While already present in pre-industrial times, deforestation and irrigation has become a critical issue today, with immense implications not only directly for global agriculture, but also indirectly for global warming. Additional costs include land degradation, groundwater contamination, and social dislocation due to displacement of small landowners, as well as costs associated with the production of pesticides and commercial energy products (Nemetz 2013:29). In addition to these factors, the global industry of harmful agricultural chemicals has emerged.

According to environmental health specialist Stephen Zavestoski (2010), companies in the agricultural chemicals sector had all the stars aligned for them when it came to the creation of new markets for their products in developing countries. The World Bank and the US Agency for International Development made loans dependent on farmers embracing the new agricultural methods. Between 1960s and 1980s, India has increased its imports of fertilizer by 600 per cent. As mentioned in Chapter 2, Union Carbide in Bhopal, who manufactured pesticides ignoring health and safety concerns, caused one of the world's worst industrial disasters.

Eventually, more people were exposed to the risks of chemical hazards, leading to the formation of global environmental health movements, and consumer protection organizations. These movements had a large effect on the way companies function as they drew connections between industrial

Figure 3.2 Agriculture (source: Engelbert Fellinger)

practices and health consequences, opening up a contentious political debate by challenging our chemical dependency, reckless use of radiation, gas-guzzling and particulate-emitting vehicles, and GM organisms. In linking ill health to corporate industrial practices, the environmental health movement challenged 'agribusiness, the chemical industry, auto production, energy companies, garbage disposal firms, and many other large sectors of the economy' (Brown 2002: 8).

However, the global environmental movement has not necessarily affected the developing countries' desire to catch up with developed countries' level of economic growth. Mattoo and Subramanian (2013) suggest that the fairest approach from an economic equity point of view would be to allow developing countries to follow the unsustainable model of Western development. However, climate change will affect developing countries more than rich ones, because of their tropical and subtropical lands. One estimate by William Cline, an economist, found that a rise of 2.5 per cent in global temperatures would cut agricultural productivity by 6 per cent in America but by 38 per cent in India (*The Economist* 2013a). This leads to a certain paradox, discussed in the case study Who is the victim of climate change? below.

Manufacturing: Fordism and post-Fordism

Henry Ford, who founded the Ford Motor Company in 1903, became famous by improving the working conditions of his factory workers. He aspired to make the car which was affordable for everybody, so low in price so that everybody would be able to own one and 'enjoy with his family the

Box 3.3 US and European subsidies

In developing countries in Africa and elsewhere, many go hungry. U.S. and European subsidies depress prices, undermining world agriculture.

For more than half a century, developed countries in the West have systematically and egregiously distorted the global production and trade of agricultural commodities through an elaborate range of domestic and export subsidies. It is naive to believe that distortions perpetuated for so long will now be swept under the carpet using the excuse of 'the hunger crisis.' Let's get some facts straight.

First, it is indisputable that the lavish farm subsidies provided by the U.S. and the European Union to their farmers distort global production and trade. These subsidies artificially depress prices, encourage inefficient producers (in the U.S. and EU) and discourage competitive producers (in the developing countries). Just look at the impact of subsidies on cotton. Some of the most competitive producers are countries in West Africa. They receive a pittance as the price for cotton because of the huge subsidies to a handful of farmers in the U.S. And exactly the same argument holds good for a host of other agricultural commodities—rice, wheat, soybeans, corn, pulses, sugar, dairy products, and so on. The bottom line: Subsidies shift production away from efficient developing countries to inefficient developed countries.

Source: Noth (2008)

blessing of hours of pleasure in God's great open spaces'. Ford's car factories became a popular symbol of the transformation to mass production and a mass consumption economy, in which anything from textiles to consumer electronics became affordable and widely available to the emergent class of 'global consumers'.

Fordism refers to production efficiency dependent on successful assembly-line methods. Fordism came to signify the mass production of affordable consumer goods. Fordism is a manufacturing philosophy that aims to achieve higher productivity by standardizing the output, using conveyor assembly lines, and breaking the work into small deskilled tasks.

Innovations in machine tools and gauging systems made possible the substitution of heavy manual labour and continuous assembly lines for mechanized efficient production. The cars – and other commodities – have indeed entered the global space by the millions. 'God's great open spaces' have shrunk as the dream of freedom on four wheels got stuck in the long traffic jams in the world capitals, causing traffic accidents, toxic emissions, and destruction of huge areas cleared to serve as roads and parking lots.

In Britain, the late Prime Minister Margaret Thatcher once said that anyone who at thirty still travels on a bus is failure, the social-status image that automobile industry is all too happy to promote. In the US, public transportation systems in the nineteenth century in most cities employed streetcar systems that provided important public transportation services to densely populated cities. A post-war phenomenon in the US witnessed the 'American Dream' driving the growing white middle class to move outside the city core to new suburbs with garages and yards. By some accounts, Ford and General Motors (GM) encouraged the 'white flight' to the suburbs and the demise of the streetcar systems in favour of private vehicles. Ford and GM bought up streetcars and railroad track to hasten this demise. This post-war suburban growth, the demise of the streetcar system, and failed attempts over the last decades to get a referendum on rail-based comprehensive public transportation system became commonplace in most of the American states. Possibly through calculated marketing efforts, public transport use became associated with poverty (Figure 3.3).

Economies of scale were produced by exploiting the division of labour – sequentially combining specialized functional units, especially overheads such as reporting, accounting, personnel, purchasing, or quality assurance, in multifarious ways so that it was less costly to produce several products than a single specialized one. Despite recent calls for responsible consumption, global consumption rates have been rising ever since and the market has expanded, giving rise to giant corporations built upon functional specialization and often hierarchical division of labour. Some observers believe that this is one of the key mechanisms that produces the present-day inequalities, as cheap labour is often equated to cheap production, greater consumption, and greater profits. Social trends of the past decades, including migration, trafficking, and indentured labour make the question of global equality all the more difficult to address.

The 1960s witnessed the internationalization of trade, and the rise of MNCs not only as economic but as political powers. The post-World War II period witnessed financial market stabilization supported by the IMF and the World Bank, with the power of both institutions soon expanding into global arenas and affecting patterns of investment everywhere. Investment in physical capital (such as commercial buildings, machinery) as well as human capital (such as education) increased, and so did investment in development projects in post-colonial countries. These two capitals were utilized in the organization of production lines and ever larger volumes of output, thereby reducing the unit costs of production.

Post-Fordism is characterized by transition from industry to services to 'experience economy'; the globalization of financial markets; and increases in global trade and exploitation of natural resources. This could be an opportunity for 'dematerialization', when consumers focus on consuming

Figure 3.3 Bike promotion misfiring (source: Helen Kopnina)

experiences, such as travel and different cultures, and sharing products, rather than simply owning products. Part of this experience relates to different means of consumption such as the Cloud to swap information rather than owning films or music as discussed in Chapters 4 and 10. Post-Fordism also signified a turn to 'just in time' production, employment, and outsourcing.

Technology: energy

Energy has been literally firing up social and economic developments since the Industrial Revolution. Certain types of energy, especially those associated with fossil fuels, have proved out to be both lucrative and controversial, as far as sustainability and social responsibility is concerned. Nuclear energy, for example, proved to be unsafe in certain conditions. The energy mix (Figure 3.4) of many advanced industrial countries like The Netherlands still relies on over 90 per cent fossil fuels.

Also, increasing demand for energy, spurred on by the population growth in developing countries on the one hand and the high levels of energy consumption of developed countries on the other hand, have resulted both in higher consumption and higher wastefulness. The developed world's habits have been eagerly imitated by the growing middle classes in the developing countries. Gwyn Prins of Cambridge University called the 'physical addiction' to cooled air in America the 'most pervasive and least noticed epidemic' (*The Economist* 2013b). Anthropologists David Casagrande and Charles Peters (2013) use an example of Phoenix, Arizona, where politicians and corporations promote the myopic consensus that metropolitan Phoenix is an oasis in the desert, that unbounded economic growth is sustainable, and that increasing demands for water and cooling can be met by more efficient use of existing resources. Publicly questioning any of these beliefs, or suggesting that federal intervention in decision making is needed, is taboo.

The rising incomes in poor countries are associated with American-style spending on air conditioning, with global warming further stoking the demand for even more air conditioning. In the Gulf, the formerly uninhibited southern littoral area is 'rimmed by the mirrored facades of office towers, gleaming petrochemical works, marinas, highways, bustling airports, vast shopping malls and sprawling subdivisions of sumptuous villas, it is home to 20 million people' (*The Economist* 2013b: 41).

Another example is biofuels. While the UK and other EU countries have heavily invested into biofuels, it appears that biofuel crops increase emissions through land clearance, fertilizer use, and by displacing other crops. When millions of hectares of land are switched from food to biofuel crops, food prices rise and food production is displaced, triggering a domino-like chain of events ending in cropland expansion elsewhere, including into the tropical forests of Southeast Asia and the savannas of South America and Africa (Phalan 2013). Displacement of productive lands for growing food implies that while production of some kinds of energy

Figure 3.4 Energy mix (source: Helen Kopnina)

can keep up with the rising numbers and needs of human population, the long-term productive capacity of land used for food production – let alone survival of non-human species – continues to be in decline. Most observers agree that this century also brought the best alternatives, particularly the 'true renewables', such as sun and wind energy. The reasons for singling out these two as the most sustainable will be elaborated upon in Part IV on Solutions.

Business responses

In response to social, economic, and technological challenges businesses have developed many strategies for addressing their responsibility. The most common way of doing so is managing the triple bottom line – a process by which companies manage their financial, social and environmental risks, obligations and opportunities. Business sustainability is intimately linked to social resilience to sustainability challenges over time as businesses' operations are intimately connected to healthy economic, social, and environmental systems. Businesses will simply fail to create economic value if the health and resilience of communities is compromised. Thus, business responses to social and economic challenges are interlinked with the notions of sustainable development, as will be further explored in Chapter 5.

Case studies

What is poverty?

Many people believe that education is the key to solving the problem of poverty in the 'developing' world. The World Bank defines 'poverty' as the condition of living on less than two dollars a day. Figures 3.5 and 3.6 are two images of children from families living on less than two dollars a day.

Questions

1   What do these pictures tell us about cash income as a measure of quality of life in the 'developing' world?
2   When we hear that education has raised someone's income level, what else do we need to know in order to evaluate whether this has been a net benefit?
3   The makers of the film *Schooling the World* have asked the World Bank how it accounts for the cash value of having a network of grandparents and aunts and cousins to help with childcare, for example, or of living in a place with clean water, clean air, and a beautiful natural environment. The honest answer from the Bank was that it simply doesn't account for

Figure 3.5 Poverty 1 (source: Jim Hurst, copyright/permission from Schooling the World)

those things. So from the standpoint of the World Bank, a family living on their own farm in an idyllic valley in the Himalayas, with plenty of food, clothing, and a beautiful house, may be 'poorer' than a family working in sweatshops and living in a slum in Mumbai. What is wrong with this view of poverty? What other factors should be accounted for to create a true assessment of quality of life?

4   When people rely on traditional subsistence livelihoods, living on their own land, using their own local resources for food, housing, and clothing, are they more or less comfortable and secure than when they rely on money and jobs in the modern economy? What are the benefits and risks of these two options?

Who is the victim of climate change?

In January 2014 the World Economic Forum declared that one of the key risks stalking the world is a renewed round of environmental shocks due to climate change. Reflecting on the Forum's declaration, Gillian Tett, a journalist from the *Financial Times*, wrote an article, 'Climate change and the V-word'.

> But as those Davos luminaries ponder the problem of climate change they should take a peek at a thought-provoking piece of research conducted by David McDermott Hughes, an anthropologist at Rutgers University. Five years ago, he travelled to Trinidad and Tobago to analyse how the chattering classes of that small island country discussed environmental problems in their national political debate and overseas dealings. Unsurprisingly, he found that the Caribbean state was deeply

Figure 3.6 Poverty 2 (source: Jim Hurst, copyright/permission from Schooling the World)

concerned about climate change. Trinidad and Tobago is surrounded by vast, capricious oceans and, in recent years, has suffered from hurricanes, droughts and fires. Since the islands are low-lying, there is also particular concern about the prospect of rising sea levels if, say, the polar ice caps were to melt.

When Hughes listened to the local debates, he noticed that the politicians repeatedly referred to themselves as 'victims' of global warming. The assumption was that the Caribbean nation was being harmed by the reckless climate abuse of other wealthier countries, particularly in the 'north' (ie the US and Europe).

But there is an irony here: Trinidad and Tobago is not just a passive victim of climate change but a perpetrator too. Most notably, the nation has offshore oil rigs and ranks 38th in the world in terms of oil production, producing more than Bahrain and Ecuador combined. In terms of carbon emissions per capita, the nation was the fourth worst offender in the world. However, this second point, Hughes discovered, was almost never explicitly acknowledged by politicians; instead, climate change was invariably discussed as something being imposed from beyond. That V-word – 'victimhood' – dominated the debate.

In the global scheme of things, this example might seem trivial. And since Trinidad and Tobago is poor, its local population certainly has reasons to feel aggrieved about the behaviour of wealthier countries over many issues, including the environment. But what is perhaps most interesting is that it is not just Caribbean nations that talk about victimhood in relation to climate change; on the contrary, if you analyse how the European and US media cover extreme weather events on their own shores, that V-word keeps appearing...

When Hurricane Sandy hit, families living on the US east coast were described as victims of climate change; so too during the recent UK floods. Environmental change is presented as something we all suffer passively, rather than actively influence. And that, in turn, illustrates a bigger question relating to the word 'victim', and the degree to which it has become a convenient cultural category in modern policy debates, both in the west and emerging markets.

(Tett 2014)

Question

Who do you think are the 'true' victims of climate change, and who are perpetuators?

Key terms

Absolute poverty, demographic transition theory, development, energy technology, Fordism, Green Revolution, inequality, medical technology, neo-colonialism, population growth, post-colonialism, post-Fordism, relative poverty.

Discussion questions

1 What does the occurrence of absolute poverty tell us about the progress of economic development?
2 What are the limitations of the definition of absolute poverty? What other factors should be accounted for to create a true assessment of quality of life?
3 Some people refer to economic development as neo-colonialism. Do you agree? Why or why not?
4 What are the positive and negative aspects of the Green Revolution?
5 Look up statistics for European consumption on the Internet. Do you think the global population can be sustained in the long term if the present level of European-style consumption is to continue?
6 What do you think is more realistically achievable: curbing consumption in the countries already used to the high level of consumption or stabilizing global population? What measures do you think are needed to achieve both of these objectives?

End of chapter summary

This chapter has focused on social and economic challenges, discussing poverty, and exploring the relationship between development and inequality. The chapter has explored the role of political and corporate elites in the process of economic development and addressed a number of causes of unsustainability, such as the consequences of the Industrial Revolution, and developments in the fields of manufacturing, and medical and agricultural technology. Finally, this chapter explored the consequences of the post-Fordist system of production with its associated patterns of consumption and population growth as the leading factors in the current unsustainability.

Further reading

Easterly, W. (2006) *The White Man's Burden: Why the West's Efforts to Aid the Rest Have Done So Much Ill and So Little Good*. New York: The Penguin Group, Inc.

Elliott, J. (2013) *An Introduction to Sustainable Development*. New York: Routledge.

Part II

Globalization, development, and business

4 Sustainability and globalization

What is meant by globalization?

Globalization is a force that shapes our contemporary world, affecting business, environment, and society. Suppliers, corporations, and consumers are linked by information, material, and capital flows as production processes become increasingly dispersed around the globe. Globalization is subject to intensive theoretical debate in contemporary socio-economic theory. The reason why it is important to talk about globalization in the context of environmental sustainability is that while over-exploitation and environmental degradation are relatively local or national in scale, they are experienced in such a large number of localities that they can be considered global. Likewise, in the context of social sustainability, notwithstanding differences in scale, issues associated with poverty, inequality, and intergenerational concerns manifest global patterns.

Recent environmental problems, such as the loss of biodiversity or pollution, are a global or 'universal' phenomenon, rather than restricted to certain cultures, societies, or countries. In the words of psychologist Peter Kahn, in fostering the human relationship with nature, we need to pay attention not only to nature but to human nature. It is helpful to distinguish between constant or universal features of human interaction with the environment, as well as 'cultural variance' factors. Universal forms are comprised of features of culture, society, language, behaviour, and psyche for which there are no significant exceptions within the cross-cultural perspective. These so-called universals are certainly not set in stone – they are rather tendencies, capabilities and propensities, which could be broadly generalized to humans. Certain capacities, such as our technical aptitude (and by implication, ability to create – and destroy – our own environment) are salient features that act in aggregate with the structural characteristics of modernity.

Perhaps we can start by asking: what is new about globalization? Travel, trade, and centres of economic, political and cultural influence have always been part of the human history. Yet, the intensity and the speed of change have greatly increased since the Industrial Revolution. In light of the ease and frequency with which people, goods, ideas, and information exchanges overcome great distances, many authors have described globalization as a fundamental change of the categories of time and space. The geographer David Harvey (1990) calls this 'space–time compression'. Anthony Giddens (1990) considers globalization as a phenomenon shaped by the forces of 'modern' capitalism: the world system of national state, world military order, and international division of labour. Manuel Castells (2001) associates globalization with the emergence of a 'network society', a social form that is historically unprecedented, characterized by a change from hierarchical, bureaucratic transfer of knowledge and power to loosely structured, social and informational networks. Many globalization thinkers have pointed out the increase in capital and labour mobility across borders, and the further integration of the global supply chains into the world's system of trade.

David Held (2004) distinguished between four main schools of globalization thinkers, namely optimistic, pessimistic, transformationist, and inter-nationalist schools. While most people find themselves partially belonging to all these schools, some central generalized ideas from each are summarized below.

Schools of globalization thinkers

Optimistic (or the hyperglobalist perspective) globalists point out that globalization has brought great social and economic benefits, and argue that environmental problems can be solved by the same technological developments that created them, pointing to the evidence that sustainable solutions are gradually emerging. For example, optimists argue that recent technological efforts at 'greening' energy supply by placing shields or growing algae testify to the human ingenuity that can combat global warming. Human ingenuity has also been brought to bear on developing a long range of sophisticated and powerful techniques for solving environmental problems; for example, pollution monitoring, restoration ecology, landscape planning, risk management, and impact assessment. Optimists further argue that today's commercial companies sometimes pioneer rather than follow inventions, and provide new insights into how economy as well as humans and nature can peacefully and successfully co-exist.

Pessimist (or skeptical perspective) globalists on the other hand argue that attempts to modify nature for the benefit of humankind have often had unintended consequences, especially in the disruption of natural equilibrium, intensification of pollution, and industrial disasters. They also point to the fact that while most commercial companies and individuals may be aware of sustainable alternatives, they often choose to ignore them, if the interest of profit is not directly served by these alternatives. Globalization sceptics, such as Walden Bello, argue that in the globalized world, increasing rates of resource use, population growth, and armed conflict have tended to magnify and complicate environmental problems that were already difficult to solve a century ago.

While optimistic and pessimistic schools of thought consider what the positive and negative aspects of globalization are in regard to environmental and social issues, tranformationalists are more interested in the complexity of effects of globalization, rather than judging whether they are 'good' or 'bad'. Transformationalists are more moderate in terms of emphasis on ubiquity and linearity of globalization, more interested in assessing its complex 'butterfly effects' or mutual interactions which are often unpredictable. The transformationalist perspective emphasizes that there is no single cause behind globalization, and that the outcome of processes of globalization are not determined.

Inter-nationalists consider globalization as still primarily nation-state dependent, as despite all the globalizing and homogenizing influences, it is still the heads of nation-states that make important decisions that affect global politics and corporate regulation, as well as domestic policies. Green investment or the lack thereof, as well as taxation systems that have indirect but salient impacts on society and environment are often sponsored by governments, and not supra-national organizations. The growing influence of MNCs does not mean that nation-states are no longer relevant for governing the flows of economic benefits as these corporations are still tied primarily to their home states or regions. In this view, national borders are human constructs that have no bearing or control over the flow of rivers, the movement of air, or natural distribution of resources. Most societies have, generally speaking, accepted policies to be done within the context of these boundaries, limiting the control to regulate or protect particular resources beyond the limits of these 'imaginary' borders. On the one hand that limits the possibilities of protecting the use of a certain resource. On the other hand, it also limits the physical area where damage can be done, for example through waste, destruction, or lack of protection. That does not, however, mean that whatever takes place within the borders of that particular country will not affect neighbouring countries or those on the other side of the world.

'Risk society'

While human ingenuity has been brought to bear on developing a large range of sophisticated and powerful techniques for solving environmental problems, attempts to modify nature for the benefit of humankind have often backfired. Returning to the discussion of technological risks and benefits, the notion of risk society refers to society preoccupied with future and safety, generating notions of risk – external and manufactured (Giddens 1990). Ulrich Beck (1992:13) referred to the risk society as a systematic way of dealing with hazards and insecurities introduced by modernization, arguing that the gain in power from the 'techno-economic progress' is being overshadowed by the production of risks.

> **Risk society** refers to a systematic way of dealing with the hazards and insecurities introduced by modernization, viewed as the probability of harm arising from technological and economic change.

Hazards linked to industrial production can quickly spread beyond the immediate context in which they are generated, as in the case of oil spill disasters or through food chains that connect practically everyone on Earth to everyone else. The risks can catch up with those who profit from or produce them.

> Everything which threatens life on this Earth also threatens the property and commercial interests of those who live from the commodification of life and its requisites. In this way a genuine and systematically intensifying contradiction arises between the profit and property interests that advance the industrialization process and its frequently threatening consequences, which endanger and expropriate possessions and profits.
>
> (Beck 1992: 39)

In the Greener Management International journal, Hanson and Middleton (2000) explicitly link risk perception to the challenges of eco-leadership. They discuss the requirements for eco-sensitive leadership, including the adoption of a long-term time frame; sensitivity to the complexity of the natural world; the adoption of non-anthropocentric viewpoints; and last but not least an awareness of environmental risk. At present, risk-management and risk-assessment calculations by many companies seem most effective when the 'no regrets' gains through energy savings or waste reduction requiring little investment are obvious. But while actions such as saving energy or transportation costs can appear to be the 'low hanging fruit' for almost all corporations, others, such as financial and particularly insurance providers, have also realized the potential in the more distant risks, such as climate change. Insuring against the effects of climate change has presently become a large trend, and risk assessment associated with the occurrence of natural disasters has become commonplace for many companies. Many businesses still see 'risk' as referring to threats to the bottom line or to reputation and brand image and will consider sustainability matters in that way.

However, sceptics wonder whether companies will be willing to neglect their prime duty to create shareholder wealth, when engaging in activities of long-term risk mitigation, and whether sustainable practices related to long-term risks will survive tough economic times. Though the business case for maintaining sustainability activities that are primarily the result of self-gain appears strong, there is also a danger that management of risk, protection of brand equity, maintenance of positive public relations, and maintenance of a position ahead of regulatory controls may be discarded if short-term gains are no longer there. In this case, if perception of risk is considered without a long-term time frame, sensitivity to the complexity of the natural world, and the adoption of non-anthropocentric viewpoints, corporate action to avoid risk is not likely to go beyond immediate requirements. While many MNCs are willing and able to seriously consider environmental risks such as climate change, their accountability to investors and shareholders remains their primary objective.

Within complex industrial societies, other priorities and risk perceptions, as well as distractions, such as sport and entertainment, take precedence over sustainability concerns. Another source of scepticism in regard to tackling climate change is the ability of companies, even the world's largest MNCs, to deal with issues that are bigger than themselves. Sustainability risks can be wilfully discounted by some corporate leaders. According to *The Economist* (2009:4), climate change is the hardest problem the world has ever dealt with as

> it is a prisoner's dilemma, a free-rider problem and the tragedy of the commons all rolled into one. At issue is the difficulty of allocating the cost of collective action and trusting other parties to bear their share of the burden...Mankind has no framework for [dealing with climate change]. The UN is a useful talking shop, but it does not get much done.

The relationship between globalization and sustainability

As discussed earlier, social and environmental problems are inherently global. For example, chlorofluorocarbons (CFCs) are responsible for the destruction of ozone molecules, regardless of where the CFCs were produced or exploited. The global commons includes resources shared by all, such as oceans, deep-sea bed, atmosphere, and outer space. The factors leading to over-exploitation of these commons are intimately linked to broader political and socio-economic processes, such as demographics, and the generation and distribution of wealth and consumption.

Increasingly, transnational companies feel the pressure of responsibility for some of this over-exploitation and are asked to consider the environmental and social problems present in their global supply chain, as will be discussed in Chapter 8. The last decades of the twentieth century witnessed a considerable expansion of supply chains into international locations, especially in the finance, automobile, IT and apparel industries, as well as increased pressures to report on the sustainability practices of their global operations. For example, apparel distributors such as Nike, Levi Strauss, Benetton, H&M, Adidas and C&A have been blamed in recent years for problems such as poor working conditions or environmental contaminations occurring during the production of their clothing. Consumption of products offered by these industries came under the close scrutiny of governments, consumers, and NGOs, as well as global competitors, as globalization of consumption became one of the key concerns of sustainable business.

Globalization of consumption

While in many poorer countries consumption is simply a matter of life's necessity, in richer segments of the population consumption (Figure 4.1) is often used as a social status marker. Humans have uniquely evolved to make tools and products, and to link their possession to their social status ('keeping up with the Jones's').

In modern times this might basically mean consuming as much – or more – than the neighbour (or in business terms, the competitor). As the nineteenth century sociologist and economist Thorstein Veblen (1857–1929) has noted 'conspicuous consumption' is spending to acquire high status goods to publicly display social status and economic power.

> **Conspicuous consumption** denotes the deliberate accumulation of goods and services intended as a means of displaying the buyer's superior socio-economic status.

Just as the newest model of the iPhone is now globally seen as a desired possession, the well-intentioned desire (or feeling of guilt) to make this product affordable to everyone presents a problem. The noble concern with

Figure 4.1 Consumption (source: Engelbert Fellinger)

the fairness in distribution of wealth, the profit-driven needs of neo-liberal economies, and the increasingly materialistic society result in the global expansion of consumer culture.

While 'raising the standard of living' may be nebulous shorthand for the worthy aim of ending severe deprivation, translated into policy the expression is a euphemism for the global dissemination of consumer culture – the unrivalled model of what a 'high standard of living' looks like (Crist 2012:141–142). Perhaps ironically, the moral call of many sustainability activists for equal distribution of wealth, leads to a greater spread of consumerist culture. Unless the consumption pattern in rich countries is somehow made more sustainable, the crisis of resources is likely to deepen.

Opportunities for sustainable consumption

Given that only a small number of consumers choose sustainable or ethical options, consumer choice editing, or denying consumers the chance to buy non-sustainable goods can offer solutions.

Consumer choice editing denies consumers the chance to buy non-sustainable goods. By eliminating consumer choice, retailers can draw attention to a range of environmental and social issues that customers may not have previously considered.

Consumer choice editing is becoming a popular form of modern retailing because retailers do not have space or capital to stock up on all available products (Blowfield 2013:282). Whether companies' decisions to restrict consumer choice are taken as a result of conscious business practices or consumer pressure, consumer choice editing sets an important standard for retailers and the long-term direction of their businesses. It also avoids the thorny issue of relying on an individual's goodwill, and assumes responsibility for products.

Another opportunity lies in the consumption of experiences rather than ownership. YouTube, Netflix and Facebook; social sharing sites for goods and services; leasing companies; and 'dematerialization' can be seen as hopeful precursors to the era of heightened global interconnectedness that could alter a nature of consumption to the less material forms.

Another opportunity for sustainable consumption lies within the types of things consumed. The new conception of the system of production design, in which waste becomes impossible, such as the circular economy, Natural Step, and C2C discussed in Chapter 11, proposes the complete transformation of production and consumption processes. Some of these processes can be found in pre-industrial systems; some are inspired by new progressive innovations. The effective, regenerative cycles of nature can provide models for wholly positive human designs and thus positive models of global consumption. Comparing the consumption and production of humans and ants, McDonough and Braungart (2002) state: 'All the ants on the planet taken together have a biomass greater than that of humans...But population density and productiveness are not a problem for the rest of the world.' The key difference with ants is that what they consume is given back to the ecosystem, and that their productiveness nourishes plants, animals, and soil. Human industry has been in full swing for a little over a century, yet it has brought about a decline in almost every ecosystem on the planet. Nature doesn't have a design problem. People do.

The good news is that corporate examples of how this can be done are plenty. The challenge is to apply these ideas on the global scale, which will be addressed further in Chapter 11.

Fairtrade

Fairtrade is an alternative approach to conventional trade and is based on a partnership between producers and consumers.

In the UK the Fairtrade market is worth around £1.3 billion and in the US$2.1 billion. Globally, the Fairtrade market has been valued in the region of US$7 billion, and consists mainly of sugar, cocoa, coffee, bananas, and flowers. The biggest markets are in the US, the UK, The Netherlands, South Korea, and South Africa. In many ways Fairtrade is an alternative riff on free trade and globalization, which is seen by many sustainability practitioners as exploiting producers in the developing world (see dependency theory discussion in Chapter 3). Fairtrade (Figure 4.2) by contrast is an attempt to ensure that producers receive a fair return on their work in terms of the prices they receive for their produce, the terms and length of their contracts, and their capacity to invest and develop their businesses. Fairtrade producers are frequently found in small co-operatives using sustainable methods and organic materials, and some clearly state that they do not knowingly include any genetically modified organisms (GMOs) in their products. They do not employ child or forced labour and allow workers to organize themselves into trade unions if they wish. Fairtrade businesses will also adhere to a certification scheme that offers guarantees to both the producer and consumer that these ethical standards have really been met.

National Fairtrade schemes do vary somewhat. For instance, the UK system certifies product material but not the labour used to produce the good which means that in the UK a T-shirt can legitimately carry a Fairtrade label but have been manufactured in a sweatshop. However, Fairtrade International has adopted a set of Fairtrade principles and core criteria which all participants must follow if they are to receive its widely recognized Fairtrade mark or logo. Many large food and beverage brands and supermarkets have Fairtrade lines and in recent years the global market for these ethically produced goods has increased significantly. Not surprisingly, fairly traded coffee has experienced a 944 per cent an increase in sales between 2001 and 2011. The number of Fairtrade growers is growing indicating that at least in certain

Figure 4.2 Fairtrade? (source: Engelbert Fellinger)

areas market-driven ethical consumption can change business practices. However, there is also evidence that growers are not always able to sell their whole crop at the Fairtrade 'premium' price leading some commentators to argue that a mixture of price competitiveness and government imposed import restrictions could strengthen the international Fairtrade network.

From an ethical perspective it is clearly important for the Fairtrade network to continue expanding but at the same time it needs to be an effective and agile entrepreneur in what is an extremely competitive environment. Businesses can and do use Fairtrade as a device for establishing more ethical supply chains and offer consumers a powerful way to reduce poverty through consumption.

There is also one larger issue the Fairtrade movement, as well as business generally, have still to confront satisfactorily and that is consumption. Ethical consumption is still consumption and is not yet a distinct and separate alternative to the culture of consumerism that characterizes most if not all developing and developed economies. As Mike Goodman (2004:909) writes, Fairtrade has yet to confront the moral issues of promoting more consumption even in its moralized form as the solution to the problems of development: 'The sheer economic and political power of Northern consumption patterns can be implicated in many of the problems alternative markets attempt to correct.'

Global organizations concerned with sustainability

Super-national organizations involved with sustainability include financial transnational institutions, as well as a number of specifically environmental or social-focus organizations and institutions, as well as NGOs, and interest and activist groups. While financial institutions such as the World Bank and the IMF are often involved in (un)sustainability indirectly through investment in specific industries, branches or entire MNCs, as well as development projects, agriculture or innovation technologies, some observers have pointed out that their global influence, due to financial leverage, is the greatest. Specific focus organizations and institutions include the UNEP and the UNDP.

Many NGOs, such as the World Wide Fund for Nature (WWF) and Oxfam, are compared in power and influence to MNCs, and in fact many of them are involved in close strategic relationships. Sometimes, the NGOs are seen to be 'selling out' by being too cooperative with corporate sponsors.

Yet, one of the great business opportunities may lie in a combination of NGO and corporate interests, as discussed in Chapter 11. WWF works with a number of large corporation such as Unilever, and also cooperates with prominent figures such as the cosmonaut André Kuipers who, by giving lectures and showing photos of the Earth (Figure 4.3) taken from the International Space Station (ISS) to corporate leaders, raises awareness of WWF's missions to protect our planet. An important part of this strategy is involving the corporate leaders in the process of positive change and alerting

Figure 4.3 Amazon from space (source: photo by ©André Kuipers http://www.flickr.com/photos/astro_andre/ with permission of WWF Karin Gerritsen)

them to their own ability to have an influence on something beyond the immediate benefits of stakeholders' loyalty.

Many NGOs and corporations are involved in international negotiations about social and environmental issues. As we discussed in the Introduction, the Earth Summit has established 'Framework conventions' on climate change and biodiversity, identifying basic aims, principles, norms, institutions, and procedures for action. These Framework conventions included the UNFCCC, the UN Convention on Biological Diversity (CBD), and the UN Convention to Combat Desertification (UNCCD). All these conventions involve financial, nation-states', corporate and non-profit sector stakeholders.

The Stern Review on the Economics of Climate Change (2006) discussed the effect of global warming on the world economy, estimating the costs of changes in climate, land, and atmosphere that are likely to lead to natural disasters, loss of harvests, and damage to natural resources. Together, the Kyoto Protocol and the Stern Review have spurred the development of regulation and increased the pressure from NGOs on governments to ensure ratification of the Protocol, as well as participation of the world's most powerful financial institutions and commercial partners.

CBD established primary threats to biodiversity, or HIPPO: habitat destruction, invasive species, pollution, population increase and overharvesting. Conservation actions included reducing the rate of biodiversity loss; promoting sustainable use of biodiversity; addressing the major threats to biodiversity; and mobilizing financial and technical resources for implementing the convention and the strategic plan, especially for developing countries. Similarly to UNFCCC and UNCCD, financial, governmental, commercial, and non-profit stakeholders were involved in the ongoing implementation of the protection of biodiversity plans. The effectiveness of multi-level stakeholder involvement in tackling a range of problems is presently hotly debated.

Globalization of sustainability concerns

Historians have argued that intellectual trends in the Western countries spurred by the Enlightenment, such as Individualism, rise in value of human life, and simultaneously a rise in living standards and consumption, are all responsible for the rise of environmentalism in the developed countries. Global concerns involve the issues of human rights, as well as concerns with anthropogenic emissions and GHGs. In the beginning of the Green Revolution (see Chapter 3) the benefits of agricultural chemicals were obvious. Yet, the higher yield meant greater demand for fertilizers to replenish the soil, resulting in poisonous substances in the monocultures of the industrially managed farms. But it also meant more people became exposed to – and eventually aware of – the risks of chemical hazards.

Some of the concerns can be called anthropocentric, or concerns with human issues such as resources (biodiversity, energy, food, etc.) and health (pollutants, etc.). The concerns about the occupational hazards in an industrial society have intensified, and the global anti-toxics movement has emerged, closely linked to the consumers' movement that arose in the late 1950s.

For some environmental activists the rights of non-human species have the same moral imperative as the earlier social movements liberating slaves, women, homosexuals, and other 'minorities' from dominant hegemonies.

> Members of the animal liberation and radical environmental movements are motivated by a belief that what they do is absolutely necessary and just. The exploitation of animals is no different from the abuse and extermination of Jews during the Holocaust, and crimes committed to end the abuse and to free animal 'slaves' are every bit as noble as the actions taken by those abolitionists who ran the Underground Railroad in the American South. Activists see attacks on governments and corporations that defile nature as just actions in defense of the Earth itself; indeed, without radical actions, including crimes, they are convinced that much of life on the planet will cease to exist. The sincerity and depth of feeling among animal rights and environmental extremists should not be doubted, and it is exemplified by ALF [Animal Liberation Front] activists who risk legal penalties and see value in freeing the smallest animal, be it a guinea pig, mouse, or snail.
>
> (Liddick 2006:82)

While economic development often entails destruction of natural habitats, destruction of property as a protest against this development by the radical environmentalists of the Earth Liberation Front (ELF) in the US in the 1990s was branded terrorism. As Ed Begley Jr. has remarked: 'I don't understand why when we destroy something created by man we call it vandalism, but when we destroy something by nature we call it progress.' This idea of ecological justice (Baxter 2005), the movement to defend all life, has been recorded on all continents where environmentalists 'speak for nature'.

Environmental concerns are not limited to the developed countries and have been shown to be a global phenomenon exemplified by the proliferation of environmental organizations in developing countries and surveys on citizen concern for the environment (Brechin and Kempton 1997). Despite the post-material values hypothesis discussed in Chapters 3 and 5, there is no empirical evidence that richer societies are more 'environmental' than poor ones and it appears that environmental concern is an exception to the post-material thesis (Dunlap and York 2008). From the business point of view this means that the globalization of environmental concerns has brought additional management challenges.

Box 4.1 The global anti-toxics movement

The global anti-toxics movement that formally arose in the early 1980s can be traced to 1971 when David Weir, working for the U.S. Peace Corps in Afghanistan, noticed that a packet of Kool-Aid he had bought listed cyclamates, a sweetener Weir knew had recently been banned in the U.S., among its ingredients. This experience triggered Weir's decade-long investigation into the problem of U.S. corporations dumping their banned products on overseas markets. His work culminated in 1981 in The Circle of Poison, a book focusing, in particular, on the dumping of pesticides. The Circle of Poison illustrated how chemical companies were protecting profits by selling, or flat out dumping, products that had been banned in their country of production in countries without the regulatory infrastructure to evaluate the risks of agricultural chemical use....

Just as the consumer movement identified multinational corporations as the primary source of new risks related to the global spread of consumer products, so too did the nascent global anti-toxics movement see multinational corporations as the driving force behind new toxic risks. In fact, the two are quite intricately related. Many environmental health threats, after all, are the result of the byproducts of the manufacturing of consumer goods, or the processing of the raw materials to make those goods. Focusing strictly on the risks related to the goods themselves, as the consumers movement was doing, was insufficient. The pesticides that individuals were consuming when eating fresh fruit and produce were also contaminating the workers who applied the chemicals. Furthermore, through drift and absorption into groundwater, the chemicals used in agriculture and elsewhere were having a much broader impact. The realization of this, however, lagged behind the initial spread of the chemical industry during the Green Revolution.

Source: Zavestoski (2010)

The greening of global supply chains

The mediation of environmental and social burden incurred during different stages of production is often referred to as greening the supply chain.

With regard to the efforts to green global supply chains, the key stakeholders might be identified as: (1) organizations, institutions, or policymakers that govern the supply chain, (2) companies that supply raw materials to be processed, (3) companies that provide direct contact to the customer, (4) companies that design the product or service offered, and (5) organizations or service providers that dispose of waste products. Many brand-owning MNCs are involved with all these stakeholders and subject to pressures to green their supply chain, as they are likely to come under pressure from consumer organizations and NGOs. Some experience with inter-company cooperation aimed at reducing the social and environmental impacts has been generated, involving cooperation between the linking companies in product chains, addressing efficient market communication, information availability, and information costs.

One of the most remarkable developments in the recent decade has been made by the Cradle to Cradle Products Innovation Institute and the Ellen MacArthur Foundation that supports circular economy. These hopeful frameworks for greening supply chains include a number of steps. First, eliminating from the economy toxins and non-renewables; second, eliminating waste; third, recreating the cycle between urban and agricultural areas, securing mutual nutrient flows; fourth, finding a dynamic balance between organic and technologically produced products; and last but not least, identifying strategic opportunities for business to engage in the closed loop production on the global scale. These frameworks will be further discussed in Chapter 11.

Most financial institutions participate in greening the supply chain through a range of solutions designed to create competitive advantages – from investment in sustainability projects including open account processing to technology innovation, to payables financing and physical supply chain visibility.

Globalization of neo-liberal democracy

In Chapter 2 we outlined a number of political explanations for the failure of environmental objectives. As government control requires a well-resourced infrastructure to 'police' the enforcement of regulations, and as stringent policies can be seen to stifle competition and block innovation, many governments have resigned control in favour of market mechanisms. One of the most difficult obstacles to sustainability involves something that most of the readers (and the authors of this book) would support – democracy. Democracy is not necessarily the best form of ecological governance, as there are other priorities recognized in society: many people in modern consumerist cultures worry more about the economy and political equality than the environment. A society governed primarily on the basis of ecological values would not necessarily be democratic (Lidskog and Elander 2009). The same is true about society governed by concerns about social equality. Simply put, it is never possible to make all people equally happy – if the government taxes the rich, the rich are unhappy; if the government taxes everybody equally, the poor are unhappy.

Also, observers have argued that democratic societies are still influenced by powerful groups, such as industrial lobbies, and that neo-liberalism dominates the global economy.

> **Neo-liberalism** a modern politico-economic theory favouring free trade, privatization, minimal government intervention in business, and reduced public expenditure on social services.

One of the consequences of neo-liberalism is the belief that market-based solutions will correct environmental problems, focusing political attention on consumer choice and lifestyles. Critics have noted that relying on individual responsibility does not guarantee sustainable choices; also consumer responsibility could be seen as a 'defense of unequal access and ultimately a strategy of the powerful to defend their ability to choose, and, therefore, to resist the regulation of resource-intensive, polluting or socially damaging products' (Isenhour 2010:457).

However, when stringent policies are in place, attempts to impose tighter regulations in one country may lead to MNCs moving operations to a country with more relaxed regulations. As for environmental regulation, neo-liberal forms of government can lead to policies sensitive to public and corporate pressures that may or may not be environmentally benign. The industrial lobbies are known to push their interests with the governments. However, as Winston Churchill once remarked, 'democracy is the worst form of government, except for all those other forms that have been tried before'.

'Groupthink' or cultural hegemony: global spread

Globalization is interlinked with neo-liberal democracy, as well as industrialism in both capitalist and socialist countries, leading to the prioritization of certain norms, values, and ideologies over others. Over the past two decades the market has increasingly been represented as the solution to issues of sustainability and conservation, leading to the reimagining of nature, and embedding market forces deeply into social and environmental policy, planning, and practice. Market forces are also entwined with the paradigm of social regulation and environmental management and with the social proliferation of such constructs as 'human resources', 'natural resources', 'ecosystems services', and 'biodiversity derivatives', as well as with new conservation finance mechanisms like 'species banking' and 'carbon trading'. The ubiquity of these constructs and approaches reflect a larger transformation in international governance and corporate self-regulation – one in which the discourse of global ecology has largely come to accommodate an ontology of natural capital, culminating in the production of what is taking shape as the cultural hegemony of global capital. One way in which this global spread of values and collective 'groupthink' is perpetuated is education.

Globalization of education

Since the early 1950s, education for all has been seen as one of the global priorities identified by the UN. The Education for All (EFA) movement has emerged in recent decades as a global commitment to provide quality basic education for all children, youth, and adults. At the World Education Forum in Dakar in 2000, 164 governments pledged to achieve EFA. There are many ways of looking at this initiative (and implications for all of us – students and instructors of sustainability and business courses – as discussed in the case study Schooling the World below).

Education as indoctrination

Education can be seen as a means to indoctrinate students in specific cultural and political dogmas. Some critics have branded the United Nations Educational, Scientific and Cultural Organization's (UNESCO's) approach to environmental education as becoming complicit in perpetuating the new 'holy grail' of the dominant political elites – namely, the expansion of consumerist culture, global markets, and other elements of cultural hegemony. The assessment criteria for business schools, for example, are how much their graduates earn.

The provocative documentary film *Schooling the World* directed by Carol Black uncovers the role of schools in the destruction of traditional sustainable agricultural and ecological knowledge, in the break-up of extended families and communities, and in the devaluation of ancient spiritual traditions.

Education as a solution

Despite the criticisms of education as indoctrination, perhaps most of us agree that education offers society as a whole huge benefits, choices, and the chance to participate in modern processes that are likely to affect the future for all. Put simply, neither Kopnina nor Blewitt would be writing this book if they did not believe in the transformative and positive power of education.

Blewitt (2013:62) has noted that, ironically, many of the authors, editors, and publishers work within the educational system they attack and wish to see reformed or overturned. This shows there is still enough space for dissenting academics to be progenitors of alternatives, if they are courageous enough to act. The same can be said about the mostly highly educated anthropologists and Indian activists in the film *Schooling the World*, who, despite their Western education, were able to develop their critical views. This critical ability is evidence that education does not destroy but perhaps can help develop students' critical ability, and offers hope that teaching a critical course to business students is indeed going to help to reach beyond the docile neo-liberal mould (Kopnina 2013).

Figure 4.4 Schooling the world (source: photo by Ben Knight copyright/permission of Schooling the World)

Specifically, environmental education and ESD initiatives offer hope for a sustainable future. Michael Bonnett (2013) has supported those ESD initiatives that are not for the indoctrination of students into economically significant 'values' but for developing a sense of intrinsic value of nature. One of the obvious advantages of education that recognizes such values is that it allows us – lecturers and students – to communicate critically with each other, express concerns, and seek mutual solutions.

Case study

Schooling the World

If you wanted to change an ancient culture (Figure 4.5) in a generation, how would you do it? The filmmakers reply: You would change the way it educates its children.

Schooling the World takes a challenging look at the effects of modern education on the world's last sustainable indigenous cultures. The film is shot on location in the Buddhist culture of Ladakh in the northern Indian Himalayas. The film examines the hidden assumption of cultural superiority behind education aid projects, which overtly aim to help children 'escape' to a 'better life' – despite mounting evidence of the environmental, social, and mental health costs of our own modern consumer lifestyles, from epidemic rates of childhood depression and substance abuse to economic breakdown and climate change. It looks at the failure of institutional education to deliver on its promise of a way out of poverty – in the United States as well as in the so-called 'developing' world. It questions our very definitions of wealth and poverty – and of knowledge and ignorance – as it uncovers the

Figure 4.5 Globalized world? (source: Ben Knight, copyright/permission of Schooling the World)

role of schools in the destruction of traditional sustainable agricultural and ecological knowledge, in the breakup of extended families and communities, and in the devaluation of elders and ancient spiritual traditions.

Schooling the World calls for a 'deeper dialogue' between cultures, suggesting that we have at least as much to learn as we have to teach, and that these ancient sustainable societies may harbor knowledge which is vital for our own survival in the coming millennia.

Questions

1   Watch the film. Do you agree that education can be seen as a form of neo-colonialism? Why and why not?
2   What do you think about the role of universal education in developing countries?
3   How do you think education relates to globalization?

Key terms

Consumer choice editing, consumer culture, education, global supply chain, globalization, neo-liberalism, 'risk society', sustainable consumption.

Discussion questions

1 Typically, people can identify themselves as both pessimists and optimists of globalization. What type of globalization effects are you optimistic or pessimistic about?
2 Do you think the current preoccupation with risks in our society is justified? What type of risks do you think are real and which ones are 'socially constructed'?
3 How do you think consumer choice editing fits within the context of neo-liberal democracy?
4 Look at the websites of the Cradle to Cradle Products Innovation Institute and the Ellen MacArthur Foundation. What do you learn from them about the currently used global supply chains?
5 If we assume that all forms of education are indoctrination, what do you think this implies about your own education?

End of chapter summary

This chapter discussed different schools of globalization thinkers and the concept of the 'risk society', exploring the relationship between globalization and sustainability. Globalization of consumption was discussed in relation to opportunities for sustainable consumption with reference to consumer choice editing. Global organizations concerned with sustainability and the universal spread of sustainability concerns were highlighted. The greening of global supply chains was discussed in the context of neo-liberal democracy. The chapter addressed the globalization of education.

Further reading

Hale, T., Held, D. and Young, K. (2013) *Gridlock: Why Global Cooperation Is Failing When We Need It Most*. Cambridge: Polity Press.
Isenhour, C. (2010) On conflicted Swedish consumers, the effort to stop shopping and neo-liberal environmental governance. *Journal of Consumer Behavior*, 9:454–469.

5   Sustainable development

What is sustainable development?

As discussed in the Introduction, the Brundtland Report (WCED 1987) defines sustainable development as: 'Development that meets the needs of current generations without compromising the ability of future generations to meet their own needs.' The Brundtland Report aimed to

1   re-examine the critical issues of environment and development and to formulate innovative, concrete, and realistic action proposals to deal with them;
2   strengthen international cooperation on environment and development and to assess and propose new forms of cooperation that can break out of existing patterns and influence policies and events in the direction of needed change; and
3   raise the level of understanding and commitment to action on the part of individuals, voluntary organizations, businesses, institutes, and governments.

The *Limits to Growth* report (Introduction) postulated that environmental protection required drastic measures, including the curbing of the human population, and fostering a 'steady state economy' (Daly 1991). Its message proved to be unpalatable to political leaders.

Rather than perceiving social and environmental problems to be solely the result of industrialist expansion, many proponents of sustainable development believe that the limits imposed by planetary bounds are not absolute but can be addressed by more efficient technologies and social organization. Sustainable development proponents seek to redress unequal distribution of global wealth and expand economic benefits to the 'bottom billion' of the world's poor (Figure 5.1).

MDGs

The international community committed to achieving eight MDGs by 2015. The MDGs commit to more equable outcomes in health, housing, gender,

Figure 5.1 Poverty (source: Engelbert Fellinger)

and sanitation that affect vulnerable groups, thus making globalization work better for the poor, as differences in wealth are seen to be crucial factors in explaining the spatial patterns of unsustainable development. Poverty is seen as a major cause and effect of global environmental problems and an obstacle to peace, security, and economic development. The MDGs have been interlinked with climate change, economic recession in many developed countries, as well as rising food, fuel, and commodity prices that impact on the poorest people.

In 2012, governments agreed at the UN Conference on Sustainable Development (also known as Rio+20 or Earth Summit 2012) to launch a set of universal sustainable development goals (SDGs). The SDGs have a potential to address climate change and the complex relationship between developed and developing countries outlined in Chapters 2 and 4.

Due to the globalization of economic development, while the emerging markets became a big part of the problem, they are essential to any solution. Aaditya Mattoo, an economist at the World Bank, and Arvind Subramanian, a senior fellow at the Centre for Global Development, suggest that the fairest approach would be to allow developing countries to consume as much energy as they need to develop to the level of developed nations, while the rich nations more or less halt their 'development'. Considering the rates of population growth and consumption in China and India, this would allow developing-country emissions to rise by 200 per cent whereas rich-country emissions would have to fall by an amount that is politically inconceivable. As a result, the ongoing negotiators have been so far unable to establish what targets if any can be applied to developing countries. Finding a solution that suits all parties will be essential to mitigating climate change in the developing world, which is most threatened by it as tropical storms and droughts are likely to effect the Global South the most. The solutions will require critical examination of economic development and innovation.

Theories of development and innovation

The implication of 'sustaining' development can be examined through the closely related theories of the EKC, ecological modernization, and the post-material values hypothesis. All three theories reflect the contested belief that economic development is positively related to improvement of environmental and social conditions and sustainable innovation.

EKC

According to the EKC hypothesis, it is believed that economic growth leads to environmental improvement.

> EKC hypothesis postulates that during early industrialization, economies use material resources more intensively, until a threshold is reached after which structural changes in the economy lead to progressively less-intensive materials use.

Critics of EKC hypothesis argue that the material saturation level of developed societies is far from sustainable if they continue at the same level of consumption (e.g. Stern 2004). For example, most developed countries at the moment are failing to reduce the level of GHG emissions and are unwilling to cut back on their consumption (e.g. Kopnina 2014a). Even if they did, it is also questionable whether it would be sufficient for developed countries to dramatically cut back on their current level of consumption without developing countries making a similar sacrifice. Neither is it realistic to expect that economic growth is to occur without causing irreversible damage to the planet's ecology. The Marxist critics John Bellamy Foster and David Harvey have written about a metabolic rift within capitalism as a result of the need for continuing economic growth. The cheaper or more efficient a production process becomes the more that tends to be produced and as capitalism requires continual economic growth the pressures on the world's resources inevitably increase too.

While 'ecological footprinting' shows that richer nations have a far greater negative environmental impact than poorer nations, this does not mean that poorer nations limit their ecological footprint out of environmental concern, but instead because of structural limitations. It does show, however, that

Box 5.1 Europe's dirty secret

While coal production and use plummet in America, in Europe 'we have some kind of golden age of coal', says Anne-Sophie Corbeau of the International Energy Agency. The amount of electricity generated from coal is rising at annualised rates of as much as 50% in some European countries. Since coal is by far the most polluting source of electricity, with more greenhouse gas produced per kilowatt hour than any other fossil fuel, this is making a mockery of European environmental aspirations. How did it happen?...

Coal is cheaper than gas in Europe and is likely to remain so, partly because Europe's domestic shale-gas industry is many years behind America's...

Germany has an ambitious plan to shift from fossil fuels and nuclear power to renewables like solar and wind (this is called Energiewende, or energy transformation). Electricity from renewables gets priority on the grid. This has allowed wind and solar to grab market share from fossil energy during the most profitable time of day, when utilities used to make most of their money and burning gas made sense. By displacing conventional forms of energy this way renewables have undermined utilities' finances...In response, companies are switching from gas to coal as fast as they can...

This coal surge is making nonsense of EU environmental policies, which politicians like to claim are a model for the rest of the world. European countries had hoped gradually to squeeze dirty coal out of electricity generation. Instead, its market share has been growing.

Source: *The Economist* 2013c:51–52

more affluence does not lead to more ecological behaviour (Kollmuss and Agyeman 2002) but is dictated by economic and political considerations. The use of controversial shale gas in America is one example of how a rich nation ignores social and environmental risks in order to make a profit. European purported 'best practices' in energy is another example illustrated in the Box 5.1.

Ecological modernization theory

Ecological modernization theory is grounded in the belief in the ability to solve problems by technological advancement. Coupled with this is the belief that environmental problems are caused by poverty and that economic growth, prosperity, and equitable distribution of resources are going to solve these problems. Ecological modernization requires the 'decoupling' of economic growth and environmental protection through constant technological innovation aimed at reducing the amount of natural resources and energy consumed and waste produced per unit of GDP. This decoupling allows the basic process of modernization and economic growth to continue as usual on an unlimited basis through the implementation of new technologies and market mechanisms (Mol 2002).

> **Ecological modernization** presupposes that while the initial stages of industrial development involve environmentally damaging and socially unfair practices, later stages lead to improved environmental and human conditions.

According to the ecological modernization theorists, what is needed in the human relation to the environment is mainly fine-tuning of the productive apparatus. Sustainable management of nature can be implemented without fundamentally challenging social relations. According to Foster (2012), this demands economic reform, with greater efficiency, but no break with the dominant structures of capitalist production and consumption or its accumulation imperative.

The weaknesses of ecological modernization theory are especially evident when it comes to climate change, and other global issues associated with the rapidly growing ecological footprint of the world economy.

Post-material value theory

As mentioned in Chapter 3, post-material values hypothesis states that while wealthier societies can 'afford' to care about the environment, developing countries worry about meeting their basic needs. Following this, environmentalism emerges when basic material needs are met and that wealthier individuals and societies are more likely to exhibit environmental awareness (Inglehart 1977).

However, the evidence is mixed. International surveys indicate that there are large differences in the willingness of individuals to make financial sacrifices to protect the environment within nations, showing individual rather than national differences in environmental commitment. Dunlap and Mertig (1997:24) demonstrate that national wealth is negatively rather than positively related to citizens' environmental awareness and concern. Dunlap and York (2008) have challenged the claim that the poor are too preoccupied with their material needs to support such 'luxury' issues as environmental protection. Witnessed by the proliferation of grassroots environmental organizations around the world, as discussed in Chapter 4, it appears that concern for the environment is an exception to the post-material thesis. There is no empirical evidence that richer societies are not more 'environmentalist' as far as their consumption levels and other sustainability indicators suggest.

In all countries, however, there is a gap between what people or governments say they will do and what is actually happening – the so-called environmental values and behaviour gap.

Sustainable development conferences

As discussed in the Introduction, sustainable development conferences have turned international attention to demographic and humanitarian aspects of sustainability. The ICPD held in Cairo in 1994 concentrated on reducing mortality and fertility rates around the world. ICPD Plan of Action included policies including sexual and reproductive health services, education, and gender equality. Health services were particularly targeted at reducing mortality. Family planning policies and higher education for women were targeted at reducing unwanted pregnancies and population pressures, as well as ensuring that most children that are born have a greater chance of survival and better future prospects.

The Johannesburg World Summit on Sustainable Development (in 2002) addressed demographic issues, but mostly from the point of view of health promotion and policies to increase economic prosperity rather than addressing the continuing high fertility rates particularly in the poorest countries. Policies targeted at reducing unwanted pregnancies and curbing population growth seemed to have been largely abandoned. Subsequent development conferences have paid increasingly little attention to family planning and contraception, focusing on health promotion and issues of economic equity instead. Aside from non-binding and non-specific references to 'promoting appropriate demographic policies', the Rio+20 Summit in 2012 did not explicitly stress the need for addressing population growth.

Two concerns can be outlined in relation to the outcomes of these conferences. First, the implication of the policies originating from such international conferences has wider implications on how population issues are treated or ignored in relation to business. Ironically, population growth may be good for business as it leads to new markets, more numerous and cheaper workforce, and more investment. Businesses can be at risk if this growth is uneven, as it may lead to threats to new markets and boycotts of products. However, when population density is high, resources get depleted more quickly, threatening mass migrations due to political instability. In other words, on the one hand, keeping the population growing and more or less wealthy might be good for business. On the other hand, the growing and wealthy population is putting an enormous strain on natural resources, creating political conflicts, and exacerbating poverty which in turn is not good for any business.

The second implication is that the conferences can offer at best inspiring guidelines, and, at worst, serve to state political goals without practical accomplishments. It was noted that conferences and summits often play a symbolic, theatrical role 'in persuading global audiences that political elites are serious about issues such as sustainable development or climate change' (Death 2011:2). Sometimes business leaders have been playing a larger role in the quest for sustainability than governments.

Business and sustainable development

Businesses that are often credited or blamed for facilitating or impeding the process of sustainable development, in relation to demands made on physical, ecological, and cultural resources. Businesses are clearly involved in changing the characteristics of technology, social organization, and production strategies that underpin the process of sustainable development, yet the overall corporate effect, as in the case of globalization discussed in Chapter 4, is difficult to assess.

On the one hand, many companies have gone beyond government regulations and have pioneered ideas or technologies that promise to make future production and consumption much more sustainable. Examples of such innovations are the circular economy, the Blue Economy, and the C2C frameworks discussed in Chapter 11. Also, as considered further in Chapter 6, strategic change involves effective strategies linking sustainability to competitive advantage, but also involve collaboration and stakeholder engagement. Throughout industry, labelling and certification to inform consumers of sustainable choices have been developed. Business ethics, discussed in Chapter 7, has also expanded much further than businesses thought was their responsibility just a decade ago. A number of not-for-profit networks have developed that support the development of consistent quality systems for reporting CSR worldwide. As mentioned in the Introduction and explored in Chapter 8, GRI is the most widely used system of reporting and includes reporting on human rights, labour, the environment, and many specific aspects of sustainable development. Last but not least, as discussed in the Introduction, sustainable development can be good business, as both good working conditions and resource efficiency provide companies with a loyal workforce and significant savings.

On the other hand, whilst many applaud the companies' commitments to sustainable development, the sceptics question the motives of corporate involvement. As discussed in Chapter 3, if economic development is conceived as a form of neo-colonialism, sustaining this development can be seen as a way for MNCs to maintain their global influence over structurally weaker post-colonial states (developing countries). The term neo-colonialism was coined by Ghanaian president Kwame Nkrumah, to describe the socio-economic and political control that can be exercised, whereby promotion of the culture and ideology of the powerful country facilitates the cultural assimilation of the colonized people and thus opens the national economy to the MNCs of the dominant country. Observers have noted that similar to the earlier forms of conversion, the crusades and colonialism, the new 'holy grail' of the West that is exported to other countries is neo-liberal democracy, egalitarianism, human rights, and open markets that in themselves contain a critique of other traditions and intolerance toward other sorts of political or economic organization.

Also, MNCs' involvement in developing countries can be seen as a form of unfair competition with local forms of production, providing MNCs with access to cheap labour and natural resources, and ensuring the continuation of market demand from expanding populations. This critique applies not only to economic development (with the associated question of whether the economic paths followed by industrialized countries of the North are viable in the long term) but often to development in terms of ideologies or political systems.

Thus, one of the most essential although very uncomfortable questions to ask about sustainability is whether social inequality and poverty can be solved through economic development. For business students this means that caution should be exercised when business expansion into new territories is seen as an undisputed good. This also implies that ethical questions associated with sustainability in relation to such complex social problems as poverty and inequality are not always easily 'solvable'. Thus, sustainability can be also about many alternative ways of living our lives and doing business, with respect and understanding of alternative ways of life. Thus it could be said that one of the largest problems of social injustice and unsustainability is precisely the idea that some of us in the position of power know exactly how to solve it.

Thus, while on the surface MNCs' investment in development projects and cooperation with humanitarian agencies may be admirable, one can question how much corporate involvement actually helps. Also, both social and environmental aspirations to meet sustainable development challenges have been labelled 'greenwashing'.

Greenwashing refers to the corporate strategy whereby cosmetic changes are made and widely publicized, yet the underlying structural problems are not addressed and the responsible consumer is exploited for further economic gain.

In addition, sceptics remain concerned as to the power of large companies to influence public thinking and even government policy regarding the changes required by sustainable development. According to Elliott (2013:161), it is well known that corporations provide huge amounts of finance to various organizations, think tanks, lobbyists, and political front groups which are opposed to progressive climate change policy and clean energy development for example (i.e. corporations who finance 'climate sceptics/climate science denial').

However evaluated, the significant role of business in the process of sustainable development and of sustainable development in the way that businesses operate is undeniable.

The WBCSD

As mentioned in the Introduction, the WBCSD was invited to compile the recommendations on industry and sustainable development and MNCs were seen to make an evolutionary leap. MNCs were no longer entities to be managed by governments, but 'had mutated into "valued partners" and "stakeholders" formulating global policy on their own terms' (Ainger 2002:21). In compiling recommendations on industry and sustainable development at the Earth Summit, the WBCSD has been successful in involving increasing numbers of corporate partners to expand their CSR practice and engage in detailed corporate reporting to shareholders, employees, and the general public on their social and economic performance along with economic activities.

A number of MNCs have announced wide-ranging plans that were to address the aims of sustainable development and the MDGs. A substantial body of WBCSD reports on various global initiatives highlights just how wide the span of corporate influence on all sectors of the economy, society, and natural resources is. The WBCSD contributed to the TEEB initiative (see the TEEB case study in Chapter 2).

Managing sustainable development in business

As discussed in Chapter 8, ISO standards provide a framework for managing sustainable development in a business district, including the evaluation, comparison, and improvement of its performance (http://www.iso.org, IWA 9:2011). It also identifies and describes factors to be considered when developing and evaluating the economic, environmental, and social performance of new and existing business districts. The Society for Business Ethics (http://sbeonline.org/) organizes annual conferences with a specific focus on sustainable development and developing countries. Some industries, such as electronics, have developed their own standards to reflect the demands of sustainable development, such as the International Sustainable Development Foundation or ISDF (http://www.isdf.org/). In terms of directly stimulating Fairtrade between developed and developing countries, Fairtrade international was developed as an alternative approach to conventional trade, based on a partnership between producers and traders, businesses and consumers (http://www.fairtrade.net) as discussed in Chapter 4.

However, the very concept and practice of sustainable development are highly contested, and despite the willingness of business leaders to address sustainable development, critical questions need to be asked, as exemplified in the sections below.

The sustainable development paradox

According to Michael Bonnett (2007), sustainable development as a term allows for such vagueness that it has enabled policymakers and commercial

Box 5.2 The WBCSD and ecosystem assessment

Ecosystem change presents both opportunities and risks to companies (as well as to their suppliers, customers and investors), such as operational (e.g. increased scarcity and cost of raw materials), regulatory and legal (e.g. public policies such as taxes and moratoria on extractive activities), reputational (e.g. relationships and image from media and NGOs), market and product (e.g. consumer preferences) and financial (e.g. availability of capital).

Focus Area on Ecosystems' current aims are to:

- Anchor the WBCSD as the preferred business partner and voice on ecosystems while maintaining a number of strong partnerships with key NGOs and conservation organizations, such as World Resources Institute (WRI) and the International Union for Conservation of Nature (IUCN);
- Develop and support implementation of corporate decision support tools to identify and respond to ecosystem risks and opportunities, such as the Corporate Ecosystem Services Review (ESR), the Guide to Corporate Ecosystem Valuation (CEV) and the Business Ecosystems Training (BET) program;
- Engage in the global biodiversity and ecosystem policy debate (primarily through OECD, CBD and UNEP), and advocate a set of clear and consistent public policy recommendations.
- Companies must anticipate that ecosystems will be more consistently incorporated into public policies, regulations, and political decisions. The UN Convention on Biological Diversity (CBD)...agreed that countries should adapt their National Biodiversity Strategies and Action Plans by 2012 to support implementation of the CBD's new 2020 biodiversity targets and other commitments...Ecosystem values will also be increasingly considered by the finance sector and business-to-business customers as they assess the biodiversity and ecosystem-related risks and opportunities of investments and supply chains.

Source: World Business Council for Sustainable Development

---

enterprises to give the impression that they are concerned with doing one thing – such as sustain natural ecosystems – while in fact attempting something quite different – such as sustain conditions for the continuance of their own, often narrowly defined, economic growth.

Giddens (2009) has noted that, semantically, 'sustainability' implies continuity, stability and balance, while 'development' implies dynamism and change. Environmentalists are drawn to the 'sustainability' angle, while governments and businesses place the focus on 'development', usually meaning by this term GDP growth. Bartlett (1994:30) has remarked that we have a spectrum of uses for the term 'sustainable':

> At one end of the spectrum, the term is used with precision by people who are introducing new concepts as a consequence of thinking profoundly about the long-term future of the human race. In the middle of the spectrum, the term is simply added as a modifier to the names and titles of very beneficial studies in efficiency, etc. that have been in progress for years. Near the other end of the spectrum, the term is used as a placebo. In some cases the term may be used mindlessly (or possibly with the intent to deceive) in order to try to shed a favorable light on continuing activities that may or may not be capable of continuing for long periods of time. At the very far end of the spectrum, we see the term used in a way that is oxymoronic.

Critics have noted that sharing wealth with the most dispossessed will necessarily include even more natural resources being consumed, higher demand, and thus deepening crises. The finite size of resources, ecosystems, the environment, and the Earth, leads to the most fundamental truth of sustainability: when applied to material things, the term 'sustainable growth' is an oxymoron.

While conventional wisdom often treats social and environmental problems as having similar causes (for example, poverty) and can be addressed by the same strategy (eliminating poverty), this book takes a more critical approach. Some social and environmental problems can indeed be solved by the same strategies. For example, access to better education for girls can lead to a better social position for women, lower mortality, and lower birth rates. Innovations within renewable energy can lead to a better quality of life for people through cleaner air and a better environment. The circular economy can be both profitable and environmentally benign, and so are other types of innovations discussed in Chapter 11.

Other types of problems cannot be solved by the same formula. Population and consumption growth are largely responsible for environmental degradation. Trying to solve social problems such as economic inequality by distributing more resources to the 'bottom billion' will lead to more natural resources being consumed, and competition for resources to intensify (Rees 2010). Slaughtering and discarding millions of cattle because of the possible risk of contamination and threat to human health might prevent a major human pandemic but also results in the waste of valuable food. Wanting to buy an organic, biological, free-range chicken might be good for human health and animal welfare, but is not as space-efficient and thus environmentally friendly, nor as cheap to produce as a 'battery-chicken' confined to a tiny indoor space, force-fed, and injected with antibiotics. The use of biofuels for the aviation industry might cut down CO_2 emissions in the short term but will result in large-scale deforestation and competition for productive land for crop growing in the long term.

As we shall further discuss in Chapter 9, expanding the 'economic pie' to include the most dispossessed will lead to even greater competition for increasingly scarce resources. Discourse on sustainable development often paradoxically singles out economic development, which might have created our current ecological problems in the first place, as part of the solution.

Sustainable development and anthropocentrism

Another key concern is that sustainable development maintains an instrumental and anthropocentric worldview and excludes consideration of an ecocentric perspective (Bonnett 2007). Sustainable development shifts the focus from solving environmental problems towards social equity issues. UNEP tend to exclude considerations of non-human species and treat the environment as a natural resource. Sustainability thinking is rarely concerned with 'not useful' species that are threatened by extinction, or the welfare of billions of animals used for human consumption.

The optimism of sustainable development tends to downplay the risks and damages to the environment outlined in the *Limits to Growth* report (Introduction), and rather focuses on solutions in the form of technological fixes (Kopnina 2012).

There is some evidence that developed countries exhibit an increased attention to the importance of green space, and the welfare of plants and animals. However, most environmental concerns are often bound with concerns for human health. For example, the quality of air is discussed in connection with the occurrence of respiratory diseases, and 'green spaces' are believed to mitigate this effect, or species of plants and animals are used for human consumption or companionship and pleasure. While there are many testimonials to citizens' concerns for individual animals or plants, there is no consistent discussion about the scale of instrumental use of other species in the process of sustainable development.

While the fate of a single rescued dolphin may capture public attention through the media, there is no consistent discussion about the millions of species 'harvested' daily, or used for medical experiments in order to serve the increasing human population (Crist 2012). Related to this is the concern for whether any modern industrial society is willing to resolve environmental problems that are not directly related to human welfare. Would environmental protection programmes targeted towards increasing productivity of land be adequate in conserving species that do not directly cater to economic needs?

Ironically, as discussed in Chapter 7, including non-human species in debates about justice requires true inclusion of humans into the conception of a united humanity, not of special interest groups such as male, female, rich or poor, developed or developing. Our altruism towards other humans has increased during the post-colonial and post-world-wars decades, expanding our concern for human lives everywhere – which is unprecedented in human history. We can hope that this recently developed concern will expand into care for all lives everywhere.

Sustainable development and inequality

As discussed in Chapter 3, development can have a number of widely ranging implications: from global progressive movements to neo-colonial practices. Many supporters of sustainable development believe that social, economic, and ecological objectives (the triple bottom line) can be addressed through economic development. Critics see economic development as a process in which the former colonial powers continue to apply existing and past international economic arrangements with their former colonies, thus seeing MNCs as the modern-day agents of neo-colonialism. The inequality produced by these neo-colonial processes underpins human insecurity, conflict, spread of illnesses, and access to medical technologies as well as resource degradation, confirming that development in its present form is not meeting the needs of current, let alone future, generations.

In the favourable economic climate of the 1970s, newly independent post-colonial nations have been allowed to borrow from developed countries at low interest rates, allowing these nations to achieve relatively high growth rates. However, in the 1980s and 1990s, due to declining commodity prices, rising costs of oil and interest rate rises, developing countries found it difficult to be able to service their debts. The IMF, WTO, and the World Bank saw the stability of the international financial system threatened by the prospect of widespread defaulting on loans to commercial banks. World economists have pondered the question: who is responsible for poverty in the Global South? And should the rich world's financial systems, with constant threats of recessions and financial instability (Figure 5.2), be universally emulated in the first place?

Critical voices have also noted that foreign aid brought by development agencies, structural adjustment programmes, and programmes to promote economic growth may have caused more harm than good in exacerbating global inequalities. As mentioned in Chapter 3, Easterly (2006) has argued that development aid made populations of developing countries largely dependent on Western handouts and have largely failed in addressing the ecological crises. In order to address poverty and inequality, the root causes of it – and the fundamental shortcomings of the system that might be responsible for their creation – need to be addressed. According to Johansson (2010), debt presents problems for sustainable development because finances leaving the country through interest payments are unavailable for internal, productive domestic investments in education, health, and infrastructure.

Thus, sustaining a faulty system based on the perpetuity of economic growth and the belief that economic development equals 'progress' makes

Figure 5.2 Economic despair in the US (source: Helen Kopnina)

this system more resilient, and its negative effects last longer. Critics have argued that the calls to address sustainable development by creating more wealth will not address the underlying faults of the system. Also, the objective of eliminating poverty and inequality might be practically impossible, as societies have been stratified throughout human history.

The difference in global power relations also dictate why unsustainable practices are still widely used, following the habit, convenience, and most often profitability of certain technologies for the powerful countries, and export of them as well as imitation by the structurally weaker countries. Wassily Leontief, who won the Nobel Memorial Prize in Economic Sciences for conducting an extensive comparison of national economic development and structure in the 1960s, has stressed the fact that the choice of alternative technologies hardly exists: 'The process of development consists essentially in the installation and building of an approximation of the system embodied in advanced economies.'

At the time of writing this book, over five decades after this statement, the Netherlands (one of the richest countries of the world where one of the authors resides) is relying on fossil energy for over 90 per cent of its energy demand. While the capacity to use alternative clean energy certainly exists, this example can bring the optimistic belief of exporting successful development models into doubt. Also, the power of the Dutch MNCs to export their operations abroad – partially to avoid environmental regulation

---

Box 5.3 International debt as a threat to sustainable development

The level of government austerity necessitated by debt servicing also has direct implications for the environment, reducing a government's capacity to deal with environmental protection and rehabilitation and to invest in environmental management. Furthermore, debts have to be serviced through foreign exchange, so that they can only be met by increasing exports, decreasing imports or further borrowing. Expanding exports can have very direct impact on the environment, particularly as the principle exports for the majority of developing countries continue to be raw materials and primary commodities. The need to increase short-term productivity puts pressure on countries to overexploit their natural resources. In the long term, this 'resource mining' raises the costs of correcting the environmental destruction inflicted now and reduces the potential for sustainable development in the future of those resources such as within agriculture and forestry. ...

Perhaps most starkly, debt raises the question of intergenerational equity: debts have to be repaid by people today in relation to loans taken on in the past by governments (and in some cases, dictators)...

Source: Elliott (2013:166–167)

---

in the home country – testifies to the fact that the power of corporate elites is not likely to be tackled by governments. While the WTO continues to assume that trade takes place between countries, the majority of trade takes place between the MNCs. Whilst MNCs are not members of the WTO and therefore have no direct power, they do have very significant economic and technical resources and make a huge contribution to domestic economies (Elliot 2013:158). In the case of MNCs' investment in developing country projects, some of these investments have a much greater impact on these countries' economies and geopolitics than direct government investment. Also, critics have argued that WTO global trade tends to disadvantage the Global South (see the discussion of dependency theory in Chapter 3).

ESD

In 1975, the UNEP and UNESCO launched a Belgrade Charter which called for the use of environmental education to develop 'a new global ethic' and combat issues identified in the *Limits to Growth* report. More recently, ESD (Figure 5.3) has emerged. Integrating the triple objective of achieving social, economic, and environmental sustainability, the UN Decade of Education for Sustainable Development (DESD 2005–2014) encouraged governments to develop their own strategies in order to reorient education and learning towards sustainable development.

Figure 5.3 Education for sustainable development (source: Engelbert Fellinger)

Many different interpretations of ESD have emerged, but the main objectives of ESD are often summarized as promoting human, social, economic, and natural sustainability. While the earlier forms of environmental education could be characterized by concern with ecological justice, and the need to address the primary causes of unsustainability, including growing population and consumption, ESD reflects the dominant neo-liberal discourse with its emphasis on continuing to promote open markets, equitable distribution of wealth, and social justice. Corporations' engagement in cooperative ventures with schools, research institutes, and universities (probably, as in the case of your own school) eagerly assure the public that their interests coincide with those of sustainable development and MDGs. Working with corporate partners as welcome sponsors, providers of desired internship opportunities, and even beacons of a successful future has become commonplace throughout the globe. Thus, while there is the need for business to get involved in ESD there is also a danger of commercial interests taking it over, rather than for companies to seize the opportunity to also learn from ESD.

Aside from the Earth Charter initiative (see Box 2.3), few programmes aimed at ESD explicitly address the paradoxes of sustainable development or consider the long-term implications of expanding population and wealth.

Box 5.4 ESD and corporate partners

A noticeable difference between the early and later years of the DESD is the private sector's interest in sustainability and capacity-building for corporate sustainability and the green economy – a movement in which ESD appears well positioned to play a key role. Whereas early on in the Decade ESD interest groups were looking for ways to connect with the private sector and VET, the reverse seems true today: the private sector and vocational schools are actively looking for new models of learning and capacity-building that can lead to greener companies and workforces. Some respondents caution that 'P' for 'profit' might dominate the other two Ps of the triple bottom line: 'P' for 'planet' and 'P' for 'people'. The new learning arising out of the business world's newfound interest in greening and corporate social responsibility is competence-based, whereby students are placed in a global context to address authentic corporate or industry sustainability challenges. Competence-based learning around real-life issues, coupled with competence-based assessment, can also be of interest to ESD in other contexts.

Source: UNESCO (2012)

More hopefully, however, technological developments that take heed of more traditional forms of 'sustainability' (as described in the Schooling the World case study in Chapter 4) or innovations that mimic natural processes such as C2C (see Chapter 11) appear more promising. Such innovations can actually draw inspiration from the pre-colonial paths of development from the Global South. This development was spiritual, cultural, and intrinsic (Figure 5.4) rather than driven by aspirations of material accumulation.

While some would oppose this 'back to the roots' trajectory, more appealing 'progressive' innovations can be exemplified by the batteries for storing renewable energy. The Joint Center for Energy Storage Research is attempting to produce the batteries, at an affordable price, which could usher in a world in which free fuel, derived from wind and solar energy, is the norm. Again, the Global South has a direct advantage as it is sunnier than the North. Another hopeful innovation would be the grid-scale storage that would revolutionize the economics of wind and solar energy, encouraging a shift from costly and polluting fossil fuels to sources of energy that cost nothing. As has been remarked in *The Economist* (2013d: 64), these innovations could be 'a manifesto for a revolution'. The question is, will the revolutionaries win, or will the Ancien Régime prevail? ESD could help to make a difference.

Figure 5.4 Back to the roots? (source: Helen Kopnina)

Case study

IUCN and Rio Tinto

The IUCN report and Rio Tinto QMM provides the first detailed site based assessment regarding Rio Tinto's progress towards achieving its Net positive impact (NPI) commitment on biodiversity – that is ensuring that biodiversity ultimately benefits as a result of a company's activities in a region. The Rio Tinto ilmenite mine in Madagascar, run by QIT Madagascar Minerals, was chosen as a pilot site to test the tools designed to achieved and quantify NPI on biodiversity.

In the report, biodiversity losses and gains are measured and forecast for the period 2004–2065 (corresponding respectively to the date of Rio Tinto's NPI commitment and the anticipated closure date of the mine), in order to determine if current and proposed mitigation activities are sufficient to achieve NPI by mine closure. The overall conclusion of the report is that given the assumptions upon which the analysis is based and the planned activities to mitigate the mine's impact, Rio Tinto QMM is on track to achieve NPI on biodiversity.

In 2013, however,

> the local inhabitants armed with spears and slingshots have been protesting against the low prices the company paid to buy their land and the employment policy at its mineral sands operation at the island's south-east tip.

They blocked workers of Rio Tinto QMM inside the site, and though some were evacuated on Thursday, chief executive Nyfanja Rakotomalala is still trapped inside with 178 others, according to company spokesman Brechard Luc Loyola.

'If the blockage persists, QMM will be in the obligation to stop all its activities,' the company said.

(*The Telegraph* 2013)

Question

Check the current situation online. What is your opinion of the conflict?

Key terms

Ecological modernization, education for sustainable development (ESD), Environmental Kuznets Curve (EKC), equality, human rights, *Limits to Growth*, sustainable development, Millennium Development Goals (MDGs), post-material values theory, poverty, World Business Council for Sustainable Development (WBCSD).

Discussion questions

1   Look up and discuss the differences between the *Limits to Growth* report and the sustainable development framework. What problems are identified and how are they framed?
2   What do you think the role of business is in the process of sustainable development? How does business relate to the ecological modernization theory?
3   Do you think the WBCSD has an influence on the process of sustainable development?
4   Do you think poverty should be the central focus of sustainable development?
5   Do you think the MDGs or SDGs are going to succeed in the next decade? Why or why not?
6   Look up the Sustainable Development 2015 website. How do you think MDGs compare to SDGs?
7   What are, in your opinion, the main paradoxes of sustainable development?

End of chapter summary

This chapter discussed sustainable development, both as an ideology and as a practice. As sustainable development is closely linked to business, theories of development and innovation such as post-material value theory, EKC and ecological modernization theory were discussed. Conferences and international agreements regarding sustainable development were mentioned, with special reference to the role of WBCSD in the Earth Summit. This chapter has inquired: who is responsible for poverty in the Global South? It also addressed ethically loaded topics such as neo-colonialism. The chapter concluded by discussing ESD.

Further reading

Blewitt, J. (2014) *Understanding Sustainable Development. 2nd edition.* London: Routledge-Earthscan.

Kopnina, H. (2012) Education for Sustainable Development (ESD): The turn away from 'environment' in environmental education? *Environmental Education Research,* 18 (5):699–717.

UNESCO (2012) *Shaping the Education of Tomorrow. 2012 Full-length Report on the UN Decade of Education for Sustainable Development.* Paris: DESD Monitoring & Evaluation – 2012.

6 Strategic change for sustainability

Sustainability and competitive advantage

Not too long ago the idea of corporate sustainability meant little more than attempting to reduce a company's environmental impact, complying with environmental regulations and saving on costs in the name of eco-efficiency. Today, many small, medium and large business organizations look to sustainability as a source of product and service innovation, a way of creating new and more responsible markets and securing customer loyalty and good stakeholder relationships. In other words, sustainability is perceived as good for business and good for achieving and maintaining competitive advantage.

> **Competitive advantage** is the term given to when a firm creates a means of securing some form of superiority, such as profitability or market share, over its competitors through offering its customers greater value.

Examples of such innovation are varied and range from such seemingly trivial things as biodegradable sunglasses (Gucci) to essential sources of renewable energy and energy infrastructure – wind, solar, hydro, and so on. Mark Vachon, who leads General Electric's Ecoimagination initiative, has argued that the renewable energy market can be valued at around US$ 1 trillion. Hewlett-Packard has stressed that efficiency and sustainability go hand in hand. Not surprisingly, intensive and consistent research and development (R&D) is important to developing a successful and competitive sustainable business.

Significantly, embedding sustainability into a business's broader strategy invariably has far greater benefits than simply offering a new product line. It can revitalize and refresh the whole organization in a vibrant and meaningful way as the late Ray Anderson, CEO of the US carpet tile manufacturer and supplier Interface, demonstrated so persuasively in his autobiography *Mid-course Correction*. Integrating sustainability imperatives into a core business strategy can lead to changes in staff development interventions, the introduction of waste and carbon reduction initiatives, development of equality of opportunity and corporate citizenship commitments, and the greening of procurement operations. Introducing sustainability can also over the long term improve financial performance in terms of return on assets, return on equity, and stock price volatility. As Eccles, Ioannou, and Serafeim (2013) discovered, an investment of US$1 in high sustainability firms in 1993 grew to US$22.60 by 2010 compared to a similar US$1 investment in low sustainability firms which grew to only US$15.40. Sustainability is therefore the key to creating value for shareholders and ensuring the long-term success of the company and of society more widely.

However, a survey conducted by Ernst and Young and the Green Biz Group suggested that many large companies are responding slowly, cautiously, and sometimes in a confused way to the challenges and risks unsustainability, for example, extreme weather events, natural resource shortages, supply chain disruptions, has caused. Investors and stock exchanges are increasingly pressing for greater corporate transparency on sustainability matters, for integrated reporting mechanisms and a positive leadership culture. In addition, the economic downturn following the financial catastrophes of 2007–2008 has led many senior executives, and some sustainability thought leaders, to focus more intently on sustainability as a means of shoring up the bottom line and enhancing a well established brand image. Many corporate actions can therefore be rather defensive, tactical, and disconnected. As a result, coherent strategy and execution is often lacking and there are perhaps three main reasons for this (Berns et al. 2009):

Ignorance: companies may not actually understand what sustainability actually means or what it could mean to the enterprise
Capability: companies may lack the capability to adequately model or even find a compelling business case for sustainability
Action: execution including institutionalization and measuring performance is frequently poor.

Consequently, companies need to think, plan and act more systematically and more proactively if they are to successfully meet the sustainability challenges of the twenty-first century, stay in business, and secure competitive advantage.

Knowledge management

To address issues relating to contemporary ignorance, lack of capability and lack of action, firms need to secure and apply valid and reliable information. This is where the processes and techniques of knowledge management (KM) are important. Data must be gathered and then processed so that raw facts and figures are turned into something more useful, namely information. This information then needs to be analysed, deliberated upon and evaluated in order for something even more valuable and useable to emerge, that is, knowledge and ideally understanding. Successful firms are those that tend to apply their KM systems holistically throughout the organization.

> **Knowledge management** is a systematic process supporting the development of individual, group, and organizational learning. It involves the creation, gathering, transforming, and application of knowledge in order to realize an organization's aims and objectives.

KM is closely connected to creativity, innovation, and learning and as such is absolutely essential for any company that wishes to embed sustainability into its practices. There are various tools that can help with this such as The Natural Step, the WWF's One Planet Leader programme, and an increasing range of auditing and certification schemes and so on. However, building a 'learning organization', a term popularized by Peter Senge (2006) in his book *The Fifth Discipline*, is not always easy. A company needs to address three critical issues before it actually becomes a *learning* organization: what being a learning organization actually means; how learning and knowledge acquisition is managed; and how the resulting change in performance can be accurately measured. Creating a more sustainable business will require learning and often radical innovation in all parts of the organization. Within this KM framework five major activities must be skillfully developed. These are:

- systematic problem solving;
- experimentation with new approaches;
- learning from past successes and failures;
- learning from the best practice of other organizations;
- disseminating knowledge quickly and efficiently throughout the firm.

To facilitate the development of KM many companies are utilizing the genuine opportunities afforded by new media technologies and digital social networks to share and stimulate ideas across boundaries within the firm, between firms, and dialogically with their various stakeholders. Information and communication technology (ICT) can help organizations shift from function- to process-orientated approaches that align knowledge systems with cooperative decision making and wider sustainability goals. As important is how companies, NGOs and governments, harness science and technology to corporate sustainability aims through developing institutional mechanisms that can traverse the boundaries between knowledge and action. Good communication can effectively enhance the significance, credibility, and legitimacy of sustainability change management processes. Boundary issues and problem-based learning methodologies can straddle policy and action, different professional and disciplinary teams, as well as an array of stakeholder groups – communities, employees, stockholders, customers, etc. – to facilitate the progress of change. The development of clean production technologies, pollution control procedures, and sustainable product design are just a few examples of actions that take place between rather than within self-contained departmental silos, and individual and group mindsets. As psychologist Daniel Goleman writes (2002:59), 'visionary leaders understand that distributing knowledge is the secret to success'.

There is a difficulty though and that is related to how change impacts are measured and evaluated. To deal with this most companies will apply some type of 'learning audit' to ensure that KM systems deliver what they promise. Clear and critical evaluation will prevent firms from seeing a new KM system as a potential magic bullet or a technical fix that will somehow put everything automatically right. It is also necessary to understand the limitations of KM and build on existing positives already present in the company, for example committed staff, growing market, trust, reputation, etc.

Creativity and innovation

As discussed in Chapter 5, sustainable development is a key element in the long-term success of business organizations. Sustainable development requires companies to think beyond the next quarterly return and embrace time frames that span decades. It requires organizations to be both strategic and systematic. Knowledge *creation*, as well as knowledge management, is key to securing competitive advantage in a sustainable economy as all organizations are now confronted by similar risks and uncertainties for which there are few historic precedents. Ecological principles and metaphors are beginning to pervade change management processes, product and service design briefs. There is a general recognition that future business success requires continuous agility, versatility, and creativity. Ikujiro Nonaka and his colleagues have done a great deal of work on knowledge generation, innovation, and the knowledge creation company. They have looked at ways in which tacit, that is, subjective or personal knowledge, can be made more explicit, that is, externalized in documents or procedures or combined with explicit knowledge to create new knowledge in a growing spiral of innovation. Dialogue, sharing, brainstorming, and other forms of dynamic interacitivity are key elements in this process. Business leaders should see that strategy development becomes a synthesizing and transcending process rather than one focused largely on logic or data analytics.

Central to this strategy development process is the need for appropriate and generative space, or *ba*. Nonaka and Toyama refer to *ba* as an organic configuration of a shared context in motion that transcends temporal, organizational, and spatial limitiations. They write:

> Although it is easier to consider *ba* as a physical space such as a meeting room, *ba* should be understood as a multiple interacting mechanism explaining tendencies for interactions that occur at a specific time and space. *Ba* can emerge in individuals, working groups, project teams, informal circles, temporary meetings, virtual space such as e-mail groups, and at the front-line contact with the customer. *Ba* is an existential

place where participants share their contexts and create new meanings through interactions. Participants of *ba* bring in their own contexts, and through interactions with others and the environment, the contexts of *ba*, participants, and the environment change.

(Nonaka and Toyama 2003: 6–7)

Ba then offers a conceptual tool whereby businesses, governments, communities, NGOs, sustainability consultants and practitioners, educational institutions, think tanks, customers, suppliers, and many others can come together to discuss, address problems, seek new approaches, and adapt and apply sustainability informed practices. *Ba* can be a physical space, or virtual or hybrid. It can become what the participants make it, and make of it. For Nonaka and Toyama *ba* is organic where the right knowledge and the right people will emerge because the whole organization has developed to enable this.

To this end some NGOs, such as the UK-based Forum for the Future, have looked at how the creative industries can work with clients to innovate for sustainability in such fields as energy, climate change adaptation, and social equity. Working with the Creative Industries Knowledge Transfer Network, Forum for the Future produced a toolkit in 2011 offering guidance on how businesses can profit from pioneering sustainability innovation. The recommendations are in many cases applicable across the business world although they all come with their own specific challenges (Forum for the Future 2011:16):

> *Share ideas openly:* The free flow of ideas is fundamental to sustainability – as there is a greater good at work here. Openness and the sharing of ideas, skills and technology need to become integral to how the creative industries work. Openly share Intellectual Property, knowledge or wisdom that may be critical for a sustainable future.
> *Add sustainability to projects*: Try asking your client if they want sustainability considerations in the project. Link them to cost savings, through efficiency and waste reduction, which clients would like anyway. Perhaps simply do them anyway – especially if they are cost neutral or positive as your client will thank you. Bigger corporate clients may also have sustainability specialists internally so join your contact, client or buyer up with their sustainability or CSR manager.

Corporate visioning

An aspect of knowledge generation invariably entails the creation of a corporate vision for the company's future and for its relationship with society or the planet at large. Whereas this vision is an important part of the intellectual capital and culture of the organization and is often perceived as the prerogative of top management, a corporate vision that embraces sustainability is often most persuasive when it is the iterative product of widespread consultation, dialogue, sharing and continuing learning with many groups and individuals inside and outside the organization. Companies frequently express their core vision and values in mission statements or vision documents.

Any lasting vision needs to articulate a central ideology, an ethical position on key issues, and an image of the future. Once having identified the core values and a vision for the company's sustainable future, the task will then be to achieve it. One method frequently adopted by sustainability organizations, international agencies and businesses is backcasting, sometimes known as reverse forecasting. Once you have decided where you want to go, the backcasting methodology will invite you to start with your end point and work backwards identifying potential problems, challenges and bottlenecks, analysing possible solutions and options, and establishing plans and actions whereby the desired future may be realized (Robinson 2003).

Collaboration and stakeholder engagement

A stakeholder is a person, group, or organization that has an interest or a concern in the operations of a business organization.

Working and collaborating with others has become an essential element in the way organizations address complex problems, promote sustainability, and develop innovative sustainability practices. Collaboration helps in the KM process by gathering and later collating views and opinions from a range of differing perspectives. This enables strategies and solutions to be fashioned that potentially have a wide range of support and agreement. For example, the construction and engineering giant Balfour Beatty states that engaging with its stakeholders in a systematic manner is a key component of what it means to be a responsible company. Its two stakeholder panels provide Balfour Beatty with an independent view on its approach to sustainability and how sustainability is integrated throughout the business. The panels review the company's sustainability strategy, its roadmaps for the future, its performance, and its performance indicators and assess the company's progress. The panels are themselves managed by the international consultancy KPMG and panel members are volunteers drawn from the firms Balfour Beatty works with, charities, NGOs, government bodies, and organizations operating within its supply chain. By 2015 the intention is for all its projects to have a stakeholder engagement plan.

Stakeholder collaboration and engagement is therefore a form of social auditing and like so many other processes there is a range of guidance on offer to all types of organizations. For instance, the AA1000 Stakeholder Engagement Standard offers a principles-based but practical open source framework for

Box 6.1 Examples of corporate sustainability vision statements

Apple and the Environment: From reporting our entire carbon footprint to finding ways to reduce that footprint, Apple takes a comprehensive approach to environmental responsibility. Product by product, facility by facility, we report on our progress every year. So you can see what we're doing – and what we've done – to make a difference.

Virgin Atlantic: Our 'Change is in the Air' sustainability programme covers two main work programmes: environment and community investment. CIITA primarily means using new technologies and fuels, and efficient operations and maintenance to make our aircraft more carbon efficient, but it also means other things too, like: engaging with others on the challenge of making our industry more sustainable; buying renewable energy for our ground operations; cutting down our ground energy use; making our ground vehicles more efficient; and reducing, reusing and recycling our waste.

Patagonia: The Sustainable Apparel Coalition's vision and purpose are based on a set of shared beliefs that:

- The environmental and social challenges around the global apparel supply system affect the entire industry.
- These challenges reflect systemic issues which no individual company can solve on their own.
- Pre-competitive collaboration can accelerate improvement in environmental and social performance for the industry as a whole and reduce cost for individual companies.
- This collaboration enables individual companies to focus more resources on product and process innovation.
- Credible, practical, and universal standards and tools for defining and measuring environmental and social performance support the individual interests of all stakeholders.

Sources: Patagonia; Apple; Virgin Sustainability Report 2012

stakeholder engagement which can be used by private and public sector bodies and in multi-agency partnerships. It also helps meet the standards criteria of other quality frameworks such as ISO 26000 – Social Responsibility (see Chapter 8 for an additional discussion on tools and standards). It is becoming apparent that companies cannot simply propound their commitments to corporate sustainability, or the triple bottom line, without understanding how stakeholders can be engaged in the wider issues of sustainable development. Company performance and the state of the wider society and the planetary environment are generally recognized as being interdependent. However, as Gao and Zhang (2006:736) note, 'engaging stakeholders through "dialogue" does not mean giving a specific stakeholder group/groups unbridled decision-making authority'. Effective stakeholder engagement cannot be productively produced in a hierarchical manner. Relationships of trust and reciprocity need to be established and *value networks* established that may lead to future knowledge generation and shared value creation.

Consequently, it is important to understand both the overall stakeholder environment and the specifics of successful engagement which include being:

- issue-based;
- pro-active instead of reactive;
- learning orientated and focused on tangible issue-based results;
- measurable in terms of a company's performance targets;
- based on a systematic methodology.

There are, in any case, very sound practical business reasons for engaging with stakeholders in a serious and authentic manner. These include:

- managing risk so that the company can operate effectively particularly in sensitive locations;
- sustainability compliance management which frequently entails (green) procurement concerns;
- development of new markets;
- product or service innovation;
- strategy development.

(Kuenkel, Gerlach & Frieg 2011)

Communication: 'talking the walk' initiatives

Communication is an area that is frequently overlooked in discussions of business and sustainability. When it is addressed it often figures in discussions of product marketing and advertising. Communication needs to take place internally as well as externally and is also an important aspect of human resource development and business leadership. But of course marketing and advertising are important to all businesses because they need to inform, persuade, and entice customers to take an interest and hopefully purchase the goods or services they offer the market.

Unsurprisingly, marketing and advertising are frequently criticized by sustainability practitioners for encouraging more and more consumption through the creation of unnecessary wants and demands that ultimately can never be satisfied. The consequences of this never-ending consumpton are irredeemably bad for the planet and for human society except when relieving material hardship. Three quarters of America's GDP consists of consumer spending. More doesn't necessarily mean being happy and fulfilled as the desire and need to shop often becomes an end in itself. In addition, some critics believe that if sustainability is to be found anywhere in a corporation it will be found in the marketing department because marketing, and its associated practices of advertising and public relations, deals with appearances rather than realities. Stories of corporate greenwash abound in the activist and academic literature and a great many have considerable substance (Pearse 2012).

In 2010 Chevron won the Rainforest Action Network's (RAN) 'greenwash of the week' award because it promoted its commitment to environmental sustainability by announcing that its Project Brightfield solar energy project in California would generate power to run its Kern River operation – a highly polluting and expensive heavy oil extraction facility. RAN also noted that Chevron is California's biggest GHG emitter and that its total renewable energy investments in 2009 made up less than 2 per cent of its capital and exploratory budget. It is therefore up to businesses to clearly demonstrate a genuine and authentic commitment to corporate sustainability and social responsibility through their communications, but they can only do this if their business operations, products, and services are sustainable too.

SC Johnson is rather different. It is a relatively small cleaning products manufacturer, with household brands Mr Muscle and Glade air refreshener, based in Wisconsin (USA) whose growing concern with transparency led it to classify and publish on the company website the environmental and health impacts of all the ingredients in its products. This transparency process started in 2001 and within 12 years its *Greenlist* became an industry benchmark. For SC Johnson, sustainability and social responsibility is integral to its way of doing business and as its 2013 Sustainability Report, *Green Choices*, indicates the company sets itself demanding sustainability targets and is very open about its progress. SC Johnson has also made significant investments in wind energy and since 2000 has reduced its GHG emissions by 40.2 per cent and its manufacturing waste by 62 per cent. However, the proverbial low hanging fruit has now been harvested, so if progress is to continue the company needs to enhance its ways of communicating its key messages to employees, customers, and other stakeholders.

One important way of doing this is through storytelling and its Green Choices website offers all manner of tips, blogs, ideas, and stories which range from money saving New Year resolutions, ways to travel in a green manner, meatless Monday recipes, car sharing services, DIY leaf bookmarks, and much more. Green Choices is therefore an attempt to win hearts and minds, to change perspectives, values and attitudes, to suggest new and better ways of living and, importantly, to convey a positive belief that sustainability is possible, fun, ethical, normal, and good business.

Many people see storytelling as an immensely important device in sustainability communications. Stories can empower, intrigue, inform, challenge, amuse, engage, and help us empathize with other people in near and distant places, in different cultures and with imagination even in other times. Stories can help us to understand the animal world too.

We make sense of the world by creating and listening to narratives. Stories can get inside our heads because we are hardwired to create and understand narrative constructions. As Jonah Sachs has shown in *Winning the Story Wars* (Sachs 2012) the digital world is re-empowering the oral tradition. New sustainability stories, such as *The Story of Stuff* series, which visually tells the story of our materialist society and our material economy, and *The Meatrix*, which is a compelling animated tale of factory farming, can go viral on YouTube and other social media platforms (see Chapter 7 for a discussion of animal rights). To be an effective sustainability storyteller it is important, as Sachs writes, to be interesting, to tell the truth and, importantly, to live the truth.

Green marketing and customer engagement

> **Green marketing** refers to a range of promotional activities that are increasingly being influenced by changes in consumer attitudes towards the environment and reflect a firm's commitment to sustainability.

For John Grant, author of *The Green Marketing Manifesto* (Grant 2008), marketing needs to do good as well as look good. Grant divides green marketing into three categories – green, greener, and greenest – and sees the essence of green marketing as making green stuff seem 'normal'. To do this he suggests green marketing should consist of 'the five I's'. That is, it should be:

- intuitive;
- integrative (of sustainability, technology, commerce);
- innovative;
- inviting (not dull, boring or simply worthy);
- informed.

Sustainability though is complex. It is systemic and dynamic. It presents businesses, customers, and citizens with something of a moving target for as we act on the world the world changes and what actions are needed to help us become sustainable will change too. Grant's position is therefore both pragmatic and principled. He suggests that change brings opportunity. If people want to eat in a more healthy manner consuming less saturated fats, then those companies who sell 'yellow fats' stand to benefit.

Green marketing needs to engage the consumer as a citizen. Green consumers–citizens and green businesses can work together through formal education, informal learning on Twitter and other social media, and through sustainable community projects such as those associated with the Transition town movement to develop responsible markets and levels of demand. New markets do need to be created which can operate for the common good and this is already evident with Fairtrade and the organic food movements. It is also important for sustainability communication to temper the gloomy scenarios of the future, presented so often within sustainability-focused news reports and documentaries, with optimism, hope, enthusiasm, fun, and a sense of empowerment. Having said that, the gloomy does play a part in communication too. Grant asks, how many people would happily eat margarine if they were not aware of heart disease? Green marketing can help generate demand for sustainable lifestyles and for sustainable change. Green consumers can have an impact on other businesses too through positively choosing to purchase green, greener or the greenest products and, also, especially in the developed world, by consuming less. However, as John Grant correctly states green and non-green consumers alike will still want the basic product attributes of convenience, availability, good price, quality, and performance.

Green shopping and market segmentation

To help customize and accurately target green marketing communications (marcom) consumers can be categorized in a number of ways including by their commitment or otherwise to shopping sustainably. A one-size-fits-all approach to communication will not work well. For Ginsberg and Bloom (2004:81–83), marcom strategies could apply the following categories:

> *Lean Green.* Lean Greens try to be good corporate citizens, but they are not focused on publicizing or marketing their green initiatives. Instead, they are interested in reducing costs and improving efficiencies through pro-environmental activities, thereby creating a lower-cost competitive advantage, not a green one.
>
> *Defensive Green.* Defensive Greens usually use green marketing as a precautionary measure, a response to a crisis or a response to a competitor's actions. They seek to enhance brand image and mitigate damage, recognizing that the green market segments are important and profitable constituencies that they cannot afford to alienate.
>
> *Shaded Green.* Shaded Greens invest in long-term, system-wide, environmentally friendly processes that require a substantial financial and non-financial commitment. These companies see green 'as an opportunity to develop innovative needs-satisfying products and technologies that result in a competitive advantage.'
>
> *Extreme Green.* Holistic philosophies and values shape Extreme Green companies. Environmental issues are fully integrated into the business

and product life-cycle process of these firms. Usually greenness has been a major driving force behind the company since day one.

Aside from reasons mentioned in the Introduction, companies tend to go green for three main reasons: competitive advantage, legitimacy, and ecological responsiveness. Increasing numbers of businesses are going green for ethical reasons that affect the organization as a whole. A new business model is developed of which marketing is an integral part but a part nonetheless. However, many firms do not always take a holistic approach to either green marketing or broader company greening. It is sometimes possible to detect a compartmentalization within marketing operations. There is green marketing of green products on the one hand and business as usual on the other.

But sustainability is something that cannot or should not be compartmentalized even though we often do compartmentalize sustainability in many aspects of our lives. Many people know and recognize that air travel is a major contributor to climate change but still fly...a lot. The market operates within society, and for marketing and business to change, environmental sustainability needs to be more than a general policy goal or vague aspiration. Change in terms of citizen behaviour, leisure, investment, industrial policy, education, taxation, and public spending is needed too. Business, society, and sustainability are interconnected and in many ways integral to the future we want.

Responsible green advertising

> **Responsible green advertising** is a type of advertising that focuses on factors relating to the environment and sustainability.

Responsible advertising may incorporate references to the way product components have been sourced, the energy or carbon expended in their production and distribution, their biodegradable or reusable qualities, and so on. Green advertising may also reference the overall sustainability and social responsibility of the business itself in terms of its philanthropic or similar activities, its concern to minimize waste and its desire to avoid excessive packaging. Responsible green advertising is closely linked to green marketing and may be developed to either expand or exploit existing green markets. Advertising is everywhere for good or ill but responsible advertising is often less apparent.

For some commentators, 'green is becoming the new black'. Environmental sustainability is becoming chic and fashionable perhaps because increasing numbers of consumers are becoming aware of the realities and urgencies of climate change, resource depletion, animal welfare issues, species extinction, excessive waste, environmental pollution, and environmental injustice issues. Levi has promoted and advertised designer jeans made from used plastic bottles with an advertising caption that reads 'these jeans are made of garbage – waste less' and Nike is selling its Flyknit shoes which the company claims has cut manufacturing waste by 88 per cent. Sustainability can become a fashion attribute but as an attribute it will itself need to be sustainable. The report *Rethinking Consumption: consumers and the future of sustainability* produced by the brand agency BBMG together with Globescan and SustainAbility (BBMG, Globescan and SustainAbility 2013) stated that 36.4 per cent of global consumers, that is, 2.5 billion people, see style, status, and environmentalism as intimately related. The average age of these 'aspirationals' is 39; 52 per cent are women, 52 per cent live in urban areas, and the biggest market is China where 46 per cent of consumers identify themselves as environmentally aware and responsible. Indeed, consumers in developing and emerging markets, rather than developed ones, are more likely to be green aspirationals. The advertising and promotion of green products in a responsible manner has a market waiting to cultivated.

Green advertising, like so much else to do with sustainability and business, is quite complex. Green advertising campaigns and green branding can certainly influence consumer behaviour and consciousness (see discussion in Chapters 4 and 11). This seems to apply to both multinational energy giants and relatively small fashion retailing outlets. However, given the unsustainable practices and frequent accusations of greenwash, green marketing and communications may in some cases be an attempt to manage risk to reputation and brand image. If green advertising can nurture environmental attitudes within society consumers must have confidence that what they are seeing is not greenwash.

One way in which trust can be gained, or in some cases regained, is by companies reducing the environmental impact of the advertising campaigns themselves. Honda and Heineken started to do this in 2010. They used a 'CarbonTrack' methodology developed by the UK advertising industry (which has an annual carbon footprint of about 2 million tonnes of CO_2) working with the green consultancy Envido and based on a carbon monitoring toolkit developed by the Carbon Trust. A year following the launch of its Sustainable Living Plan in 2010, Unilever announced it would quantify the carbon impact of its digital advertising. This is a good positive step but Unilever's customers will need improve their act as well (see discussions in Chapters 4 and 11). As Jack Neff (2011) noted in *Advertising Age*, the single biggest environmental impact in Unilever's value chain is neither manufacturing or marketing but the energy and water consumption of its customers when they use its products. An American woman, Neff remarks, typically spends 11 minutes having a shower.

Green consumers' intent is not always translated into actual purchasing choices. Green messages are mediated in different ways by different groups, or market segments, and individual scepticism is often an important factor in doing nothing, but green advertising can be more effective if it concentrates on how individual consumers can help to make a small but meaningful difference by taking some easily accomplished action. That is far better than framing advertising messages generically in terms of saving the planet or applying a broad green brush to the company brand.

However, brands are important too for brands are about trust.

Brand value and sustainability

According to the UN's World Intellectual Property Organization, a company's brand can account for up to 50 per cent of a company's marketized capital value (WIPO 2013). Today, the value of a brand is invariably influenced by the role the brand plays in the wider media culture. Brands have a purpose and they perform a function. They appear on TV and in movies, become associated with cultural and sporting events, are printed on peoples' T-shirts, and are an emblem of success, taste, lifestyle or metaphysical meaning. And, it is not only goods and services that articulate a brand's meaning. Individuals, particularly celebrities, help cultivate a brand's aura or cultural resonance.

The writer and consultant Seth Godin (2009) defines a brand as

> ...the set of expectations, memories, stories and relationships that, taken together, account for a consumer's decision to choose one product or service over another. If the consumer (whether it's a business, a buyer, a voter or a donor) doesn't pay a premium, make a selection or spread the word, then no brand value exists for that consumer.

Brands invariably take the form of a particular image, design, and especially a logo. No major public event is complete without a parade of corporate and sometimes NGO, university, and governmental departments' logos. Ideas and ideologies also become instantly recognized with a logo or a particular image that has gained an iconic status within popular culture. Even sustainability and sustainable development has succumbed. Just consider how images of wind turbines and saplings are used as visual tropes to convey ideas of regeneration and sustainability. The famous photograph of a floating blue planet in a sea of blackness taken by an Apollo astronaught has been used tirelessly to signify the fragility of planet Earth to the point of becoming cliched.

However, logos and brands can at times turn into an end rather than a means, often concealing as much as they reveal. As Naomi Klein showed in her best-seller *No Logo* (Klein 2000) there is a problem when companies like Nike want, and to a degree succeed, in becoming associated with personal transcendence through selling sports/leisure/fashion ware rather than simply being seen as a commercial organization selling stuff to make a profit. Sustainability could become a way of just shifting more merchandise.

Nevertheless, for many sustainability practitioners in business and outside the question is not so much whether to brand sustainability but how it can be done. If brands have become less a product and more of a signifier of a way of life or of cultural meaning, then why not brand sustainability? Many of the big corporations that have to a lesser or greater degree embraced sustainability such as Walmart, Nike, Unilever, Marks and Spencer, Coca Cola, Xerox, IBM, McDonalds, Procter & Gamble, Apple, and Johnson & Johnson have worked with big brand NGOs such as WWF of giant panda fame to further develop their strategic sustainability commitments. Many have greened their supply chains and improved their reporting mechanisms. Most apply tools such as supply chain tracing, product life cycle assessments, and supplier audits to detect illegal sourcing or human rights abuses; big brand companies have reduced their exposure to criticism and gained social legitimacy (see Chapter 8). Walmart, for instance, forestalled much future criticism from campaign groups when it announced that it would tell its 100,000 suppliers that they had to cut their carbon footprint by 20 per cent by 2015. Global big brand buyers also help to commercialize new technologies like solar energy and smart metering and their economic power can lead to pro-environmental changes in developing countries where environmental regulations are weak or poorly enforced.

Sustainability is perhaps on the threshold of becoming mainstream. Accenture and the UN Global Compact published the results of a survey in 2010 which stated that 90 per cent of CEOs see sustainability as crucial for the strategic success of their organization. However, three years later Accenture reported that many CEOs felt that the sustainability efforts of big corporations had levelled off and despite deeper awareness and commitment many companies were unable to make the pro-environmental changes necessary to address global challenges and ensure business success.

For Dauvergne and Lister the reason is clear: the big brand business model is inherently unsustainable. They write:

> Brand companies are implementing sustainability governance on their own terms to improve competitiveness and business value. Their aim is to leverage sustainability for business growth while focusing on reducing the intensity of environmental impacts. Consequently, the on-the-ground results of big brand efforts have not been able to reverse – or even measurably slow – the net environmental consequences of rising global consumption on ecosystems such as the global climate, tropical forests, or oceans. The underlying objective of this form of governance – more corporate growth and more consumption of retail goods – inherently limits its capacity to reform a growing world discount economy of consumption that is driving global environmental change. As a result, many of the specific measures and mechanisms end up increasing the overall stress on the global environment even as the impact of producing and consuming some products declines marginally.
>
> (Dauvergne and Lister 2012:43)

Green consumption and consumerism is still consumption and it is the amount of stuff we produce and consume that is the problem. Green marketing and advertising must do more than simply give a green tinge to existing practices. They need to help fashion values more in accord with ecosystem limitations and help foster demand that can motivate the development of new business models. If this occurs business and sustainability, and sustainability and society, could co-evolve in the way they need to. In the world of digital social media, brands are shaped by consumer opinion and demand and there are plenty of instances where media users have named and shamed corporations which have harmed the environment or used sweatshop labour. Nike and Apple have both experienced and responded positively to public criticism. Perhaps corporations, consumers, and citizens can together help reshape brands, lifestyles, business models and social relationships (see discussions on the circular economy in Chapters 1 and 11).

Case study

Walmart greenwashing the supply chain?

In 2010 the mega retail corporation Walmart announced it would reduce 20 million tonnes of GHG from its global supply chain within five years. Working with the Carbon Disclosure Project (CDP), it would engage actively with its largest supplies to reduce their carbon footprint. Suppliers would report all their climate data to CDP. They were also provided with a framework to help them understand the business risks associated with climate change.

In 2012 Walmart requested carbon disclosures from 3000 of its suppliers of which 1100 responded. 58% of these reported carbon reduction activities. In 2013, Robert Kaplan, a senior sustainability manager at Walmart, said: 'we are on track with our projections to achieve the goal and we're developing partnerships with key suppliers to curb GHG emissions throughout the life cycle of the products we sell'. GreenBiz.com noted that this reducing of supply chain emissions would amount to little more than a rather large carbon offset scheme.

Having made this announcement Walmart has continued to expand its operations and its own carbon emissions have increased. Walmart's 2014-2015 investment plans anticipate the construction of 516 new stores in the U.S. with up to 28 million square feet of store expansion in other parts of the world. In addition, by simultaneously pressurizing its suppliers to cut costs, the quality of many of the products Walmart sells has suffered. Their clothes, for example, tend to wear out faster inducing consumers to more regularly dispose of purchases in order to buy new cheap replacements. In 2013, Stacey Mitchell wrote a report *Walmart's Assault on the Climate* for the Institute for Local Self-Reliance. In it Mitchell noted that in 2012 Walmart reported a 1.3% reduction in GHG emissions which was about the average in the US retail industry during the economic downturn. In terms

---

Box 6.2 Apple: the No1 global brand of 2013

With the customer at the nexus of everything it does, Apple continues to respond to emerging needs, improve its products, and break new ground in design and performance...The company has announced that the Mac Pro will be assembled in the US, which demonstrates that Apple has taken criticism over Foxconn worker conditions in China to heart. The brand's environmental commitments also appear to be growing: Apple is still the only company in the tech industry whose entire product line exceeds US Energy Star specifications and a new solar facility – the largest privately owned solar array in the US – is now fueling its North Carolina data center. The company plans to achieve 100 percent renewable energy for its data centers and facilities worldwide and already has a second solar facility scheduled to be operational by the end of the year. In a move that may further shore up its reputation, Apple hired former US EPA chief, Lisa Jackson, as its first VP of Environmental Initiatives.

Source: Interbrand (2013:22–23).

---

of its GHG intensity however, that is, the volume of pollution per $1m in sales, Walmart's record was far worse than competing chains such as Costco.

Walmart does not report all its carbon emissions to CDP such as that produced from shipping. The company is one of the USA's biggest importers. Nearly five per cent of all containers heading for the US are Walmart's and cargo ships tend to burn dirty 'bunker' fuel which significantly adds to air pollution and impacts on climate change. Additionally, Walmart has not altered its business model to seriously reduce the distance goods travel from where they are made to where they are sold in its retail outlets. And, as for reducing GHG emissions, Walmart has certainly promoted its program to cut energy usage and waste streams in some small Chinese factories, but it has also, and more quietly, moved much garment production to Bangladesh to take advantage of the lower costs resulting from Bangaldesh's poor environmental, labour and safety standards. Stacey Mitchell (Mitchell 2013: 11) concludes, 'Behind all of Walmart's slick greenwashing is a business model that is fundamentally unsustainable. It depends on a highly polluting, far-flung global supply chain and a network of sprawling supercenters.'

Case study sources: Kaplan (2013); Kho (2012); and Mitchell (2013).

Key terms

Competitive advantage, green marketing, greenwash, knowledge management (KM), responsible advertising, shareholders, stakeholders, sustainability and brand value

Discussion questions

1　How can sustainable business practice contribute to gaining competitive advantage?
2　How can creating and innovating be nurtured within a business?
3　What is the point of visioning in a business context?
4　What is the value of engaging with all stakeholders in fashioning green business practice?
5　Does green marketing and responsible advertising just reinforce the ideology of consumerism? Do you agree or disagree and why?
6　Why is brand image and brand value so important to sustainable businesses?

End of chapter summary

This chapter has discussed the relationship between sustainable business practice and achieving a competitive advantage. This has a great deal to do with how information is gathered, turned in to knowledge and applied in a wise and innovative way. Businesses continually need to improve and innovate. To do this effectively, sustainable businesses must engage with all of their stakeholders and through their communication practices, specifically marketing and advertising, to be perceived by their customers as offering needed, valuable, and environmentally responsible goods and services. In doing this, a company will be able to fashion a respected, trusted, and attractive brand image. A company's overall valuation is often closely related to how the brand is perceived. To get to that stage companies will need to envision and strategize ways of realizing triple bottom line goals and be fully honest and transparent in the process.

Further reading

Klein, N. (2000) *No Logo*. London: Flamingo.
Pearse, G. (2012) *Greenwash: Big Brands and Carbon Scams*. Collingwood, Australia: Black Inc.
Porter, M.E. (2004) *Competitive Advantage*. New York: Free Press.
Sachs, J. (2012) *Winning the Story Wars*. Harvard, MA: Harvard Business Review Press.

7 Business ethics

Linking sustainability and ethics

Executives confront ethics and business practice issues internally within their companies and externally in their dealings with suppliers, clients, competitors, government agencies, professional asociations, employees, customers and, of course, in relation to environmental regulation and fundamental moral norms. Business ethics involves practical reasoning and reflection using theoretical models as a guide to action but also involves being able to understand and perceive issues from the perspective of various stakeholders such as employees, suppliers, customers, and so on. Ethics involves being able to understand what is right and what is wrong and being able and willing to select, and morally justify, courses of action accordingly. However, there are often grey areas which lead businesses to take what they consider to be the 'least worst decision'.

In many ways, sustainability is a moral issue as well as a practical, environmental, political, economic, and social one. Individuals, groups, and businesses have pursued their own goals too often at the expense of the planet and have often made a great deal of money doing so. The ethical question is: should they have? Another is: should they continue to do so? For many people, and not just sustainability practitioners, the answer is a resolute *no*. Business ethics, therefore, involves how people in business relate to the wider social and ecological environment in such a way that sustainability becomes a key business principle, that is, one that characterizes an organization's culture and values and acts as a guide to action. Considering ethics involves answering all sorts of further questions too. Should companies pollute the environment even if this is cheaper, i.e. will increase profitability, than installing a clean production process? Should companies bribe government officials in order to secure lucrative public contracts? (Should public officials accept bribes?) Should company directors recieve huge bonuses when their company profits are falling and other employees are losing their jobs or having their pay cut and working conditions worsened?

Business ethics is an applied form of ethics that addresses principles and problems that arise in doing business. Business ethics can refer to the action of whole organizations and to that of groups of individuals.

So, how do we balance what is right with what is profitable, or what may be considered a reasonable profit? How do we choose whether or not it is 'right' to invest in poor nations? Should the poor nations have the right to rapid economic growth even if that leads to increased GHG omissions that exacerbate climate change? Considering that the poor nations suffer disproportionate consequences of climate change and considering that the rich nations have been historically responsible for higher levels of GHG (see Chapters 2 and 3), is it fair for the rich nations to support the unsustainable development trajectory of developing nations? Is elevation of poverty a moral imperative? Should concern for animal rights be considered on the par with human rights? There many specialist texts on business ethics that explore these issues. In this chapter we will explore a few key concerns relating to sustainability.

There are many organizations that deal with ethics in business, such as the Global Council on Business Conduct, or Society for Business Ethics, or Ethical Consumer. The Society for Business Ethics, for instance, is an international organization providing a forum for research, teaching, and the practical application of ethical principles and concepts to the management of businesses. Thus, theory and practice is entwined. It is important to have a grasp of some ethical theory even if it takes the form of asking some awkward and ostensibly simple questions. For instance, should we judge the rightness or wrongness of a decision or action on the basis of the consequences of that action or the intentions behind it? What if the intentions were admirable but the consequences terrible? In business, these questions often relate to costs and externalities. So what criteria should we use to guide our actions as business people and to judge the actions of others? We can help ourselves to some extent by identifying different categories of ethics such as:

- *Consequentialist ethics* refers to whether a policy, practice, or specific action results in a net benefit to a business, or the wider society.
- *Deontological ethics* bases the rightness or wrongness of policy, practice, or specific action on broad ethical values or principles such as fairness, honesty, rights, justice, responsibility, respect for other human and non-human creatures, or property.
- *Virtue ethics* focuses on the moral integrity, intentions, and motivations of the actor, say a company or business person, rather than the action or perhaps policy itself.

Ethics is about corporations being and acting responsibly.

CSR

> **Corporate philanthropy** can be defined as the generous donation of money, goods, personnel, and services to good causes.

CSR refers to corporate initiatives to assess and take responsibility for a company's effects on the environment and its impact on society as a whole. Conceptions of CSR differ according to where you are and what the culture of a country may be but CSR is generally considered to be about businesses behaving ethically and contributing to the economic and social good while doing business, that is, creating value. It may be also perceived as building capacity for sustainable livelihoods or simply businesses 'giving back' to society.

> **CSR** is the continuing commitment by business to behave ethically and contribute to economic development while improving the quality of life of the workforce and their families as well as of the local community and society at large.

CSR has developed in response to many value-based criticisms of business practice which have articulated concerns over climate change, depletion of the natural resources, environmental pollution, excessive waste, species extinction, biodiversity loss, poor working conditions, and human rights abuses. CSR has emerged as a way of tempering the 'business of business' values promoted by neo-liberal economists such as Milton Friedman. As Ian Davis states (*The Economist*, 2005), a 'business of business' outlook puts at risk billions of dollars of shareholder value, because it blinds companies to the impact of social issues and outcomes (or shifts in their implicit social contract) which often could have been anticipated.

The growth of CSR has initiated a shift from treating pollution and waste as 'externalities' to including them among all the costs incurred by business when engaged in market activity. CSR has led to companies accounting for their environmental and other impacts in financial and moral terms. This has seen some businesses moving beyond simple compliance with environmental regulations and directives to more generally doing good through their mainstream business practice. Companies may act morally in a number of ways, from being modestly philanthropic to being good corporate citizens.

CSR has therefore helped to introduce the relatively new concept of *corporate citizenship* which since the 1990s has largely taken three forms (Crane and Matten 2010):

A limited form similar to philanthropy, i.e. undertaking charitable deeds and making charitable donations.

An equivalent form, i.e. to CSR, involving managing stakeholder engagement but not moving too far away from traditional business practice.

An extended form, i.e. incorporating the liberal notions of citizenship and social, civic, political, and increasingly, environmental rights.

Although within the liberal philosophical tradition rights pertain to individuals, and by extension the corporation which has the legal status of an individual albeit without the same responsibilities, rights may also be ascribed to human social groups, flora and fauna, and the Earth itself.

Some companies have attempted to create an ethical leadership role for themselves in both established and emerging economies, with rights in mind such as literacy development, poverty alleviation, disease control, and women's education, while simultaneously nurturing new markets. The US communications company AT&T, for example, has garnered many CSR awards over the years including 'best place to work', 'best company for diversity', and 'best corporate citizen'. Coca Cola has also worked strenuously to cultivate a reputation for good with donations of US$2.5 million cash and in kind contributions to the Philippines following the typhoon in November 2013. The company has also donated US$1 million to the Global Fund financing HIV/AIDS programmes in Africa, and has contributed to active forest conservation projects in the Amazon and clean water projects in Ethiopia and Burkina Faso. It has also promoted campaigns and new products lines nearer home to tackle the growing problem of obesity.

There are darker tales to tell too. Coca Cola has also taken over a number beverage brands marketed as natural foods as its traditional soft drinks products have dropped in popularity and those for healthier products have increased. The US market for natural and organic products has tripled in recent years to about US$91 billion and Coca Cola has used the profits from its healthy products to fight campaigns advocating the labelling of all foodstuffs containing GMOs. Pepsi and Kellogg have done likewise. In addition, Coca Cola has also faced serious criticisms for its labour practices in Columbia, Guatemala and Turkey, earning the epithet 'Killer Coke' for its violent physical attacks on trade union leaders in Latin America (Foster 2008).

There are clearly some contradicitons in Coca Cola's record. Coca Cola's water extraction in its plants in India have significantly reduced the water tables in a number of places. The desire to do good and to be seen as a good corporate citizen is sometimes in tension with the need to increase profits and shareholder value. Can the two be reconciled? The ethical issue may be either one of intentions or consequences or the application of due diligence governance procedures (see below). Companies, like individuals, are of course fallible and mistakes can be made unwittingly, or otherwise. Inevitably perhaps, many executives see CSR as a product or service itself which will generate returns to the business and some academics have produced a 'virtue matrix' to help businesses calculate such returns.

Is CSR just a corporate myth?

This leads a number of critics to see CSR as a myth or simply a means by which corporations seek to manage risk and reputational damage incurred by doing business as usual. American business academics Michael Porter and Mark Kramer (2006) see much corporate responsibility as largely reactive and unfocused and despite the huge communications efforts still basically separate from the core business agenda. Without clear business benefits, CSR is often hard to sustain and justify particularly to stockholders. Nonetheless, Porter and Kramer also argue that social development and company competitiveness are mutually dependent and greater practical synergies between economic and social objectives need to be sought. Competitive companies create wealth, create jobs, and produce needed and desirable goods and services. Consequently, there are a number of shared value opportunities in both the developed and developing worlds that can be exploited through technological and infrastructure innovation, energy efficiency, ethical/sustainable procurement, and good quality stakeholder partnerships including local communities, government bodies, and NGOs. Healthy competitiveness can only be sustained within a healthy society and healthy environment. CSR is therefore in everyone's interests.

The best corporate initiatives involve far more than giving money for they also need to ensure, measure, and evaluate real impact. This often means getting directly involved. For example, in the 1990s General Electric adopted a number of underperforming schools in the US, giving money, in kind donations, and encouraging General Electric managers and employees to work with school administrators to assess needs and mentor students. This led to significant improvements in graduation rates in 80 per cent of the schools involved. Education achievement is good for the individual, good for the community, and good for the economy. It is important that companies make an effort: to find shared value in operating practices and in the social dimensions of the market economy. Companies have the ability to foster economic and social well-being but to do this their work and that of NGOs and governments need to be more closely integrated.

From CSR to corporate citizenship

> **Corporate citizenship** means acting honestly and transparently, and recognizing the rights and needs of all stakeholders.

There have been a number of international initiatives designed to promote CSR and corporate citizenship. In 1976 the OECD published its first iteration of its *Guidelines for Multinational Enterprises* and in 2011 they were revised for the fifth time. These guidelines consist of voluntary recommendations in areas such as employment and industrial relations, human rights, environment, information disclosure, and consumer interests.

Box 7.1 Categorizing CSR issues

Porter and Kramer argue that companies though will need to prioritize what social issues they engage with and these can be categorized as follows:

- *Generic social issues*: important socially but are neither affected significantly by company operations nor are able to influence a company's long-term competitiveness.
- *Value chain impacts*: are significantly affected by a company's routine business activities.
- *Social dimensions of competitive context*: factors in the external environment that significantly affect the underlying drivers of competitiveness in those locations where the company does its business.

In 2000 the United Nations Global Compact (UNGC) was launched as a strategic initiative aimed at aligning business operations and strategies with ten universally accepted principles in the areas of environment, anti-corruption practice, labour and human rights. The UNGC's intention is to support inclusive economic development, new technological, economic, and social benefits as well as enabling organizations to develop a positive ethical identity and culture through what may be termed a living code of ethics. Many critics point to the voluntary nature of reporting for signatories to the UNGC but the recent 'delisting' of companies not complying with Global Compact's ethical requirements has resulted in greater interest from businesses wanting to join and a rapid decline in those just signing up for PR purposes.

A key question, and sometimes confusion, for many is whether CSR is actually a latter day form of corporate philanthropy or something more. True philanthropy perhaps means giving according to need without expecting any form of pay-off and much corporate giving certainly has great PR value. There are a number of well known corporate philanthropists who have given away part of their huge wealth to good causes for reasons other than prestige, making even more money or assuaging a guilty conscience. Andrew Carneigie, Paul Getty, and today Bill Gates are just three well known names among a gallery of business philanthropists. However, for many critics and indeed business leaders, it is important to move CSR beyond philanthropy or charitable giving so that it becomes an integral part of what it means to do business and to be a business. This requires distinct leadership and concerted action. John Browne, former CEO of BP and currently CEO of the fracking company Quadrilla, and Robin Nuttall of the global consultancy firm McKinsey, suggest that it is important for corporations to publicly demonstrate how doing business delivers value to society as well as to itself. Unilever's Sustainable Living Plan, for example, has the twin goals of doubling sales and reducing environmental impact, which also serves to lay the foundation for improved brand image and cultural changes within the organization. To do this effectively, companies need to learn what their stakeholders want and how much and where they may be prepared to compromise. This takes time and will involve monitoring the Internet and social media, having in-depth conversations with some people, and undertaking research maybe at a corporate level on strategic issues and concerns. Unfortunately, few companies rarely understand or profile their stakeholders in sufficient depth, although in-depth understanding is a key to positive engagement.

Positive engagement requires that employees have the right skills, particularly of negotiation and communication, to develop and maintain trust. The engagement process must also be clear and adequately resourced. External communication must not be propagandist or hollow. Unsubstantiated claims should not be made and actual outcomes should be measured and made publicly available.

Plenty Foods Ltd, a subsidiary of Ceylon Biscuits, has worked with a network of 10,000 farmers/producers and 106 company distributors and retail outlets in Sri Lanka to ensure that local rural communities benefit both economically and nutritionally from its products. Its flagship cereal brand, Samaposha, has achieved a number of quality assurance certifications and rural areas are a significant and growing market for this product. Corporations can therefore actively go beyond philanthropy if they develop sound partnerships with community enterprises which usually have democratic and participatory governance structures which empower both individual members and communities. These community enterprises can offer corporations a great deal if the relationship is viewed by the corporation as an asset and a source of future learning and knowledge rather than as something entered into as an act of charity. Companies and communities should therefore focus on shared value and capacity building, and celebrate their joint achievements.

The Vodafone Foundation in India has identified three priority areas for its action on corporate citizenship – the environment, the emancipation of women, and education. In December 2013, it launched a book, *Women of Pure Wonder*, which celebrates the stories of sixty women from ordinary backgrounds who have achieved exceptional things

Human rights

Businesses need to respect human rights – the rights to life, to shelter, to food, to security, and so on – for reasons of fundamental justice and equity rather than charity and philanthrophy. The Vodafone example above directly refers to human rights just as the Killer Coke campaign also does

Box 7.2 Vodafone's *Women of Pure Wonder*

Anita Rana, the demure Jat housewife from Meerut...was shattered by her husband's sudden death 16 years ago from a heart attack. 'I knew little else than cooking, jhadu-pocha (cleaning) and that he was doing good work to serve the people through his NGO.' Defying her family, she stepped out of purdah, took over the NGO and is today the recipient of many national and international awards, 'including one from the British parliament'.

Her goal is to work relentlessly against female foeticide. 'Do you know in Meerut and Baghpat the sex ratio is 1,000 boys to 865 girls?' Through a children's helpline and working with likeminded people, she tries to bust clinics that perform sex selection scans, and takes in abandoned female newborns and places them in adoption. 'I want to tell women that if there is a sudden tragedy or setback in your life, don't be despondent. Get up, go out and work, and you'll be rewarded.'

Sunita Dhairyam, Founder of Temple Tree Designs, is a wildlife photographer and artist who returned from the US in 1995, bought a barren piece of land – now not so barren – along the border of a national park in Chamarajanagara district of Karnataka, on which she runs a medical clinic for the needy. 'It's a constant struggle to raise the money because we also give compensation to those whose cows are killed by the tigers, but I raise money through my art, selling T-shirts I design.'

The focus is always on using technology through mobile phones to make a difference, particularly in education – teaching English – or helping members of organisations such as SEWA improve their sales. 'Our CSR is through actual participation, we never do chequebook philanthropy,' adds Rohit Adya, Vodafone India's Director, External Affairs.

Source: adapted from Bhagat (2013)

but in another way. With the end of World War II, and the creation of the UN, the international community vowed never to allow atrocities to happen again. The Commission on Human Rights, at its first session early in 1947, authorized its members to formulate what it termed 'a preliminary draft International Bill of Human Rights' and in 1948 the UN published the Universal Declaration on Human Rights.

The first two principles of the UNGC, a UN initiative aiming to persuade businesses to adopt socially responsible and sustainable practices, are inspired by this 1948 Universal Declaration:

1   Businesses should support and respect the protection of internationally proclaimed human rights.
2   Businesses should make sure they are not complicit in human rights abuses.

The Global Compact has worked with Monash University in Australia to publish a very helpful business guide to human rights. Complementing this, the International Labour Organization (ILO), another body associated with the UN, has published eight conventions covering fundamental principles and rights at work: freedom of association and the effective recognition of the right to collective bargaining; the elimination of all forms of forced or compulsory labour; the effective abolition of child labour; and the elimination of discrimination in respect of employment and occupation.

The rights of indigenous peoples to their land and livelihood is an important element in the ongoing debate around human rights and these rights are of particular relavance to the heavy extractive industries working in Africa, South America, Australia, and elsewhere. CSR policies of companies such as BHP Mining, Rio Tinto (see case study in Chapter 5), and Shell have had to accommodate the land rights of indigenous peoples by publicly demonstrating that their business operations benefit the local communities and ensuring any environmental harm incurred is remedied effectively once operations have ceased.

Other good practice examples include: a participation agreement between Argyle Diamonds and the Gidja, Malgnin, and Woolah aboriginal peoples in Australia recognizes the indigenous peoples as landlords for Argyle's mine as it resides on their ancestral land. It is sometimes difficult to accurately assess the progress of the global mining industry in realizing the goals of social responsibility and sustainability because of a considerable variability in reporting practices. This can make it very difficult to compare the performance of one company with another. Meaningful measures addressing the application of policy statements to practice are also often lacking. Unfortunately, there are many accounts of bad practice too. Sometimes this seems to been through wilful neglect and at other times because of poor management and planning. There are also many challenges regarding the wider development role private firms can effectively play in the Global South. In many cases local communities do not have the skills, knowledge, or confidence to engage effectively with big corporations on CSR and this raises concerns as to the best way companies can be held accountable for their actions.

'Soft law' litigation can act as a protective mechanism which although legally non-binding does help to develop the precepts of corporate responsibility in such a way they could become incorporated into binding domestic 'hard law'. In other words, soft law is a reflection of social norms and social expectations of what corporations should and should not do and increasingly these norms are informing a corporation's social licence to do business. This approach is clearly expressed in the UNGC's *Guiding*

Principles on Business and Human Rights which has been produced by John Ruggie. It emphasizes several positive aspects of CSR in regard to human rights and in particular:

*   *Due diligence* obligations on the part of corporations to respect human rights.
*   *Respect plus* suggesting that in certain circumstances, such as when operating in conflict zones, it will be incumbent on corporations to do more than protect or respect human rights.

In addition, a concept known as the 'sphere of influence' relates to a business's reach, influence, and 'complicity' so that proclaiming ignorance of unwelcome consequences is not a sufficient justification or excuse. Companies can be deemed complicit if it is evident that they 'should have known'.

Labour issues: poverty, pay, and working conditions

The economic recession, the financial crisis, and the climate problem have combined to make life even more difficult for many working people. Even before the crisis, wage growth was stagnating and the proportion of people on low pay was increasing. As the ILO's *Global Wage Report 2010-11* stated, an income redistribution from wages to profits and from median to high earners has obviously occurred. Those with higher incomes tend to save more and in many countries household consumption has only been maintained by increasing numbers of families going into debt. This has led to various campaigns for 'a living wage', that is, an income level sufficient to support a household at an acceptable standard of living. Of course, this standard may vary according to place but definitions are often qualified with terms such as 'frugal comfort', or 'existence worthy of human dignity' or with concepts such as minimum or necessary.

In the five years following the global economic crisis of 2008, 39 million jobs have been lost and global unemployment is likely to remain at 6 per cent or more for the foreseeable future. In 2012 197.3 million people were without a job. Global youth unemployment is high too, currently at 12.7 per cent and is expected to rise to 12.9 per cent by 2017, and the employment to population ratio is the lowest it has been for over 20 years. In 2011, 1.52 billion workers were in vulnerable employment. The ILO currently estimates that 397 million workers are living in extreme poverty with a further 472 million workers unable to meet their basic needs on a regular basis.

Additionally, the number of working poor is also growing steadily leading the ILO (2012:9) to state:

> ...to generate sustainable growth while maintaining social cohesion, the world must rise to the urgent challenge of creating 600 million

productive jobs over the next decade, which would still leave 900 million workers living with their families below the US$2 a day poverty line, largely in developing countries.

Investment in job creation and action to address the mismatch in skills and occupations is urgently required. The problems of the advanced capitalist economies have severely affected developing countries. There is sound evidence that in response to the plunge in demand for exports, price volatility and the falling rate of profit, multinational firms have intensified processes of organizational restructuring, introducing new work patterns that increase labour productivity. This means employees are often working harder for less pay, their employment is precarious, and often to cut costs companies may neglect health and safety in the workplace. Long-term unemployment, short-time working, and temporary lay-offs in many manufacturing sectors have increased too. Indeed, the impact of this intensified labour exploitation has moved beyond the confines of the workplace. Wage cuts have meant that the workers can no longer even afford to cater for basic household and family needs including proper and adequate food. Sharp increases in the workload of employed workers has resulted in increased dangers such as 'accidents' at work leading to a real decline in workers' general health and well-being. In developing countries, a slowing down of the shift from low productivity to high productivity employment has weakened a key driver of quality job growth.

Despite the under-reporting of occupational accidents in some countries, records show that every day in the region of 960,000 workers suffer injury at work and 5,330 die as a consequence of work-related diseases. Excessive fatigue, stress, and stress-related illnesses are becoming increasingly common, resulting in higher levels of absenteeism due to sickness. The extra need for, and costs of, medical care further compromise the basic human rights of many households to decent food, adequate shelter, and children's education. Finally, as the quality and standard of living declines, the life expectancy of many working people and their families is likely to decline too. The question here is whether some businesses are operating at the expense of their employees. If so, is it a consequence of unfortunate but necessary actions or deliberately intentional simply to increase profit? To put it bluntly, the welfare of working people has been sacrificed on the altar of a global market economy that does not work. Neo-liberal deregulation over the last 30 years has certainly licensed serious attacks on labour activists and the environment in the name of economic growth, energy security and job creation.

Accompanying the degradation of work and fall in working people's living standards, business and government leaders increasingly call for economic growth – not always acknowledging that growth is not the solution to everything. Global poverty and inequality has been increasing markedly in recent years. The 'trickle down effect' is a myth, as much of the 'wealth' that was created in the good times was not real – just numbers on a screen – and it is the rich rather than the poor who have benefited. At the same time, too many business organizations still see the natural environment as something to be exploited, just as ordinary workers are and have been.

> **Neo-liberal economic theory** is an ideology emphasizing the efficiency of private enterprise, free trade, and open global markets. It seeks to maximize the role of the private sector and private profit in all aspects of social and economic life.

Despite the growing public prominence of CSR and corporate sustainability many of the bad old ways persist as costs, competition, and growth continue to figure prominently in debates on the future development of business. However, organizations like the Fair Labor Association (FLA)

Box 7.3 The Fair Labor Association

The Fair Labor Association is a collaborative effort of socially responsible companies, colleges and universities, and civil society organizations. The FLA creates lasting solutions to abusive labor practices by offering tools and resources to companies, delivering training to factory workers and management, conducting due diligence through independent assessments, and advocating for greater accountability and transparency from companies, manufacturers, factories and others involved in global supply chains.

The FLA provides a model of collaboration, accountability, and transparency and serves as a catalyst for positive change in workplace conditions. As an organization that promotes continuous improvement, the FLA strives to be a global leader in establishing best practices for respectful and ethical treatment of workers, and in promoting sustainable conditions through which workers earn fair wages in safe and healthy workplaces.

Hours of work

The regular work week shall not exceed 48 hours. Employers shall allow workers at least 24 consecutive hours of rest in every seven-day period.

Compensation

Every worker has a right to compensation for a regular work week that is sufficient to meet the worker's basic needs and provide some discretionary income.

Source: http://www.fairlabor.org/

---

work with a growing number of companies to ensure workers are treated and rewarded fairly. Companies involved with the FLA include Adidas, Apple, H&M, Nestle, Nike, Patagonia, and Puma.

Business and poverty – 'bottom of the pyramid'

Many sustainable practitioners have noted that development aid alone will not be enough. If the 'bottom billion', the world's poorest people, are to be 'lifted out of poverty', developed countries may need to do more than pour in money (see discussions of poverty in Chapters 1, 2, 3 and 9). Some critics have even suggested military intervention might be required in extreme circumstances and many have looked to business to play a bigger part in poverty alleviation.

Undoubtedly, business is a driving force in the world economy and low wages a significant source of poverty, and although increasing numbers of people are being lifted out of dire absolute poverty global inequality is increasing too. If the poor are getting less poor, the rich are getting richer and at a much faster rate. This is an equity issue, just as increased global affluence among a rising global population will inevitably place greater pressures on the Earth's natural resources. But this is not all. Some people have argued that it is possible to alleviate global poverty by treating the global poor as if they were simply another market. There is money to be made from the world's poor if the poor are treated ethically, sensitively, and in a businesslike way. Harvard academics CK Prahalad and Stuart Hart have argued that a very good business case can be developed for corporations wishing to practically address global poverty. Unsurprisingly, doing business with the world's poorest 4 billion citizens, that is with those at the 'bottom of the pyramid' (BOP), requires radical technological innovations, new business models, and a re-evaluation of price–performance relationships. It also involves new methods of financing and higher levels of capital efficiency in many cases.

Despite corporate commitment to development through BOP initiatives it is important that the Western economic model of production and consumption is not transposed to the Global South. Increased consumption, even if undertaken in a more eco-efficent and socially just manner, will still need to respect the ecological carrying capacity of the planet even if poverty is addressed successfully. A new economic development and business model is therefore of primary significance (see Chapter 11). Rudiger Hahn (2009:320) writes:

> By an improvement of the living standard at the BOP and the hereby rising demand for food, water, energy, resources, disposal potential and so forth the pressure on the environment and the resource base will grow further. Therefore a development of the BOP on the basis of the western model of living is ecologically not acceptable mostly due

to the limited resources and assimilation capacity. In the same way the threat of an overly excessive exploitation of nature beyond the carrying capacity already becomes apparent just through the pressure of a further growing world population. This leads directly to damages for coming generations and thus negatively affects the intergenerational justice in terms of sustainable development.

There are also other businesslike concerns about the BOP idea. Many companies including DuPont and Procter & Gamble have failed to generate a healthy return on their investment despite otherwise healthy market penetration rates. Critics have suggested a new BOP venture will probably need an impractical start-up penetration rate of over 30 per cent to guarantee success although this has been achieved on occasion by companies such as SC Johnson in its promotion of its anti-malaria insecticide in rural Ghana. However, what is important here is that this BOP venture is an aspect of SC Johnson's overall CSR commitments. BOP consumers are not 'ordinary' but in many ways quite vulnerable consumers and there are serious ethical concerns regarding very rich and powerful corporations making even more money from the world's poorest. Perhaps, there is an irreconcilable contradiction or dilemma at the heart of BOP, and perhaps in CSR more widely. Kirk Davidson (2009:28) asks:

> When Procter & Gamble sells a sachet of detergent or an individual disposable diaper to a BOP consumer in Mexico or India, what happens to the profit P & G derives from the sale? If it is immediately repatriated to Cincinnati, little has been done to raise the income level of the BOP and 'eradicate world poverty.' The poor consumer has simply substituted buying the detergent or the diaper for rice or beans or some other essential product. To what extent is the seller willing to reinvest those profits in the BOP community?

Many people argue correctly that it would be unjust to prevent poor people from spending their increased income to improve the standard and quality of their lives even if this does entail consuming more goods and services, natural resources, energy, etc. This leads to wider political issues relating to the contraction of economies in the Global North and an acceptance of their responsible expansion in the Global South. Ultimately, these broader political issues engage notions of corporate and global citizenship, government and governance, and practical policies aimed at an economic development understood as human and ecosystem well-being rather than just the production and consumption of more and more stuff. The planet cannot afford further ecological deterioration and although there is continuing talk of the need for trade-offs between the environment and economic development, there are also many voices who deny the efficacy and legitimacy of such trade-offs. Whatever the case, sustainable development certainly requires an enabling global political culture involving long-term and substantial reductions in the consumption and ecological impacts of the minority at the top of the pyramid.

Environmental ethics and animal rights

In Chapter 2 we discussed anthropocentrism. Anthropocentrism can be deeply embedded within the ethical fabric of society as discrimination against other species is considered to be a non-issue. For example, while ethical assumptions underlying sustainable development condemn practices like child labour, gender, class, ethnic and racial discrimination, daily mechanized slaughter of farm animals for human consumption is rarely disputed.

Thus, the overwhelming ethical concern for *all* humans propagated as the most common sense moral basis of post-industrial societies seems unprecedented in human history. Related to this unprecedented reification of human life – including that of unborn children – is the increased concern with *resources* rather than sentient beings. In a 1972 paper titled "Should Trees Have Standing?" Christopher D Stone proposed that if corporations are assigned rights, so should natural objects such as trees. This was a rallying point for the then burgeoning environmental movement, launching a worldwide debate on the basic nature of legal rights that reached the US Supreme Court. Including animal and plant rights into core moral principles, will have a number of fundamental implications. If animal life had been placed on an existential par with human life then their exploitation and that of their homelands would become morally unfeasible (Crist 2013).

Convention on International Trade in Endangered Species of Wild Fauna and Flora and animal welfare

The global market for animal products is huge. Many national diets involve a massive consumption of meat, particularly in the US. Meat consumption is also an indicator of globalization, or at least 'Westernization', and has increased significantly among the more affluent classes in India and China. Even the Japanese are now eating more red meat than ever before. Animal products are also extensively used for clothing, fashion, and luxury goods and this has led to a resilient, often illegal, trade in animal skins, ivory, and rhino horn which apparently when ground into a powder is assumed by some to have aphrodisiac qualities. Traditional Chinese medicines and many Western cosmetic products rely on animal products.

The Convention on International Trade in Endangered Species of Wild Fauna and Flora (CITES), for example, came into force in 1975 and now has a membership of 179 countries. The Convention text states that the trade in specimens from rare and endangered species as listed in the Convention's two appendices should be subject to strict regulation and can only be authorized in exceptional circumstances.

Unfortunately, organized crime syndicates and rebel militia have become increasingly involved in this wildlife crime, with 22,000 African elephants being killed for their ivory in 2012 alone. There are many profitable legal, semi-legal, and illegal business opportunities stemming from the slaughter of rare, endangered, and other less vulnerable species. The trade in python skins is currently worth US$1 billion per annum and one large rhino horn can sell for up to US$500,000 on the black market. The trade in tiger skins and endangered reptiles is equally vibrant and legitimate businesses have been enlisted to help deal with this growing problem. There are also ethical concerns that relate to the right or need to respect the health and well-being of other creatures too which go way beyond seeing them as an economic resource, fashion accountrement, cosmetic, or an enticement to a fun day out on a killing field. In 2013 wildlife experts worked with forty European entrepreneurs and business coaches to develop a system that could effectively trace the origin of wildlife products from the collection of say a python to its ultimate transformation into a handbag. ASKING is a smartphone app that can contribute to the sustainable use of animal products by enabling consumers to undertake their own supply chain audit. John Scanlon, Secretary-General of CITES, has argued that private sector businesses could establish a technology and innovation fund (the CITES Technology and Innovation Fund or CTIF), that could help attract investors and entrepreneurs to develop other technologies which could help enforce CITES' work.

Animal well-being is a controversial area of medical experimentation by the pharmaceutical and cosmetic industries, health bodies, universities, and some government agencies. This activity has generated a great deal of debate, publicity, and a considerable amount of sometimes quite violent protest. Although many people argue that much of this animal experimentation is strictly unnecessary and often produces inconclusive results and have suggested a range of alternative methods, others have argued the complete opposite (see Chapter 2).

However, societal attitudes towards animal welfare have slowly changed and although experimental practices continue, private and public sector bodies often go to great lengths to soothe public fears animals are being treated cruelly or callously. The CSR and sustainability reports of many research labs and drug companies publish strict ethical codes articulating a broad concern for animal well-being, although often falling short of stating that animas have rights, the way animal rights campaigners such as Peter Singer and Tom Regan have argued. The Eurogroup for Animals is a leading NGO within the EU campaigning against animal testing and has argued persuasively that animal welfare ought to be a key component of CSR, and corporate responsibility more generally. Many well known supermarket chains and other retailers have become active promoters of animal welfare issues. Superdrug's CSR and Environment policy states for instance that it is committed to ending all testing on animals for cosmetic and toiletry products and increasing awareness and action on environmental issues. The international pharmaceutical-led health and cosmetic retailer, Alliance Boots, is also committed to an end to animal testing, although its 2008 Animal Testing policy admits,

> We recognise that until satisfactory replacements are available, some animal tests will be carried out by others to meet regulatory requirements and protect public health. These safety tests sometimes involve ingredients used in products manufactured and sold by subsidiary businesses.

In March 2013 the EU enacted a law which made illegal the marketing, importing, or selling of animal tested cosmetic products in its 27 member states. However, according to a number of campaign groups, many big brand companies, including Nestle, Unilever, Procter & Gamble, Hellmann's, and Yakult, still engage in animal testing.

Some have argued that non-human species have been granted a greater degree of moral standing in post-industrial neo-liberal societies than was previously the case. The rise of ethical vegetarianism and concern with treatment of pets and farm animals suggest a decrease in the objectification of animals among some segments of society. While there are many testimonials to citizens' concerns for individual animals or plants, there is no consistent discussion about the scale of instrumental use of other species, and proportionally insignificant political representation of advocates for the rights of non-humans. The scale of human use of animals or plants has increased exponentially with human population growth and increase in consumption (Crist 2012). While the fate of a single rescued dolphin may capture public attention through the media, there is no consistent discussion about the millions of species 'harvested' for consumption, or used for medical experiments.

Ecological restoration and pollution control

Heavy extractive industries such as drilling for oil, coal mining, and stone quarrying involve processes that seriously degrade the environment. Occasionally, there may also be avoidable but devastating disasters that hit the global headlines. In April 2010 BP's Deepwater Horizon's rig experienced a blowout causing a massive oil spill in the Gulf of Mexico. The consequent ecological and economic damage was immense. The oil discharge continued for 84 days with an estimated 800 million litres of oil being released in to US waters. The economic, reputational, and political fallout for BP was huge and billions of dollars have been paid in compensation.

However, huge compensation is not always secured by those affected. Joe Berlinger's 2009 documentary, *Crude*, charts the strenuous efforts of the Cafan indigenous peoples, with their NGO allies in Ecuador and the US, to seek financial compensation and a substantial pollution clean-up from Texaco (now Chevron) after decades of environmentally destructive operations on their lands. There have been similar compensation campaigns regarding Shell's activities in Nigeria for many years, leading to genuine attempts by the oil company to improve its practice. Despite this, in 2013, Amnesty International argued that there were systematic flaws in Shell's system for investigating oil spills in the Niger Delta which combined with a lack of transparency and the publication of inaccurate data has renewed distrust in what has become known as 'Big Oil'. Amnesty's *Bad Information* report (Amnesty International, 2013:12) states:

> Women, men and children living in the Niger Delta have to drink, cook with, and wash in polluted water; they eat fish contaminated with oil and other toxins – if they are lucky enough to still be able to find fish; the land they use for farming has been contaminated; after oil spills the air they breathe reeks of oil, gas and other pollutants; they complain of breathing problems, skin lesions and other health problems, but their concerns are not taken seriously and they have almost no information on the impacts of pollution.

The controversies surrounding proposed (and actual) drilling for and mining for rare earth metals (including uranium) in Arctic areas such as Alaska, northern Canada, and probably in the very near future Greenland too have caused many corporations to produce detailed EIAs, clean-up and future ecological restoration strategies.

Other well known companies are already involved in ecological restoration or conservation projects, often in partnership with NGOs. Coffee is a staple and fashionable drink throughout the world and coffee shops like Starbucks, Costa, and Cafe Nero adorn many high streets and some university campuses. Coffee is a major Fairtrade product and coffee beans can and are being cultivated under the canopy of newly planted forests.

The ecological systems services provided by our natural environment are the basis for economic development, social prosperity, and ecological well-being. Damaging these 'services' has serious economic, ethical, and practical as well as environmental and human rights implications. Willem Ferwerda (2012) has suggested establishing an international mechanism that could create Ecosystem Restoration Partnerships. These would involve university business schools, NGOs, scientists, businesses, farmers, and local people restoring millions of hectares of land worldwide. Sustaining, restoring, or conserving ecosystems and biodiversity can be integrated into CSR with equal weight being given to the three 'Ps' of People, Profit, and Planet. Ferwerda argues that businesses, governments, and communities should do this. His prescribed course of action and an ethical position necessitates integrated cooperation and a radical shift away from the business of business is business mentality. In restoring natural capital and nature's resilience, businesses can contribute to the long-term environmental and economic good, add value to society, and see a return on investment (ROI). Potential ROIs may accrue

Box 7.4 Starbucks, coffee and climate change

In 2011, the NGO Conservation International (CI) renewed its long term partnership with Starbucks Coffee Company, a key corporate partner since 1998. This new two year agreement, worth US$3million, will promote coffee production practices that conserve biodiversity, maintain healthy ecosystems and support economic and social development in coffee production landscapes.

Starbucks began featuring CI's new logo on bags of whole bean and ground coffees from suppliers independently verified through the C.A.F.E. Practices program. In 2008, Starbucks and CI agreed to address the most important issue in the world – global climate change. The same forests that produce the world's best coffee and sustain millions of farmers also extract and store vast amounts of carbon dioxide. In fact, when they're destroyed, these forests release dangerous greenhouse gas into our atmosphere.

Healthy, productive forests are in everyone's best interest, and they're at the heart of this renewed partnership. In addition to shade grown coffee, Starbucks and CI are now investing in and supporting communities across coffee-growing landscapes who engage in climate-friendly activities, including protecting existing forests and helping to restore degraded landscapes.

Source: Adapted from Conservation International

from developing new green markets, carbon credits, biodiversity offsetting, biofuels and from enhancing corporate brand value, trust and reputation. Money can therefore be made from respecting planetary boundaries and the lives of other creatures.

Corporate governance

At the centre of ethical business practice must be good corporate governance which refers to the way that the company is governed. The governance of a company will broadly determine whether it does business in a sustainable or unsustainable manner or in a just or unjust way. Governance is multifaceted, dealing with social, economic and political accountability, financial probity and public transparency.

Ethical corporate governance refers to the processes and policies a company has which addresses issues relating to its administration, management, and the conduct of its day-to-day business.

Ethical corporate governance has increased in public importance particularly since the major scandal surrounding the demise of the massive US energy company Enron in 2004, whose blatantly corrupt and illegal practices triggered a large number of other corporate controversies concerning bribery, pollution, fraud, and price rigging. The failure of the major banks in 2007 and 2008 has added to these concerns. Well known companies such as Barclays Bank and BAE Systems have come under the media spotlight. Barclays was fined £290 million by British and US financial regulators for fixing bank lending rates.

Corporate wrongdoing has sometimes been exposed by whistle-blowers who as a result have frequently experienced corporate retribution in the form of dismissal, personal vilification, and blacklisting. The issue of whether a company employee should make public the wrongdoing of his/ her employer is both ethical and highly personal. Where does the loyalty of an employee lie and for that matter where does the company's loyalty lie – to its shareholders or its wider network of stakeholders and the wider social and ecological environment? Many national governments and international bodies such as the EU have recognized the social and corporate value of disclosing wrongdoing and have consequently passed laws protecting whistle-blowers and requiring companies to produce whistle-blowing policies and open and just procedures whereby allegations can be fairly investigated. Confidentiality guarantees and whistle-blower protection from company retaliation have been central to these initiatives, ensuring corporations act fairly and openly. All this is part of good or ethical corporate governance and there are a number of high profile guides company directors can consult. The OECD's *Principles of Corporate Governance* (OECD 2004) was first published in 1999 and is generally regarded as an international benchmark and universal model of good practice. In 2012 the EU published a new *Corporate Governance Action Plan* which focused on three fundamental aims, of which the first two are primarily ethical in nature:

- *Enhancing transparency*, which encompasses board diversity, risk management practices, governance reporting (including explanations for not applying ethical code provisions), shareholder identification, and disclosure of institutional investors' voting and engagement policies and voting records.
- *Engaging shareholders*, encompassing disclosure of renumeration policies and individual remuneration of directors, better shareholder control over related party transactions, improving transparency regarding conflict of interest with advisors, clarification of the meaning of 'acting in concert', and encouragement of the policy of employee share ownership.

The third aim is related to supporting growth and competitiveness.

Good corporate governance codes, plans, and principles must also be fully integrated with corporate sustainability policies and practice, sustainability reporting initiatives, and broader CSR commitments. Sustainability and ethical good practice are now fundamental concerns of the board of directors of any small, medium, or large enterprise claiming to be responsible. Good governance plays an important part in the realization of sustainability and socially responsible business strategies, and in turn is an excellent indicator of authentic and effective leadership too.

Case study

Tata Steel, ethics and sustainability

Tata Steel's vision is to be the global steel industry benchmark for value creation and corporate citizenship. Since its formation in 1868, the Tata Group has been driven by five core values which define the company's ethical position. These are: integrity, understanding, excellence, unity, and responsibility. For Tata Steel, sustainability is a core value extending across all its activities – economic strategy, environmental action, social support, and governance. Tata Steel's managing director is its chief ethics officer. Improvements in environmental performance are identified by sustainability assessment tools such as life cycle assement and comprehensive management systems. Employee welfare and health and safety are key concerns and aim at a zero fatality rate. Recognized trade unions are engaged and free collective bargaining respected. Equal opportunities and workforce diversity are also ensured. No person under the age of eighteen is employed by Tata or any of its suppliers. Wherever possible the company purchases goods and services from local entrepreneurs ensuring local economies benefit from its operations. Tata Steel has integrated reduce, reuse, and recycle in all its processes, extracting iron and carbon by reusing many residual materials, and reducing its consumption of primary raw materials. Tata Steel India reported an 18 per cent decrease in specific water consumption between 2002 and 2012.

Tata Steel's 2012–2013 Annual Report states:

> Responsible businesses are increasingly seen as corporate citizens who must set examples, actively contribute to the well-being of society, not just in economic terms, but also through actions that are aimed at conserving the environment and contributing to the growth of society. As boundaries of responsibility are redefined, businesses must be proactive, they must define and drive a vision that welds the goals of the society in which they function, with their own aspirations for growth.

Tata Steel aims to go beyond legal compliance with environmental laws and regulations and to make a positive contribution wherever possible.

Key terms

Business ethics, corporate social responsibility (CSR), good governance, human rights, partnership, poverty, trade, work.

Discussion questions

1 What are business ethics?
2 What has business ethics got to do with sustainability?
3 Is there a difference between CSR and philanthropy?
4 To what extent are low wages a cause of global poverty?
5 Why should businesses concern themselves with animal rights?
6 Why is good corporate governance so important to creating a more sustainable and ethical business environment?

End of chapter summary

Achieving a more sustainable world and certainly more sustainable business practice are both practical and ethical concerns. An important part of making this happen is when companies adopt policies that directly address social responsibility and environmental sustainability. Global poverty, labour exploitation, and environmental degradation are clearly moral wrongs, and businesses, like individuals, can be and have frequently been culpable. Just as an individual ought to act in a fair and just manner so should a company, especially one as big as BP, Tata Steel, Starbucks, or Apple. Most large businesses do try to act ethically and responsibly and many are looking to develop business models that move CSR beyond philanthropy. To do this involves adhering to those principles and practices advocated by the UNGC and much of the consequent activity addresses a whole range of human and other rights, making poverty, environmental protection, and restoration and respect for the well-being and lives of other creatures important elements of doing good by doing good business.

Further reading

Crane, A. and Matten, D. (2010) *Business Ethics: Managing Corporate Citizenship and Sustainability in an Age of Globalization*. Oxford: Oxford University Press.
Fleming, P. and Jones, M. (2013) *The End of Corporate Social Responsibility?* London: Sage.
Trevino, L. and Nelson, K.A. (2010) *Mangaging Business Ethics*. London: John Wiley.

Part III
Critical evaluation

8 Creating sustainable business practice

Government regulation and policy

It is often believed that the EU is far greener and far more culturally sympathetic towards the environment and sustainability than the US. America's refusal to ratify the 1997 Kyoto Protocol on climate change, its enthusiastic embrace of GMOs, fracking (the hydraulic fracturing of underground areas to extract shale gas), and its continuing dependency on 'Big Oil' seems to confirm this picture. The US has the highest per capita level of GHG emissions and a smaller percentage of its land devoted to organic agriculture than any other country in the world.

In Europe the application of the Precautionary Principle has generally made environmental regulation more risk averse than the US and public opinion tends to support this approach. However, American regulations regarding the handling of potentially carcinogenic substances are far stricter than in the Europe, However, it is not unknown for US companies to respond quickly and publicly to consumer fears related to GMOs. Since 1999 McCain Foods, the world's largest producer of chips (French fries), has adhered to a policy that its foods would not include GMOs. Other major US-based companies have been at the forefront of promoting the assumed environmental and other benefits of GMOs. More recently, environmental policy and regulation in the US and EU seems to have reversed positions, with European regulation today more relaxed than the US in some areas, with the US now becoming a little stricter.

In 2009 President Obama pledged to reduce America's GHG emissions by 17 per cent by 2020 and in 2013, in a keynote speech, he indicated that the environment would figure prominently in his second administration. He announced a number of executive orders empowering the US Environmental Protection Agency (EPA) to institute tougher regulations in a number of fields such as fuel efficiency standards and pollution controls. He also pledged federal funds to support the development of renewable energy initiatives. There are also growing areas of US and EU cooperation. In January 2013 the EPA and the EU renewed the Energy Star Agreement for a further 5 years which encourages the use of a common voluntary label

Box 8.1 Remarks by President Obama on climate change

Georgetown University, Washington, D.C., 25 June 2013

Today, we use more clean energy – more renewables and natural gas – which is supporting hundreds of thousands of good jobs. We waste less energy, which saves you money at the pump and in your pocketbooks.

And guess what – our economy is 60 percent bigger than it was 20 years ago, while our carbon emissions are roughly back to where they were 20 years ago.

So, obviously, we can figure this out. It's not an either/or; it's a both/and. We've got to look after our children; we have to look after our future; and we have to grow the economy and create jobs. We can do all of that as long as we don't fear the future; instead we seize it.

And, by the way, don't take my word for it – recently, more than 500 businesses, including giants like GM and Nike, issued a Climate Declaration, calling action on climate change 'one of the great economic opportunities of the 21st century.' Walmart is working to cut its carbon pollution by 20 percent and transition completely to renewable energy. Walmart deserves a cheer for that. But think about it. Would the biggest company, the biggest retailer in America – would they really do that if it weren't good for business, if it weren't good for their shareholders?

Source: The White House, available at: http://www.whitehouse.gov/the-press-office/2013/06/25/remarks president-climate-change

and a consistent set of energy performance indicators on electrical goods such as computers, monitors, printers, and multi-function devices. The intention is that this Agreement will boost the global demand and supply of energy efficient office equipment and stop manufacturers being deterred from eco-innovation by multiple and sometimes confusing labelling systems. At the time of writing, many of President Obama's promises have still to be acted upon.

In recent years a number of key sustainability principles have to varying degrees gained acceptance in a wide range of international treaties, regional agreements, and the legislation of nation-states. These agreements and regulations aim to control the environmental impacts of businesses, government bodies, and other organizations within a broad framework of a free market global capitalism which often attenuates their potential effect. These principles address:

- environmental sustainability;
- social equity and human rights;

and include:

- the Polluter Pays Principle;
- the Precautionary Principle;
- the Participatory Principle.

Polluter Pays Principle

In 1972 the OECD introduced a principle stating that those organizations which pollute the natural environment should pay, through either fines or taxation, for the measures needed to reduce or clear up that pollution. Since then much environmental legislation in the US, Japan, and the EU has virtually become synonymous with the Polluter Pays Principle.

The Precautionary Principle

The Precautionary Principle usually follows the definition published in the 1992 Rio Declaration on Environment and Development namely that 'where there are threats of serious or irreversible damage, lack of full scientific certainty shall not be used as a reason for postponing cost-effective measures to prevent environmental degradation'. However, the Precautionary Principle has been quite controversial and has not gained broad agreement on any one definition, interpretation, or even on its value as a way of informing risk regulation. Cass Sunstein (2005) of Harvard Law School has been a persistent critic suggesting that the principle can impede innovation, development, and effective regulation without necessarily offering the degree of protection its supporters claim. However, the UNGC argues that, considered as a means for generating preventative rather than remedial action, the principle does have important benefits for business, such as:

- environmental clean-up often costs a great deal of money and harms brand image;
- investing in unsustainable production and poor environmental methods gives sub-optimum returns;
- R&D in environmentally friendly products can have significant long-term benefits.

The Rio+20 Earth Summit reviewed the Precautionary Principle as a result of the wide range of interpretations and debates it has engendered, but it still remains of paramount importance to the future of sustainability in business and elsewhere as a means of inducing developers and innovators to reflect deeply on what they are doing.

Extended Producer Responsibility

Since 2002, the OECD and national governments have refined and extended the Precautionary Principle so that manufacturers and businesses are more effectively liable for the environmental damage they cause. This extended principle encompasses the whole produce life cycle including both upstream and downstream impacts.

The OECD defines Extended Producer Responsibility (EPR) as a concept where:

> ...manufacturers and importers of products should bear a significant degree of responsibility for the environmental impacts of their products throughout the product life-cycle, including upstream impacts inherent in the selection of materials for the products, impacts from manufacturers' production process itself, and downstream impacts from the use and disposal of the products. Producers accept their responsibility when designing their products to minimize life-cycle environmental impacts, and when accepting legal, physical or socio-economic responsibility for environmental impacts that cannot be eliminated by design.
>
> (OECD Extended Producer Responsibility (EPR) Fact Sheet)

In the US the application of EPR has mainly concentrated on hazardous materials or products that have low recycling rates such mercury switches and fluorescent lamps, but in the future EPR may also include paper and packaging. Some studies have suggested that nearly 70 per cent of American households have access to paper recycling facilities and those that argue for a business-led EPR system for packaging and printed paper argue that many companies have a significant financial interest in recycling more.

The Participatory Principle

The Participatory Principle, and similarly the Precautionary Principle, requires public engagement, consultation and debate on social, economic and particularly environmental policy, practice and implementation. Participation is a key feature of democratic environmental and sustainability governance. For instance, EIAs, a formal process of evaluating the impacts a proposed business, construction, or other project may have on society and the environment, often require public participation through consultation. Unfortunately, these consultations are often accused of falling short of a genuinely meaningful public involvement in decision making processes. Sometimes the rather inadequate attempts by governments and businesses to enter into dialogue with local communities, NGOs, and other civil society bodies may be the product of a lack of skills and capacity rather than will, intention, or a basic understanding of how dialogues should proceed, be managed, or integrated into wider business procedures.

Environmental management systems: Eco-Management and Audit Scheme

In the last 20 years there has been a considerable increase in the number of new environmental policy instruments such as eco-taxes, market-based initiatives, voluntary agreements, and environmental standards such as Europe's Eco-Management and Audit Scheme (EMAS) and informational devices such eco-labels in OECD countries.

> **An environmental management system (EMS)** is a tool for managing the impacts of an organization's environmental impacts by providing a clearly structured approach to planning and implementing environment actions.

EMAS is an EU voluntary environmental management initiative that has been operating since 1993 and is designed to improve a company's environmental performance, articulating a belief that a proactive approach to environmental challenges is a sign of a successful and responsible organization. Participation in the scheme is available to any public or private sector organization that wishes to reduce its environmental impacts and improve its overall environmental performance. EMAS can cover multiple sites within a single EU country and by the beginning of 2014 over 4,500 organizations and about 8,150 sites had registered with the scheme worldwide. The independent nature of EMAS ensures its reliability and validity. Organizations are required to publicly disclose the nature of their performance against a series of performance criteria and indicator statements. When an organization secures EMAS accreditation it can display the EMAS logo to promote its commitment to be environmentally responsible and a good corporate citizen. For SMEs a simpler scheme has been devised.

The EMAS Easy methodology covers all the EMAS requirements as well as those produced by ISO, a global federation of national standards bodies, namely its ISO 14001. EMAS Easy is based on an eco-mapping concept which encompasses a business's location and internal processes, offering participating organizations a clear and distinct set of guidelines, aids, prompts, and tables.

Many published evaluations of EMSs have consistently demonstrated that they have a positive impact on a firm's environmental performance. For instance, EMAS has led to improvements in many companies' pollution control, environmental planning, and has had indirect and beneficial environmental impacts on waste, packaging, transportation and, to some extent, the supply chain and R&D. The adoption of EMAS may also lead to improvements in innovation capacities and overall competitiveness. Many studies have shown how reducing environmental impacts, energy consumption, waste, and so on can significantly reduce costs and can increase the market valuation of the company. Other benefits include: better risk management, efficiency savings, better relations with local communities, improved public image, assured legal compliance, new business opportunities, improved quality of workplaces, and reduced carbon emissions. Unfortunately, SMEs are often unaware of their own specific environmental impacts as well as changes to environmental legislation and regulation. However, many companies operating in an international setting adopt EMSs as a way of demonstrating their external legitimacy, and, in the case of many Chinese companies, as a way of gaining entrance to international markets.

Sustainable supply chain management

A **supply chain** is a system including businesses, information, and resources linking raw materials, components, or services from a supplier to a business that fashions them into an end product and then delivers them to the end customer.

As discussed in Chapter 4, in a globalizing world, many companies have extended and diverse supply chains. Such long and complex supply chains increase the risk of reputational and commercial damage when a link in that supply chain is involved in unethical practices. Outsourcing and offshoring has exacerbated these dangers and certain states can have quite relaxed labour and environmental standards. Many well-known brand names, such as Nike and Apple, have suffered reputational damage when suppliers have been shown to use sweatshop labour or have used raw materials emanating from areas characterized by conflict and human rights abuses.

The electronics industry, and particularly those companies involved in producing digital media and communications technologies, have in many cases responded swiftly to allegations that rare earth metals – including tantalite, cassiterite, wolframite, gold, or their derivatives – used in manufacturing processes originate in war zones like the Congo.

Public debates and campaigns by NGOs like Greenpeace on 'conflict minerals' have led Hewlett-Packard, IBM, Cisco, and Apple to review their supply chains, often in cooperation with NGOs or as a member of the Electronics Industry Citizenship Coalition (EICC). Other companies such as Nintendo, which according to *Ethical Corporation* magazine still use conflict minerals in its game consoles, have (at the time of writing) still to act; otherwise they are in danger of losing credibility, especially in Europe, as a good corporate citizen despite the success of their products (see discussion on business ethics in Chapter 7).

Complex supply chains are particularly vulnerable to 'natural' disasters too. When floods devastated Thailand in 2011 causing 800 deaths and costing the Thai economy US$45 billion dollars, the price of hard drives rose steeply in high street stores for months afterwards as two thirds of manufacturers are located in this region. Hitachi, Dell, and HP all felt the impact and this caused CEOs in other sectors to start talking the language of sustainability too. They decided that when dealing with supply chain vulnerability they should require their suppliers to adhere to rigorous environmental, social, and employment standards. Many businesses are now linking the increasing incidence of extreme weather events to anthropogenic climate change.

Reviewing the supply chain inevitably involves working with stakeholders, including other companies dependent on the same or similar supply chains, and such networking has proven to be an effective way of reducing business risk and improving performance. Many large companies work with NGOs or environmental consultancies to do this. In 2013 Coca Cola announced it would extend its partnership with WWF to 2020, having already improved its water efficiency by 20 per cent and reduced its carbon emissions. The intention is to go further and to reduce the embodied carbon in its drinks by an additional 25 per cent. The company intends to work with the WWF to review its manufacturing processes, packaging, delivery methods, refrigeration, and ingredient sourcing. This will entail cooperation across the company's entire supply and value chain. However, such action is not necessarily easy to accomplish. Many companies will almost certainly experience internal and external barriers to greening the supply chain. These barriers may include cost, inadequate regulation (lack of the proverbial 'level playing field'), inadequate management information systems and/ or management of the transformation of materials, and poor supplier commitment. However, jointly dealing with uncertainties and environmental issues in a proactive and positive manner can and does produce effective, trusting, cooperative relationships among all those firms in the supply chain. Sustainable supply chain management is clearly a complex activity requiring a conscientious and critical appreciation of ecological and ethically focused business practices. Linton, Klassen and Jayaraman (2007:1080) write:

> Sustainability stretches the concept of supply chain management to look at optimizing operations from a broader perspective – the entire production system and postproduction stewardship as opposed to just the production of a specific product...In addition sustainability introduces less quantifiable considerations relating to the natural environment and in some cases social issues – what the business ethicists and the accounting fields refers to as the triple bottom line.

Localizing production, reducing transportation times and distances, and shifting consumption practices to support local business and local food growing can render supply chain management less complicated and make it inherently more sustainable. With globalization, production is often distributed in many places thousands of miles apart and foodstuffs are often transported huge distances, which inevitably increase carbon consumption and reduce economic opportunities for small local businesses, retailers, and growers. Working in partnership with environmental NGOs enables firms to draw on established and credible knowledge and expertise. As Peter Senge told the *Harvard Business Review* (quoted in Prokesch 2010:71):

> People don't trust the business-as-usual mind-set – for good reason. I don't think it's so different in the U.S. If a credible NGO certifies your product, your brand can gain hugely if you are willing to change your practices. NGOs can also provide knowledge. No business knows what Oxfam knows about the plight of farmers or what WWF knows about biodiversity and watersheds. The best businesses don't just hire the sharpest people; they also keep expanding their expertise by partnering with NGOs that have deeper and broader knowledge.

Life Cycle Assessment

Life Cycle Assessment (LCA) involves taking an analytical approach to the production of a good or service from the cradle to the grave. It covers everything that is significant environmentally (and socially) from the extraction of raw materials, their transformation in the manufacturing processes, to their ultimate disposal which may include reuse or recycling rather than simply dumping unwanted stuff in landfill sites. LCA facilitates the direct measurement of environmental impacts and fundamentally emphasizes the idea of futurity in the assessment of business performance. Around 80–90 per cent of the total life cycle costs of a product have been traced back to the final design stage making product design a key element in sustainable business practice.

LCA involves a number of stages (Welford 1998) namely:

- the identification of areas of environmental impact;
- the quantification of energy and material inputs, emissions, waste outputs, etc.;
- an assessment of the environmental impact and impact mechanisms involved in the inputs and outputs;
- the establishment of options and strategies for improving each stage of the product's life cycle.

There are generally four agreed stages in the LCA methodology which include:

- inventory and data gathering;
- impact analysis including effects on the environment, habitat modification, and human health;
- impact assessment which involves classification of impact categories, e.g health, ecology; characterization, quantification and aggregation of impact data; and valuation often involving comparative analyses and some degree of subject assessment;

- improvement and interpretation leading to better product or service design or manufacturing processes.

Closely related to LCA is Life Cycle Design (LCD) which incorporates LCA concepts into the design process and is consequently very similar to eco-design. Life Cycle Management (LCM) refers to a largely integrated approach to managing the life cycle of these products and services, which will include engaging with partners and stakeholders involved in the supply chain. An effective and sustainable LCA and LCM can lead to improvements in competitive advantage, strategic decision making, product/service design and value, securing new business opportunities, markets, and risk management processes.

There are numerous business guides to life cycle thinking and its associated C2C methodology. For example, UNEP worked with the Society of Environmental Toxicology and Chemistry (SETAC), which set the first LCA standards in 1990, to produce a great deal of detail valuable information (UNEP, 2007). There are a great many consultancies, NGOs, and other bodies also offering EMS and LCA expertise. ISO first standardized the LCA framework in its series of EMS ISO 14040 certifications in 1997/1998 and revised them in 2006 (Figure 8.1). The LCA methods prescribed in these standards often minimize the problems associated with discrepancies and/or variations possible in data gathering and interpretation.

LCA can be applied to any product or service from the manufacturing of hand drying equipment, detergents, building products, smartphones to seemingly sustainable fuels such as bioethanol. An assessment of fuel ethanol production from sugarcane in Brazil showed that what might seem to be at first glance a highly sustainable product and process includes aspects that pose

Four different phases of LCA can be distinguished:

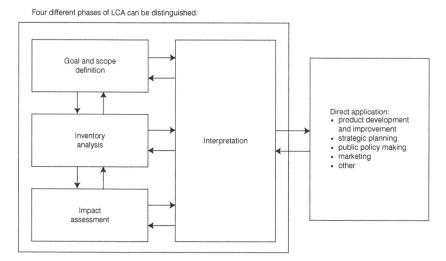

Figure 8.1 LCA framework as designated by ISO 14040

uncomfortable questions for many sustainability practitioners. In an interesting study Ometto, Hauschild and Roma (2008) concluded that the life cycle impact of fuel ethanol was high for it consumes a high quantity and diversity of non-renewable resources including an intensive use of pesticides, nutrients, and diesel during the largely mechanized cultivation of the sugarcane. The burning of diesel at harvest time also contributed significantly to air pollution. Inputs of renewable resources, particularly water, are high too. Thus, life cycle assessment clearly demonstrated that producing bioethanol in Brazil undoubtedly contributed to global warming, ozone formation, acidification, nutrient enrichment, eco- and human toxicity.

The Natural Step: change management

The Natural Step (TNS) framework for strategic sustainable change, education and communication, sometimes referred to as a Framework for Strategic Sustainable development (FSSD), starts from a scientifically based definition of sustainability centred on four key principles (or four system conditions) (Figure 8.2).

In a sustainable society, nature is not subject to systematically increasing

- concentrations of substances extracted from the Earth's crust;
- concentrations of substances produced by society;
- degradation by physical means;

and in that society

- people are not subject to conditions that systematically undermine their capacity to meet their needs.

TNS methodology is based on systems thinking and is an important tool for organizational planning and for mainstreaming sustainability in business and society. Importantly, it provides a way for businesses to see risks as potential opportunities and its ABCD analytical approach facilitates a clear apprehension of a sustainable business model. The four-phase ABCD analytic refers to:

- *Awareness* – aligning the business around a common understanding of sustainability.
- *Baseline mapping* – of the major inputs, outputs, and impacts of the business and how they can be managed more sustainably in accord with the four system conditions.
- *Creating a vision* – inviting decision makers and stakeholders to create a persuasive long-term vision for a sustainable business.
- *Down to action* – encompassing step-by-step implementation, prioritization of goals, and evaluation of progress and necessary modifications.

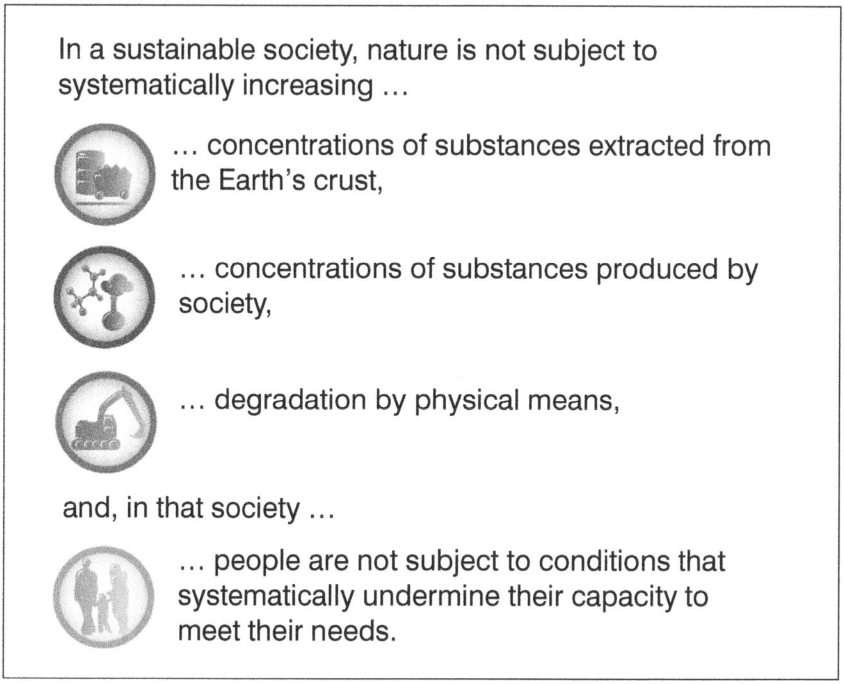

In a sustainable society, nature is not subject to systematically increasing …

… concentrations of substances extracted from the Earth's crust,

… concentrations of substances produced by society,

… degradation by physical means,

and, in that society …

… people are not subject to conditions that systematically undermine their capacity to meet their needs.

Figure 8.2 The Natural Step (source: www.thenaturalstep.org, permission of Scott Perret)

TNS employs a technique known as backcasting which is a cooperative, non-hierarchical methodology requiring widespread engagement with many stakeholders and a capacity to learn socially from others. At the end of the backcasting process an action plan is usually developed which will form the basis for implementation and future R&D. In this way, backcasting forms an important element of TNS's strategic framework for sustainable change.

Many companies, such as IKEA, Interface, Scandic Hotels, Mitsibushi, McDonalds, Volvo, Panasonic, Dow Chemical, Electrolux, and others have successfully adopted TNS to improve their sustainability performance and profile (Nattrass & Altomare 2001). Local governments and neighbourhood communities have also engaged successfully with TNS process. There is also a close relationship between EMAS, ISO 14001 and TNS for both the ISO and EMAS certification schemes provide additional structure when applying TNS principles which, for some critics, are primarily educational guides to facilitating structural and cultural change within organizations and the wider society. Its fundamental educative message is one of planetary limits and ecological citizenship.

Eco-labels

EMSs and certification schemes now exist for most business sectors and with these schemes come logos, kitemarks, and other publicly visible marks of quality, authenticity, and responsibility. When comparing similar products, eco-labels can inform sustainable purchasing decisions because they confirm a product has met a wide range of environmental performance criteria.

> An **eco-label** is a voluntary identification of the product developed by governments, manufacturers, and third-party organizations.

The first eco-label scheme, the Blue Angel, was launched in Germany in 1978 but today the eco-labelling approach to environmental certification is practised globally. A wide range of eco-labelled products are available on the market exhibiting 'green', 'biological', 'organic', 'fairtrade', or 'sustainable' symbols or claims. Not surprisingly, environmental performance labels and declarations vary greatly and the growing number of environmental claims made by companies led the US Federal Trade Commission (FTC) to issue 'Guides for the Use of Environmental Marketing' ('Green Guides') to provide detailed and accurate information and guidance on claims for biodegradable, compostable, recyclable, recycled, ozone-safe, and climate-neutral products.

In Europe, the EU's Ecolabel voluntary scheme was launched in 1992 and participation in the scheme enables a company to use the Ecolabel on a specific group of products. By the end of 2011, 1,300 licences had been awarded with the logo appearing on 17,000 products. In 2014 the Ecolabel Index, the largest global directory of eco-labels, tracked the existence of 445 eco-labels in 197 countries across twenty-five industrial sectors. This has led increasing numbers of people to ask how green any given eco-label might be. The debate is particularly vigorous within the 'sustainable' fishing industry but is not confined to that sector.

In the North American construction industry, the Leadership in Energy and Environmental Design (LEED) certification scheme has led the field for some time, although it now faces competition from the rival Green Globes scheme. This means that there is no overall agreement on a single definition of what makes a building 'green' or green enough, although a high rating such as in the UK being awarded a Building Research Establishment Environmental Assessment Methodology (BREEAM) 'Excellent' or 'Outstanding' is generally recognized as very valuable and does bring with it considerable green kudos. In the US, Joel Makower, founder of GreenBiz. com, has noted that prior to LEED anyone could say what made a building green but now, at least for buildings, LEED has established a comprehensive set of standards and has been credited with the sharply increased demand for green building. By creating a unified standard, it has enabled product manufacturers, architects, developers, city planners, landlords, and tenants alike to speak the same language and operate on the same playing field. LEED has now certified over 20,000 construction projects and according to GreenBiz the new LEEDv4 performance and transparency requirements is likely be a global incentive for construction firms to be more sustainable.

Although eco-labels appeal to and are highly valued by green consumers and have certainly raised general public awareness, the market share for eco-labelled products remains fairly small. Without engaging in other more conventional marketing practices which are concerned with product and brand positioning, price, place, and general promotion there is a danger that potential new markets for green products may not be created to the degree they could and should. In the report *Signed, Sealed... Delivered?* published by SustainAbility in 2011 there is a recognition that the proliferation of eco-labels, combined with some corporate game playing, probably requires a rethinking of what eco-labels are, what they should do and how they should do it. Echoing our discussions in Chapters 4, 9 and 11, the report states (SustainAbility, 2011: 44):

> If the move to a more sustainable world requires new trading relationships and new forms of consumption – such as services, sharing, re-use, and yes, less consumption – a product-by-product focus may end up missing the larger point. Too much focus on any one product may distract from the greater imperative to keep production and consumption within environmental limits and to ensure sustainable livelihoods for all.
>
> We urge a shift towards a new, systems-focused model based upon increasingly demanding and pre-competitive standards, above which brands compete, collaborate and partner with civil society to embed these standards into business models and to transform supply chains and consumer behavior – and where civil society and government evolve more effective and efficient ways of holding business accountable.

Interestingly, the WWF has noted that for many business executives the value of eco-labels lie more in increased operational effectiveness than in promoting sustainability.

Corporate reporting

Sustainability must not only be practised but must be *seen* to be practised. Many people argue that firms should publicly account for and report on what they do, what at other times would have been treated as externalities. Environmental pollution was frequently considered by business to be an 'externality' and not really its business. Today pollution and other externalities are definitely a company's business and corporate reporting now includes information on the social, environmental, and other impacts and most importantly on the improvements companies have undertaken. This accounting and reporting, of course, needs to be accurate, measured, and verified otherwise allegations of greenwashing could cause reputational damage whether or not they are borne out by the facts.

Consequently, many companies issue regular bulletins on their social responsibility and sustainability performance, going into considerable detail in their annual corporate sustainability reports. Shareholders need to be convinced their investment is worthwhile not least because bad labour practices, failure to comply with government regulation, or poor environmental performance can swiftly and negatively impact upon the financial bottom line. Unless a company is fully transparent in its reporting processes and procedures it is very difficult for shareholders and other stakeholders to have a clear view of a company's health. Corporate reporting is now the norm in Europe and the USA although the quality and detail of this reporting does vary. KPMG has reported a dramatic increase in corporate reporting in the Asia Pacific region and it is now mainstream business practice throughout the world. Among the world's largest 250 companies, the corporate reporting rate is 93 per cent.

For the global consultancy PWC, corporate reporting is often not taking into account the complexities of the modern business world and a new integrated reporting model needs to be developed but, for PWC, first a number of barriers to change need to be addressed:

- stakeholders tend to perceive and analyse parts of the whole rather than the whole system;
- the current focus is too firmly on data, rather than people, culture and behaviours;
- more disclosures tend to be bolted onto the old model rather than to recast in a new model on the basis of what's important and relevant;
- there is inertia about the complexity of changes that could increase liability.

At the core of corporate reporting is financial reporting which, at the very least, needs to apply generally accepted accounting principles (GAAP) but also needs to cover governance, executive renumeration, corporate responsibility, and sustainability, It must also include critical contextual and non-financial information that aids understanding, such as market position, performance and future prospects, known as narrative reporting (PWC 2011). Integrated or systemic (as opposed to analytic) reporting connects information on all of these elements, thereby presenting an organization's performance holistically. Business performance cannot be separated from the wider society, the environment, or the economy (Table 8.1). The International Integrated Reporting Committee (IIRC) has developed a framework, the Integrated Reporting Framework (IRF), that largely does this and reflects the social, economic, and environmental context in which the firms operate.

KPMG believes that, although few companies currently generate integrated reports, such reporting will increase in the future. In 2013 the Sodexo Group, a global leader in quality of life services, issued its first

Table 8.1 A comparison of analytic and systemic approaches to corporate reporting

Analytic approach	Systemic approach
Concern with definition of parts	Concern with understanding the whole
Focus on elements rather than their interaction	Focus on interaction of elements
Focus on internal structure of the system	Equal focus on the internal structure of the system and its interaction with the wider business environment
Produces a static model	Produces a dynamic model
Tries to disguise complexity	Encompasses complexity

Source: Adapted from PWC (2011:9).

integrated report reporting on the progress it has made since it published it *The Better Tomorrow Plan* in 2009. Sodexo's CSR website provides a great deal of information in an attractive and accessible manner, including videos, graphs, diagrams, key performance figures, testimonials, and case studies. As Neil Barrett (Barrett 2014), Vice President of sustainable development at Sodexo, wrote in *GreenBiz*,

> With a supply chain that includes 10,000 suppliers ranging from large multinational companies to family firms, our commitment to sustainability means we have to think locally and globally. While you might expect us to source locally in remote and hard-to-reach places, which we do, we'll introduce you to a local producer who grows vegetables that Sodexo serves 40 minutes from his farm in the very heart of Paris; a family-owned food distributor in the United States who connects us to three dozen local farms; and 1,000 technical experts who are part of the Roth (a Sodexo company) business model that deploys them to serve our clients across the United States.

GRI

The GRI, referred to in the Introduction, was set up in 1997 to provide organizations with a comprehensive voluntary sustainability reporting framework. GRI is currently used around the world by over 11,000 companies and has witnessed a steady take-up by companies involved in oil, gas, mining, and pharmaceuticals. In May 2013 GRI issued its fourth iteration (G4), shifting its focus away from levels of sustainability to value chain materiality. Its design is now more user-friendly and universally applicable to all organizations. The G4's emphasis on what is material encourages organizations to provide only information that is of critical relevance to businesses and their stakeholders, with disclosure coming in two forms – core and comprehensive. The general and specific standards that were revised for G4 pertain to the supply chain, governance, ethics and integrity, anti-corruption, public policy, GHG emissions, and energy. GRI guidance comes in two parts, namely Reporting Principles and Implementation, which, recognizing the importance of clear communication, includes advice on presentation and report formats. GRI is also closely aligned with other frameworks including the OECD Guidelines for Multinational Enterprises, the UNGC's Ten Principles, the UN Guiding Principles on Business and Human Rights, and the ISO 26000 guidelines on social responsibility.

GRI has had considerable entrepreneurial successes in promoting sustainability reporting and the triple bottom line but there are some critics who doubt whether GRI and similar initiatives, such as SustainAbility's biennial reports or KPMG's triennial surveys, do actually offer sufficient conditions for organizations wishing to effectively contribute to global sustainability. Milne and Gray (2013:24) write:

> Through the practice of incomplete TBL (aka sustainability) reporting many organizations seem to confuse narrow and incomplete, partial reporting with claims to be *reporting on being sustainable*, actually *being sustainable*, or more commonly, with claims to be *moving towards sustainability*. These claims, we contend, are further exacerbated through the institutional developments [which] may amount to little more than soothing palliatives that, in fact, may be moving us towards greater levels of un-sustainability.

Not surprisingly, scepticism of corporate intentions continues as increasingly sophisticated and detailed reporting is contrasted with regular revelations of corporate secrecy and wrongdoing, bribery, price fixing, inadequate R&D disclosure, aggressive mergers and acquisitions, or failure to compensate for past actions. Many critics suggest that corporate reporting can still mask corporate malpractice and some of the giants of the pharmaceutical industry who profess adherence to GRI guidelines, such as Pfizer, have sometimes been singled out for sharp criticism (Goldacre 2012). Pfizer's efforts to prevent 'counterfeit' drugs appearing on the market is often perceived as simply a way of maintaining their own commercial dominance even if it is at the expense of human health in the developing world. It took 15 years for some Nigerian families to receive compensation for the death of their children from meningitis after a controversial drug trial conducted by a Pfizer subsidiary, despite becoming the subject of a bestselling book by John Le Carré and a Hollywood movie, *The Constant Gardener*, released in 2005.

Green accounting systems and investment strategies

For all the GRI and other schemes' failings, many businesses have become more sensitive to the need to act in a socially responsible and sustainable manner. Progress may be relatively slow and subject to barriers and hesitations that retard momentum but increased transparency and increasingly accurate reporting does enable actual and potential investors to screen companies and direct their funds to those companies that do act sustainably. NGOs such as Friends of the Earth and other groups such as the Climate Institute and the Asset Owners Disclosure Project have campaigned vigorously in recent years for ethical, green, and socially responsible investment. The Global Initiative for Sustainability Ratings (GISR), a joint initiative of Ceres and the Tellus Institute, was launched in May 2013 with the intention of creating a standard for sustainability ratings that would help mainstream sustainability concerns in the financial markets and so hopefully direct investment capital towards companies making a genuine effort to go green. TNS has a similar scheme known as the Gold Standard Benchmark for Sustainable Business.

It has also been estimated that there are possibly over one hundred sustainability ratings currently in existence including those compiled by very well-known brands such as the Dow Jones Sustainability Index and the FTSE4Good Index. Many reports and surveys indicate that an increasing number of institutional investors, such as pensions funds, are contemplating switching their resources away from oil, coal, gas, alcohol, gambling, and arms to more sustainable enterprises. The Global Compact 100 Index tracks the stock market performance of a representative group of GC companies on both adherence to the Ten Principles and leadership commitment and profitability. The deciding issue in many cases, despite the attractiveness of a more value-driven investment strategy, is simply maximizing or at least optimizing ROI.

In 2013 the ethical research firm Eiris showed that the money held in UK green and other ethical funds had increased to £12.2 billion and other research has shown that ethical investors are fairly heterogenous. There seems to be a wide variation in the degree to which an investor is willing to sacrifice an improved financial return for ethical performance (Berry and Yeung 2013). Investors will frequently screen out the very worst firms in preference to selecting the very best for this reason. However, there has recently been a growing global interest in the principles of Islamic finance in many parts of world. The Islamic Bank of Britain, a Sharia compliant retail bank, states that each of its financial products 'are derived from trade, entrepreneurship and risk-sharing in which the customer and Islamic bank work together as partners towards a mutually profitable end', that is, in a fair, ethical, and socially responsible manner. Interest payments on loans are not Sharia compliant, so the Islamic finance principles of co-ownership, or Musharaka, with leasing, or Ijara, are applied to the banks' mortgages. This means that the bank and the customer purchase the property in partnership. The customer will then pay rent on the bank's share in the property. Thus, as Joel Makower (2013:28) writes, the world of ethical finance and investment is not simple and although there are grounds for optimism it is necessary to be realistic:

Few investors – particularly the large pension funds and other institutions that can move financial markets – have viewed sustainability as a relevant investment criterion. Even when shown studies that sustainability leaders outperformed their peers on key financial indicators and ratios, including stock price, most analysts and fund managers haven't been impressed. Only hard core 'socially responsible investors' new to the theory.

Accompanying the movement for green and more ethical investment is a growing interest in green accounting backed by such global brands as Walmart, Tesco, Google, and some big oil corporations. Puma, the sportswear company, has estimated the financial value of the ecosystem services it benefits from – water, GHG emissions, land use, etc. – as being about US$145 million.

There are growing numbers of green accountancy firms and academic interest in the field fuelled by the work of Tim Jackson, John Elkington, and others who have persuasively advocated the need for new methods of sustainability accounting and for governments to move away from economic growth measures such as GDP and GNP which simply measure the volume of economic activity irrespective of whether this activity damages people or the environment. Sustainability accounting in business aims to create and provide high quality information systems which will help a company become sustainable. It is necessarily related to corporate sustainability reporting, which is basically a means of communicating performance to stakeholders and the general public.

Putting a price tag on nature or appending a financial valuation to ecosystem services does engage business, although it also enrages many others who feel the natural environment should not be subjected to the dictates of a profit and loss account. The financial valuation of forests, fresh water, air quality, and chlorinated hydrocarbon (CHC) and GHG pollutions which harm the atmosphere's ozone layer and contribute the climate change, makes a deal of sense when this is presented to CEOs in terms of billions, or more likely trillions, of dollars. Global sustainability tools, standards, and protocols are essential guideposts for businesses and communities but are often inadequate, fiercely debated, or undermined and too frequently ignored. Nevertheless, TEEB reports (see TEEB case study in Chapter 2), produced collectively by GRI, IUCN, PWC, UNEP, and the WBCSD, have suggested how the development of new business models, using sensitive financial valuation criteria, could conceivably deliver both biodiversity and ecosystem service benefits while promoting private investments, entrepreneurship, and wider corporate social responsibility. The TEEB business guide (TEEB 2010) offers a number of small case studies of corporate engagement to demonstrate this. For example, British American Tobacco (BAT) has widely promoted improved, and profitable, agricultural practices including soil and water conservation, a responsible

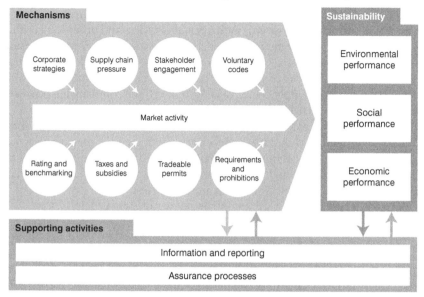

Figure 8.3 A market-based approach to sustainability (source: adapted from TEEB for Business Coalition Prospectus, 2012)

use of agrochemicals, environmental standards in tobacco processing, and local and sustainable afforestation measures which help farmers who need wood for tobacco curing. Even though BAT has won numerous awards for CSR and sustainability reporting, many people question the ethics of a company whose product is harmful to human health and potentially lethal. In addition, critics argue that there is a long way to go before green accountancy and the accounting profession in general is able to move beyond thinking predominantly in terms of creditors, investors, lenders, and market-based mechanisms to resolve the many environmental problems that have been caused by the market itself (Figure 8.3).

Case study

Intel and a conflict free supply chain

In 2009, Intel asked its suppliers to complete a survey on the origin of metals used in its supply chain. The results demonstrated there was great variance in the amount of information suppliers knew about the metals used in their supply chains. In response to this finding, in 2009, Intel conducted its first on site conflict minerals smelter review; this was also the first to be conducted in the electronics industry. As of May 2012, Intel has conducted on-site reviews of over 50 smelters in 13 different countries and will continue with smelter validation audits in the future.

To ensure a holistic approach is taken to conflict minerals, Intel is committed to collaborating with industry stakeholders and others on conflict minerals. Intel has convened conferences and workshops on the topic and has also promoted cross sector collaboration. For example, Intel convened a 'Responsible Gold Sourcing Summit' which aimed to promote responsible sourcing in the gold supply chain. On a local level, the company has also sent staff to the Eastern DRC to gain firsthand insight on the issue.

Intel has learnt that in order to address the issue of conflict minerals, collaboration with stakeholders is necessary. By doing this, the company has gained invaluable knowledge which has helped it understand the operating characteristics of each smelter and determine the gaps in its ability to trace the source of ore from specific mines and countries.

Source: http://supply-chain.unglobalcompact.org/site/article/121

Key terms

Audit schemes, corporate communication and reporting, eco-labels, ethical investment, green accounting, regulation.

Discussion questions

1 How can government motivate green business through regulation?
2 To what extent should the greening of business be left to businesses alone?
3 How can EMSs facilitate change management practices within business?
4 How can green accounting systems and ethical investment make businesses more sustainable?
5 How can complex supply chains be managed more sustainably?
6 Why are there so many different reporting systems? Is this a problem?

End of chapter summary

This chapter has explored a number of practical actions and strategies businesses, governments, and communities can adopt in creating more sustainable economic and commercial arrangements. All actions, tools, frameworks, and strategies that exist, such as government regulations, environmental systems, eco-labelling schemes, sustainability reporting initiatives and green accounting processes, for businesses and society tend to change. There are plenty of examples of good practice but not enough and they really need to be scaled up to make the powerful impact they must. Communicating all this as both a distinct possibility and as a credible way of doing business is developing through increasingly effective corporate reporting, green accounting, and ethical investments. Governments can aid and further motivate these changes through passing green legislation and regulation. In addition, consumers can adopt more responsible and greener practices themselves too.

Further reading

Elkington, J. (2012) *The Zeronaughts: Breaking the Sustainability Barrier*. London: Earthscan.

Jackson, T. (2011) *Prosperity with Growth: Economics for a Finite Planet*. London: Earthscan.

Nattrass, B. and Altomare, M. (2001) *The Natural Step for Business*. Gabriola Island, Canada: New Society Publishers

PWC (2011) *Tomorrow's Corporate Reporting: a critical system at risk*. London: Tomorrow's Company.

9 Key challenges for making sustainability a reality

The changing global business environment

One key factor determining the long-term success of business is how well it recognizes significant sustainability challenges, and identifies changes in the business environment and adapts to them. Some changes are so dramatic that everybody notices them (such as scarcity of certain precious metals); others are subtle but can threaten industry if ignored for too long (such as climate change or population growth). It has been estimated that US$2 trillion of economic output could be put at risk if businesses do not respond to 'peak metal', putting pressure on profits and risking the operations of those businesses that do not adapt (World Economic Forum 2012).

Considering that sustainability has become mainstream, consumer needs require not only cheap or better quality products, but also products that are socially and environmentally responsible. What is less obvious is in how much corporate leaders and consumers are informed about sustainable choices and in how much sustainability can be 'made to work' in a new global business environment. A key question then is not whether efficiency strategies will be implemented, but whether we can accelerate their adoption so that ecological overshoot can be slowed and, ideally, reversed (Tennant and Brennan 2015). Below we shall outline the paradoxes of sustainability, focusing on the practical and ethical challenges that businesses face in the globally changing environment.

Paradoxes of sustainability

Charity paradox

Similar to the sustainable development paradox discussed in Chapter 5, the 'charity paradox' outlines conflict rather than complementarity in social and environmental interests (Figure 9.1). While on the surface of it environmental and social-focus NGOs appear equally altruistic, the paradox arises from their conflicting objectives. For example, the survival of a mere

Under Pressure

Madagascar's wildlife are under threat from a growing human population. The Malagasy people's need for croplands and food, combined with a global desire for minerals and other products found in the region, are taking away habitat for fossa, lemurs, tortoises, lizards and fish.

Denver Zoo cares for several species of endangered Madagascar animals and works with conservation partners in Madagascar to work on meeting the needs of the people while saving these rare, unique animals.

Figure 9.1 Charity paradox (source: Helen Kopnina)

3,000 tigers in the wild depends on combating poaching and destruction of natural habitat associated with the expansion of human settlement. A charity organization combating AIDS, for example, will have very different priorities from a charity concerned with the survival of tigers. While one charity sees saving every human life and raising welfare as the highest moral priority, another one might be concerned about the expansion of agriculture in the last remaining habitats for endangered species, considering extermination of other living beings on Earth morally equivalent to genocide.

Another side of the charity paradox is exemplified by the dependency theory, discussed in Chapter 3. We shall recall that according to the dependency theory, developed countries continue to exploit developing countries through foreign debt and disadvantageous trade, and development aid, making poor countries dependent on handouts. NGOs promoting development do not address the very development enterprise that might have caused poverty in the first place. In this view, charity may be seen as actually prolonging the faulty system.

As discussed in Chapter 5 it is questionable whether poverty can be adequately addressed by putting even more pressures on the existing

Box 9.1 Slavoj Žižek on poverty and charity

Indeed, the remedies are part of disease

They try to solve the problem of poverty, for instance by keeping the poor alive or in the case of very advanced school, by amusing the poor

But this is not a solution. It's an aggravation of the difficulty.

The proper aim is to try and reconstruct society on such a basis that poverty will be impossible

And the altruistic virtues have really prevented the carrying out of this aim

The worst slave owners were those who were kind to their slaves

and so prevented the core of the system being realized by those who suffered from it...

It is immoral to use private property in order to alleviate the horrible evils that result from the institution of private property ...

Question

Watch the whole video. Do you agree or disagree with this view? Why and or why not?

Source: Excerpt from Slavoj Žižek – *First as Tragedy, Then as Farce* (2010)

resources. The fact that most charity donors are not consciously aware of this potential conflict has wider implications for businesses.

Economic growth or conservation?

A number of difficult questions need to be asked. Let us use the example of the tigers in the Box 9.2.

Progress or return to the roots?

While sustainability embodied by traditional communities may be an attractive ideal (see the Schooling the World case study in Chapter 4), 'return to the roots' is hardly realistic, given the current striving towards 'progress', in which economic development is seen as the greatest good (Figure 9.2).

Just as the car was seen as the greatest good for human mobility, or just as asbestos was seen as the 'miracle material' in the construction industry, and plastic was invented as the greatest durable material, so we have seen how many 'progressive' things have backfired. Nonetheless, we are still not prepared to return to riding horses or camels and drinking from the mud-

Box 9.2 How much does the dead tiger cost?

Should we choose for conservation of tigers and preservation of the last pristine habitats in favour of ecological justice or should we promote only human welfare? Would conservation of tigers also not bring economic benefits to the nearby communities that could profit from eco-tourism if the tiger population survives in the long term? As most zoo owners know, keeping a live tiger brings in more profit than a skin of a dead one. Should the zoo owners invest more into anti-poaching programmes? Yet, as some animal rights organizations inquire, is it ethical to keep great cats caged for profit? Do the zoos' breeding programmes and protection they offer from poachers not overweigh this concern?

In the wild, the remaining tigers are endangered as Chinese medicine uses tiger parts for its lucrative trade. Is the Western pharmaceutical industry well placed to defeat the myth of tiger product healing and simultaneously wipe out competition for its own products?

The paradox is that hardly any long-term economic growth can be achieved without conservation of natural resources, be it tigers, or water, or land; but this conservation is conditional on combating the effects of economic growth.

cups made from clay. Although either of these actions could make a huge difference in sustainable living, we tend to seek newer and more 'advanced' designs, rather than see ourselves as 'going back in time'.

As we shall further discuss in Chapter 11, many innovative ideas, such as the circular economy or C2C, are not 'new'. Yet, in order to reintroduce

Figure 9.2 Progress or return to the roots? (source: Jim Hurst, copyright/permission of Schooling the World)

these ideas, one of the explicit strategies (that can be very lucrative as well) is presenting these as progressive inventions.

Possibility versus dream

How realistic are certain sustainability solutions, given the world's political, economic, and current ideological climate? How much can be actually be achieved, and how much sustainability is an idealistic dream? We may need both – the dreamers and the doers, best of all combined. The pessimists could instruct us on what the limitations are, and the optimists could inspire us to look ahead and break the boundaries. Since the Industrial Revolution occurred only 300 years ago (which is nothing in comparison to the millennia-long history of human civilization), the reversal of some features of industrialization that have turned out to be simply disastrous should not require a great effort or a substantial compromise to our pride. This is both the challenge and the opportunity for business.

Practical challenges

As discussed in Chapter 5, sustainable development objectives can be found empirically questionable in propagating the oxymoronic goal of maintaining economic growth and redistribution of wealth and simultaneously keeping the health of the ecosystem intact. Few businesses realize the relationship between population growth, economic expansion, and efficiency gains. After an initial period of exploitation efficiency gains are usually marginal and are unlikely to match the extra demand placed on consumption by a growing middle-class population (Tennant and Brennan 2015). Realizing this has significant implications for business that wants to go beyond the status quo.

Disputing the mainstream theories of sustainability

As we have discussed in Chapter 5, sustainability and sustainable development embodies a number of paradoxes that need to be understood before ways forward can be devised. Economic development continues to depend on exploitation of natural resources, and inequality in access to resources has been a persistent feature of past development processes. Yet, if inequalities are to be addressed by raising the consumption level everywhere to the level of 'developed' consumers, the Earth's capacity to sustain the current human population of 7 billion – and growing – will become all but impossible (Rees 2010). Instead, current development is compromising the opportunities of future generations. Thus, the idea that sustainability is about 'lifting' the poor to the level of the rich, without the rich changing their unsustainable practices, appears to be one of the greatest myths of sustainability.

Eco-efficiency might not be the long-term solution as it only works to make the destructive system a bit less so (McDonough and Braungart 2002). In the worst cases, eco-efficiency can make the system that results in over-exploitation become more pernicious, because its workings become more subtle and long term. For example, the sustainability initiatives such as Shell's eco-marathon (competition for inventors of more fuel-efficient car engines) allow the company to sustain its core business, oil. Fossil fuels cause problems ranging from climate change to skewed geopolitical relationships and dependency on 'oil states' and thus are fundamentally unsustainable. If car motors become more efficient, that would imply that an unsustainable product would last longer, and no fundamental change to alternative sources of energy would be made.

Critique of the mainstream business models

At present, much of business is simply about profit, and environmental impacts are rarely decoupled from economic growth. To be restorative implies that businesses have a positive environmental impact, yet this is particularly difficult to implement in the context of contemporary manufacturing. Obsolescence is a strategy that is well integrated into the idea of volume sales business models: if products are designed to last for a certain number of months or years, then a manufacturer has reason to believe that it will be able to sell more of his product in the future. A durable product, however, comes with no guarantee of repeat sales and so manufacturers must conceive of different ways to make money in the long term, before the market becomes saturated.

Going on with a system that generates massive amounts of waste in the endless spiral of production and consumption, only prolongs the faulty system (McDonough and Braungart 2002). Strategies relating to the flows of materials within industrial value chains, for example end-of-life management (EOL) and EPR, have historically focused on the management of products at the disposal phase and are still largely wasteful. Whilst these approaches attempt to resolve the issue downstream they have limitations due to the impact of decisions made during product design. Implementing most of these strategies will often require product design changes that should occur at the beginning of the manufacturing process.

A consequence of poor design is seen in the many cheap consumer goods that are economically unattractive to take apart and repair. If parts cannot be accessed to facilitate any type of maintenance it is likely that the product value will be lost well before the real end of its life cycle, as discussed in Chapter 8. On the other hand, many packaging materials could potentially last for hundreds of years (think of plastic and glass), and yet they contain one-time use consumable products only, with most packaging being disposed of afterwards. Recycling of packaging results in downcycling.

Cradle-to-grave

McDonough and Braungart (2002) outline a number of fundamental problems with the typical cradle-to-grave production system: the use of 'one size fits all', 'brute force', and 'culture of monoculture'. An example of 'one size fits all' is an international style architecture – found everywhere in the world – a rather unimaginative block building that requires a lot of electricity to keep it lit at night, warm in the winter or cool in the summer.

As will be discussed in Chapter 11, by contrast, C2C buildings are similar to pre-industrial designs in that they use local materials, like the mud huts of the Bedouins, which are naturally cool during the hot days and keep in the warmth at night, without any use of electricity. Obviously, different world regions will use different (local) materials, utilizing geographic and climatic differences, materials, and the knowledge of traditional construction.

The example of the use of the use of 'brute force' is dishwashing detergents, or any kind of chemicals used for agriculture and human waste treatment facilities. As discussed in Chapter 2, such measures have a tendency to misfire and have severe side effects.

The obvious example of a 'culture of monoculture' is agricultural crops or plantations used for biofuel production that have taken an increasingly larger proportion of originally biologically diverse land. Without noticing, we live in an absurd and increasingly globalized world where everyday urban planning prohibits any natural growth:

> The average lawn is an interesting beast: people plant it, then douse it with artificial fertilizers and dangerous pesticides to make it grow and to keep it uniform – all so that they can hack and mow what they encouraged to grow. And woe to the small yellow flower that rears its head!
>
> (McDonough and Braungart 2002)

Burning garbage (Figure 9.3), for example, to generate energy, may seem 'green', but it is only one step removed from the cradle-to-grave model, as discussed in the Introduction.

McDonough and Braungart (2002:18) summarize the negative consequences of industrialization as a system of production that puts billions of pounds of toxic material into the air, water, and soil. It produces materials so dangerous they will require constant vigilance by future generations and results in gigantic amounts of waste. The existing system creates prosperity by digging up or cutting down natural resources and then burying or burning them, and erodes the diversity of species and cultural practices.

This wastefulness is prevalent in everyday life. A typical example of everyday urban living is the dog owners' wrapping up their pet's excrement in plastic and throwing it in mixed garbage containers. Another example is modern funerals, when the body together with the coffin and many other valuable materials literally goes up in smoke. All these examples do not testify

Figure 9.3 Waste to energy (source: Helen Kopnina)

to any kind of natural cycle or regeneration that could offer a profoundly more hopeful vision of sustainability. While nobody would suggest that dog excrement or dead bodies should be left lying on the ground, there are much more intelligent ways of disposing of them so that they become part of something new, nothing less than regeneration of life.

The prevailing economic paradigm, McDonough and Braungart contend, is based on short-term thinking encouraging rampant consumption and environmental destruction for the sake of economic development. Since the time of the Industrial Revolution, most products, from milk packages to non-renewable energy, were designed not to last, and most have built-in obsolescence. When products are recycled they may be 'upcycled' or 'downcycled'. Both usually refer to the repurposing of waste products and materials, but whereas upcycling increases the value of the product, downcycling decreases it by shredding, melting or crushing and destroying any inherent value that the product may have had. Cradle-to-grave products usually end up as toxic landfill, in an incinerator, or downcycled into the low-value products.

> **Downcycling** is the process of converting waste materials into new materials or products of lesser quality and reduced functionality.

Think of your typical rubbish bin. If you live in a rich country, most of the contents of this rubbish will be burned to generate new energy for running our factories and cars, and heating our houses. A small percentage of your rubbish might get recycled. Some might go into the biodegradable compartment, some in paper, some in glass recycling. If you live in a poor country, most of the rubbish will go to the landfill – just be dumped in the ground or in the ocean. The Pacific Ocean Garbage Patch is such an example.

According to Braungart (2013), recycling is a form of downcycling that involves transportation, energy, and often other resources such as water. Something that has once been a tree will be reduced to slow 'death', either quickly in the incinerator, or slowly, by extending its 'life' by recycling. For example, the so-called 'Waste to Energy', widely recognized as promising 'green technology' incinerators that burn waste to create energy in the form of electricity, contribute to environmental degradation and climate change (see Figure 9.3).

This cradle-to-grave industrial system does not possess an adequate long-term goal. While being eco-efficient may indeed reduce resource consumption and pollution in the short term, the system does not address the deep design flaws of contemporary industry. Rather, it addresses problems without addressing their source, setting goals and employing practices that sustain a fundamentally flawed system. It inspires one to do less bad. McDonough and Braungart (2002:62–63) question the 'general goal of efficiency that is largely destructive… Being less bad isn't good enough.' Better alternatives are discussed in Chapter 11.

Critique of the triple bottom line

In Chapter 5 we briefly discussed the EKC hypothesis, ecological modernization, and post-material values theory. It is implied by all three theories that technological advancement and prosperity would create environmental awareness and tools for environmental repair and sustainable use. Yet, the challenges of sustainability will require major changes in the way members of the political and corporate elites perceive and address environmental and social issues. Petter Næss (2011) has argued that capitalism and long-term environmental sustainability are incompatible. The scope for decoupling growth in production and consumption from environmental degradation is limited and the decoupling is unable to keep up with unlimited growth. Thereupon, economic growth is indispensable for capitalism. Without growth, the capitalist economic system is prone to run into more and more serious crises. Since capitalism depends on the natural environment as a resource base, its environmental non-sustainability will in the long run lead to a serious crisis in capitalism itself. This is a real tension in any discussion of capitalism per se, although socialist or Communist countries, such as China, have also adopted a capitalist market model of production.

Regardless of whether governments respond to the economic crisis through additional stimulus packages or reduced government spending, environmental and resource constraints remain. Sometimes the three P's (People, Profit, and Planet) simply cannot be balanced, as it is impossible to have your cake and eat it too.

Critique of sustainable consumption

An easy solution of 'sustainable', 'responsible', ethical', or 'green' consumption may seem like the silver bullet. Yet, even the most environmentally minded consumers find it difficult to consume less or consume sustainably. In *Confessions of an Eco-Sinner*, Fred Pearce (2008) surveys his home and then sets out to track down the people behind the production and distribution of everything in his daily life, from his socks to his computer to the food in his fridge. He discovers that awareness of unsustainability is not enough to lead a sustainable lifestyle. Examples of unsustainable products include green beans grown in Kenya for Marks and Spencer, or prawns being mass produced in Bangladesh, or cotton grown in Kazakhstan, made into textiles in China and manufactured in other countries to be sold in Western Europe.

In 2007 Colin Beavan performed a public experiment of extreme environmental living in the middle of Manhattan. The project had been intended to question and look for alternatives to the typical American's consumption-based way of life. It was aimed to be a 'vehicle to help bring broader public attention to the range of our environmental crises – from ocean depletion to species extinction to climate'. The resulting popular book (Beavan 2009) and a film *No Impact Man* has brought concerns about social dimensions of 'truly sustainable consumption' to the fore. One of the most acute observations was how Beavan's family and friends reacted to what they saw as his extremely odd or even depraved way of living without electricity or running water (using rain water), and not buying anything (growing his own vegetables).

In examining the case of sustainability-minded consumers in Sweden, Isenhour (2010) notes that contrary to the contemporary dominance of theories which link sustainable action to awareness, the most significant barrier is not lack of information but rather concerns with conformity, equality, and fairness. Purchasing decisions are made in part because of people's inherited or learned habits (e.g. children often following the parents' consumptive patterns), acquired habits (e.g. what they have bought before), beliefs and assumptions (e.g. that a product is good for their health), emotions ('retail therapy'), social influences (e.g. what their peers buy), and conformity to class expectations (e.g. products aimed to enhance one's relational social standing). The case study at the end of this chapter will illustrate the strength of these mechanisms in everyday life.

Objects (and in modern times, consumer products) are not simply goods in their own right, but symbolic objects through which we communicate our social status. Businesses that sell goods are facilitators of symbolic communication attributed to goods, and hence much is expected of them

Figure 9.4 Mass consumption (source: Engelbert Fellinger)

when it comes to sustaining this aspect of our lives (Blowfield 2013:66). As anthropologist Richard Wilk (2009) has inquired: 'What makes human wants and needs grow? How do things that were once distant luxuries— say, hot water—become basic necessities that people expect on demand for civilized life?' While we may not know the answer to these questions, various retailers have discovered that triggering global consumption (Figure 9.4) is relatively easy, despite religious, ideological, moral, and political barriers that at various times and places are used to discourage consumption. Another concern is pricing and price sensitivity of sustainability goods, and the question of whether sustainable choices can be made available and affordable on the global scale.

In Chapter 2 we discussed the problematic relationship between neo-liberalism and environmental protection. What is most significant in the case of consumption is that it is businesses and the governments that are the largest consumers of all consumer products and individual consumption decisions are insignificant in proportion. Thus, many consumption decisions are not made by consumers at all, but by governments, regulatory agencies, and businesses (Wilk 2009). Focus on individual responsibility reflects the dominance of neo-liberalism whereby governments delegate responsibility to consumers and thus avoid politically unpopular decisions that would actually regulate or limit consumption (Hobson 2002). These issues were also discussed in sections on green marketing, brand value, and responsible advertising in Chapter 6. Wilk (2004: 27) has argued that responsible consumption is not necessarily about 'reducing consumption' per se, but about making sure that the 'goods and services people buy, use and throw away' consume fewer resources. For a very small segment of Western consumers, ethical consumption means not consuming anything socially or environmentally damaging at all, as in the case of vegans or customers buying Fairtrade products only. Whether such responsible behaviour can be voluntarily adapted by society as a whole is questionable. It is also questionable how 'responsible' the majority of consumers are when they choose between what is cheap and what is 'right'. If left to open market mechanisms, sustainable consumption is likely to fail.

Rebound effect

Some studies point to the irony of trying to solve the problems associated with over-consumption with even more consumption, regardless of how green and efficient production processes become (Isenhour 2010).

> **Rebound effect** refers to consumer response to the introduction of new eco-efficient technologies or products which tend to offset the beneficial effects by perpetuating or actually increasing consumption of these products.

The rebound effect, also known as Jevons paradox, generally focuses on the effect of technological improvements on energy consumption. The rebound effect is generally expressed as a ratio of the lost benefit compared to the expected environmental benefit when holding consumption constant. The contemporary emphasis on 'green consumerism' might also be driving more consumption as it aims to absolve consumers of their guilt by offering 'responsible' products (Žižek 2010). According to the rebound effect 'green' items are purchased to appease the wealthier consumer's conscience, driving more resource depletion and waste (Greening, Greene, and Difiglio 2000).

Even though cars may be more efficient, drivers often rationalize driving more often and farther because of these fuel efficiencies, offsetting gains. The increasing affordability of energy efficient vehicles also drives demand for resource extensive production of new cars, regardless of the functionality of existing automobiles (Isenhour 2010:459). Electric cars still use space (roads, parking), and require materials for making them. The direct rebound effects for cars: (1) an increase in the number of vehicles; (2) an increase in fuel consumption in response to increases in technical efficiency; and (3) an increase in vehicle miles travelled (Greening, Greene, and Difiglio 2000:392).

Ethical challenges

In Chapter 7, we outline a number of the more difficult challenges associated with sometimes conflicting interests and practical (im)possibilities. Realizing the ethical and practical paradoxes can be both daunting and exceptionally rewarding. The resulting actions are more likely to be carefully thought through and balanced, with the potential to reach beyond conventions. Just appearing to be doing good without clear regard for the complexity of sustainability challenges is not likely to shift corporate responsibility beyond the status quo.

Intergenerational justice

Which states, corporations, organizations or citizens are currently prepared to drastically reduce their consumption and transport for the sake of future generations (Lidskog and Elander 2009)? Meat eating and the need for dietary change is part of the sustainable lifestyle challenge. Cattle produce a lot of methane that contributes to climate change. Meat eating has spread into traditionally vegetarian societies, such as Hindus in India, moving them towards American-style meat consumption. Obesity (Figure 9.5) is one of the global health problems likely to be inherited by future generations.

Another challenge has to do with the type of climate our children will inherit. Wijkman and Rockström (2012) demonstrate that political and corporate leaders are in denial about the magnitude of the global

Figure 9.5 Looking into the future? (source: Engelbert Fellinger)

environmental challenges and resource constraints facing the world. Despite the growing scientific consensus on major environmental threats as well as resource depletion, societies are largely continuing with business as usual, at best attempting to tinker at the margins of the problems.

According to a new report by the EU's Joint Research Centre (JRC), global CO_2 emissions increased by 45 per cent between 1990 and 2010, reaching an all-time high of 33 billion tonnes. The fifth such assessment published by the IPCC (known as AR5) has stated that it was found that as a planet, we cannot exceed the combustion of one trillion tonnes of carbon if we want to limit increases in global temperatures to less than 2 degrees Celsius (Chapter 2). Currently, we have consumed approximately 570 billion tonnes, or 57 per cent, of that trillion tonnes of fossil fuels in the past three centuries (IPCC 2014). Under the Protocol, emissions from developing countries are allowed to grow in accordance with each country's needs. The last decade has seen an exponential increase in emissions in many countries in Asia and Africa, threatening future generations.

Biospheric egalitarianism

To which extent should only the loss of human life and welfare be the basis of political action? Should climate policy also take into account the consequences for non-human species and plants (Lidskog and Elander 2009)?

> **Biospheric egalitarianism** concerns the rights of other species independent of human interests.

As we have mentioned in the discussion of ecocentrism in Chapter 2, biospheric egalitarianism is concerned with the value of non-human life. Non-human species: those that we directly depend on (e.g. farm animals and plants), like to enjoy (e.g. pets, zoo and circus animals, house plants, botanical gardens, parks, etc.), indirectly depend on (e.g. animals used for medical experimentation, plants for pharmaceutical industry) and those that we do not depend on (see Figure 2.5). Biodiversity protection is not necessarily contingent on social and economic interests (Kopnina 2014b). Mass extinction could conceivably come to pass without jeopardizing the survival of the human species, which could be sustained by agricultural monocultures.

Some scholars have argued that there are many ways in which animals have been granted a greater degree of moral standing in post-industrial neo-liberal societies than was previously the case. However, the scale of human use of animals or plants – directly for consumption or indirectly through actions such as forest clearings – has increased exponentially with human population growth and increase in consumption.

Environmental justice versus ecological justice

One of the objectives of sustainability is to achieve global justice. Yet, global justice can also conflict with the aim of solving some of the environmental problems. In order to explain this, let us return to different types of justice described in Chapter 2.

> **Environmental justice** refers to inequitable distribution of environmental burdens to vulnerable groups such as ethnic minorities or economically disadvantaged populations; or to developed and developing countries' unequal exposure to environmental risks and benefits; or to intergenerational justice between present and future generations; or to ecological justice.

First, proponents of environmental justice seek to redress inequitable distribution of environmental burdens such as hazardous and polluting industries to vulnerable groups such as ethnic minorities or the economically disadvantaged populations (e.g. Carter 2007). The EPA defines environmental justice as the fair treatment and meaningful involvement of all people regardless of race, colour, national origin, or income with respect to the development, implementation, and enforcement of environmental laws, regulations, and policies.

Second, environmental justice refers to developed and developing countries' unequal exposure to environmental risks such as the consequences of climate change. Global warming is believed to affect the world's poor – those least able to protect themselves against crop failures and rising sea levels. This is due in large part to the fact that the poorest people tend to live in the most polluted environments since in rural areas of the developing world, they have been forced onto marginal areas by the process of enclosure, leading to deforestation, soil erosion, and agricultural failure (Singer and Evans 2013). A related concept is environmental racism.

> **Environmental racism** refers to the enactment or enforcement of any policy, practice, or regulation that negatively affects the living environment of low-income or ethnically marginalized communities at a higher rate than affluent communities.

The dilemma in regard to this type of justice can be exemplified by the current deadlock between developed and developing countries in regard to issues such as the international post-Kyoto Protocol negotiations on climate change. As discussed in Chapters 2 and 3, while the developing countries recognize environmental issues as global, they want developed countries to pay for solutions. Poor nation-states fear that international agreements will limit their attempt for economic growth whereas economically powerful nation-states refuse to make substantial reductions of their GHG emissions if developing countries do not make a similar sacrifice. Developing countries inquire whether developed countries have any right to ask them to curb their economic growth while they themselves are enjoying the benefits of it.

Third, temporal environmental justice refers to the issues associated with intergenerational justice – concern for future generations of humans. The fate of future generations may be uncertain due to the present growth and consumption patterns.

In sum, all three types of environmental justice are largely anthropocentric. As discussed in Chapter 2, anthropocentrism can have a positive effect on the environment (for example, when people are concerned about the local rivers being polluted because of the negative effect on human health). Protection of nature for the sake of humans also provides business opportunities such as continuous exploitation of natural resources, and ecotourism.

By contrast, proponents of ecological justice identify anthropocentrism as one of the mechanisms which marginalizes the question of justice in relation to other species.

Ecological justice refers to justice between all living species.

The ecological justice perspective suggests that anthropocentrism is woefully inadequate as it fails to guarantee the protection of those who are not instrumental for human well-being. If concerns for non-human species or non-living things like water, soil, rock and air are to be recognized, existing policies will need to be radically revised. It means that a host of issues ranging from biodiversity protection to animal rights will need to be integrated into all laws, the way other forms of human rights and non-discrimination measures are currently integrated within national and sub-national legal systems. Taking into account the long evolutionary history of human ethics, and recent milestones such as the successful inclusion of human rights, minority rights, women's rights, etc. into standard practice offers hope for this ethical switch toward biospheric egalitarianism. The urgent need to protect (endangered) species is not likely to be adequately addressed in the current global paradigm that prioritizes social justice only as it applies to humans.

The question of demographics

Perhaps the greatest challenge to sustainability remains the 'elephant in the room' – population growth and economic growth. The co-founder of the sub-discipline of environmental sociology, William R. Catton (2012), argues that modern people have become not only hypernumerous but also hypervoracious. They now inhabit the planet with no regard for carrying capacity limits for the human population, let alone for non-human species. As Paul Ekins (1991) has noted, a sustainable consumer society is a contradiction in terms.

Figure 9.6 Two primates, one caged (source: Helen Kopnina)

Some people argue that the size of the population does not matter as long as the sustainability challenges outlined above are met. They argue that since most of the population growth happens in developing countries and in economically disadvantaged populations whose consumption is negligible in comparison to the wealthier segments of the population, we should not be worried about the negative effects of population growth. However, there are a number of reasons why these opinions can be relegated to the realm of myths.

First, the challenges outlined in the sections above are by no means met within the present social and political circumstances. As we discussed in Chapter 3, if we argue that the growing population of the poor does not have as heavy a 'footprint' as the rich, this argument is only valid in a short-term perspective and totally misses the point in the longer term. It is the question of well-recognized ethics, discussed in Chapter 7, that all people born on this planet have the right to decent living conditions. Since the poor justly aspire to the same standard of living as the rich and the lifestyle of the rich is by no means sustainable, this leads to complicated ethical and practical questions that are presently unanswered by mainstream advocates of population growth (Chapter 5).

The smaller population can perhaps live in relative balance with its environment and continue to consume at the present rate. It becomes harder and harder to do so with the larger population. Large population scales up other challenges. While the obvious solutions to this were proposed – addressing population growth *and* reducing consumption, neither of these seems desirable given the current political and social climate.

Thus, the very large challenge for business, if it attempts to be 'really' sustainable, is realization of this socio-political context, rather than tinkering at the margins of the problems. As mentioned in Chapter 2, investment in institutions that advocate family planning can have a much more significant impact than developing a product that uses 10 per cent less plastic than its competitor.

The role of decision makers

The threats to the external business environment include competitors, who may introduce new, superior methods of production, pioneering best practices in sustainable production, or extend their target markets to include less sustainability-minded customers, or find new ways of attracting key employees. One of the key roles of corporate decision makers is how to balance the challenges outlined above with the demands of their main stakeholders: governments, consumers, and shareholders. While new government policies may require changes in how businesses operate, including restrictions on importing environmentally damaging products, or establishing requirements for a minimum wage and working hours as well as tougher health and safety requirements, it is largely the MNCs or consortiums of commercial partners that decide what happens within the context of the transnational spaces where they operate. As will be discussed in Chapter 11, businesses that realize potential conflict and seek reconciliation have a greater capacity to fundamentally address rather than muddle through sustainability challenges.

Case study

Smartphones at school

One of the authors of this book has recently been to a parents meeting at her 14-year-old daughter's school, in a well-to-do area of Amsterdam, The Netherlands. The mentor of the class has initiated the discussion of class disturbances caused by the use of smartphones by schoolchildren. The parents have responded that they indeed experience great problems getting their children to do homework and ignore their smartphones, which many see as 'addiction'. Some parents have reported that their children are constantly distracted by WhatsApp and Facebook messages, fail to make direct social contact, and sleep badly because of the ongoing messaging and game playing. Some parents reported devising rules that limit their children's exposure to smartphones, instituting strict time limits on phone use, switching off Wi-Fi or asking their children to leave the phone outside the bedroom at night.

Yet, all but two parents did give their children smartphones. The one parent whose child did not have a smartphone received curious and sympathetic comments, such as 'Oh, but doesn't your daughter miss the phone?', and 'But how can she communicate with her friends?' One particularly concerned mother has asked 'Would it be OK if we gave her the phone for her birthday?' implying that perhaps the parent of the smartphone-less child could not afford to buy one.

Other than the above-mentioned problems with their children's use of smartphones, the parents did not discuss the social or environmental costs of smartphones. Neither of these highly educated parents were aware or willing to consider these costs and to deprive their children of, in the words of one mother, 'modern necessities'.

Perhaps a solution to this is the acquisition of technologies that have social credibility and environmental integrity. The Fairphone is marketed as a 'seriously cool smartphone that puts social values first'. It has the chic design and technical specifications of other smartphones but unlike these rivals is manufactured in a closed loop system using conflict-free resources, by workers who receive a decent wage, and it will have a buy-back system that will both reduce e-waste and reduce the number of smartphones in circulation. Now that surely is cool.

Questions

1 Consider ecological modernization theory and post-material values hypothesis discussed in Chapters 3 and 5. If parents were fully aware of the negative social and environmental consequences of making the phones, do you think they would still choose to give their child a smartphone?

2 Consider that purchasing decisions are not always rational but based on relational contexts, such as inherited and acquired habits, beliefs and assumptions, emotions, social influences, and conformity to class expectations. What kind of pressures do you think the parents and children are under to purchase the phones?

3 Do you think Fairphone offers a sustainable solution?

Key terms

Biospheric egalitarianism, charity paradox, conservation, ecological justice, environmental justice, global business environment, intergenerational justice, rebound effect.

Discussion questions

1 What do you think are the greatest paradoxes of sustainability? Provide both the summary of the text above and your own ideas.

2 Consider the questions in smartphones at school case study. What another examples are there of consumer purchasing decisions that are not consistent with sustainable consumption?

3   Give your own example of the charity paradox.
4   What do you think is the practical difficulty with the triple bottom line for business profitability?
5   Give your own example of the rebound effect and discuss it in relationship to business.
6   Since the future generations are not born yet and non-human species cannot speak for themselves, how do you think intergenerational justice and biospheric egalitarianism be addressed in democratic systems?
7   How do you think population growth can be addressed?
8   How can the critique of eco-efficiency be related to the critique of charity by Žižek (Box 9.1)?

End of chapter summary

This chapter outlined a number of challenges to mainstream views of sustainability. We put forward the argument that sustainability cannot be met by simply tinkering at the margins of the current economic system, but requires major changes in the way political and corporate leaders perceive and address environmental and social issues. The changing global business environment requires understanding of the paradoxes of sustainability and necessary choices between growth and conservation. This chapter disputed the triple bottom line and outlined the shortcomings of eco-efficiency and sustainable consumption. The chapter has outlined a number of ethical challenges concerned with intergenerational justice and biospheric egalitarianism. The role of corporate and political decision makers is stressed as the key to the resolution of those challenges.

Further reading

Beavan, C. (2009) *No Impact Man: The Adventures of a Guilty Liberal Who Attempts to Save the Planet, and the Discoveries He Makes About Himself and Our Way of Life in the Process*. New York: Farrar, Strauss and Giraux.
Greening, L.A., Greene, D.L. and Difiglio, C. (2000) Energy efficiency and consumption—The rebound effect—A survey. *Energy Policy*, 28:389–401.

Part IV

Solutions

10 Human resource management, green jobs, and a greener economy

Knowledge and skills: human resource development

Human resource management (HRM) is a relatively young discipline and is a particular approach to employment management aimed at securing competitive advantage for the organization. It attempts to do this through the effective and efficient deployment of committed and capable employees by applying an integrated set of approaches, techniques, and interventions. An important part of HRM involves the design, organization, and delivery of learning and development (L&D). This L&D is often referred to as human resource development (HRD) and within an HRD context, development may be understood as the growth or realization of individual, group, or team abilities as well as the nurturing of future capacities for learning.

> **Human resource management** is a process including the selection, recruitment, appraisal, training, and development of staff in accordance with employment legislation and the welfare needs of employees.

L&D can take the form of formal classes and training schemes or more informal, basically experiential, learning on the job approaches. L&D can also involve collaboratively working within interdisciplinary and inter-professional groups who are tasked to address key problems, issues, and ambitions. Thus, learning, combined with development, is concerned with initiating relatively permanent changes in knowledge, attitude, values, skills, performance, and by extension organizational culture. From a strategic perspective HRD means being proactive and systemic, which is achieved through clear planning and initiating changes to organizational culture.

HRD recognizes that value frequently resides with or within employees whose skills, knowledge, and capabilities in turn constitute a large element of a company's 'intellectual capital'. Strategic HRD will therefore enable the following:

• the organization to respond to challenges and opportunities through the identification and delivery of various interventions;

- information to be disseminated explaining the need for and opportunities of training, education, and development;
- employees to understand the goals and objectives of the organization;
- individuals, supervisors, line managers, and top managers to be informed of their roles and participate in HRD delivery;
- the continuous improvement of employee and company performance.

HRD inevitably helps to support and develop ethical leadership and consequently has an important role to play in helping businesses to be both learning organizations and sustainable and responsible ones too.

Sustainability and HRM

The integration of ecological sustainability with strategic HRM marks a recent but important shift in how many HR professionals see their role. The employee is now seen as both a source of value, a potential change agent, and as a value-orientated leader. HRM activities frequently seek to encourage value formation within organizations through continuing professional development (CPD). This means the introduction of ecological sustainability as a value set is essentially within the traditional L&D function of a company's HR department. Having said that, sustainability as an HR concern is not as yet widespread, although this is changing as increasing numbers of companies start to modify their business model.

Sustainable HRM and HRD will focus on social, environmental, and financial outcomes and are emerging as integral parts of many businesses' HRM strategy. Many aspects of a sustainable human resource policy address wider societal concerns such as climate change, carbon footprint, personal health and well-being, work and life balance, and lifelong learning in uncertain economic markets. Unless sustainability informs HRM and HRD, it is possible that employees could be impediments to sustainable change rather than agents and leaders of it and, as such, would not realize the value they possess or can produce.

Recognizing this, the Society for Human Resource Management Foundation defines 'sustainable HRM' as 'the utilization of HR tools to help embed a sustainability strategy in the organization and the creation of an HRM system that contributes to the sustainable performance of the firm' (Cohen, Taylor & Muller-Camen, 2012:3). These tools include:

- attracting and selecting new employees committed to the goals of corporate sustainability and social responsibility;
- designing training, development, and reward systems supportive of sustainablity goals;
- creating an organizational culture and climate that enables sustainability practices to develop;
- instituting clear processes and procedures to support managers and communicate effectively throughout the organization.

Box 10.1 Triple bottom line strengthens company culture and employee engagement

What does our way of doing business – balancing financial, social, and environmental decisions – mean for our employees?

Our people are crucial to our success. When the values inherent in Triple Bottom Line become part of our fabric as a company, they weave a strong corporate culture. This, in turn, energizes a workforce with the will to champion the company – secure in the knowledge that Novo Nordisk is committed to not only its success as a company, but to their own success as well. In general, our employees believe that the culture within Novo Nordisk is strongly aligned with the spirit of our Triple Bottom Line principle and that the company creates an attractive place to work. Employee satisfaction and engagement scores, which are measured through annual eVoice surveys (Figure 10.1), have been high since 2006. In a survey of US employees conducted for this case study, 80% expressed that our Triple Bottom Line principle has a significant positive impact on our company's reputation. What's more, those surveyed believe that a sound reputation contributes positively to overall performance and strong stakeholder support.

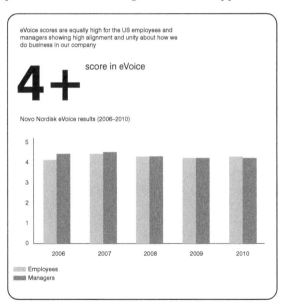

Figure 10.1 eVoice scores showing alignment between staff and company values at Nordisk. Source: Novo Nordisk (2012) The Blueprint for Change Programme January 2012.

continued ...

Box 10.1 continued

Among '100 Best Companies to Work for'.

External stakeholders have also recognized our corporate culture. In the United States, Novo Nordisk has made the Fortune '100 Best Companies to Work for' list 3 times since 2009 and the 'Best Places to Work in New Jersey' list 6 times since 2005.[1] The Great Place to Work Institute, which creates the Fortune list, surveys employees on 5 key attributes: credibility, respect, fairness, pride, and camaraderie...In the United States, our unwanted [employee] turnover rate has fallen from 7.3% in 2005 to 3.4% in 2010, allowing us to retain a highly qualified work force.

Source: Adapted from Novo Nordsk in the USA: Triple Bottom Line strengthens company culture and employee engagement

[1]   Novo Nordisk is a Danish pharmaceutical company and a leading supplier of insulin.

HR and the social ecology of the organization

Ethical values are a signficant element within all organizational cultures whether they are explictly acknowledged or not, and a shift towards sustain0ability necessarily involves transformative changes in a company's value base and value chain. Dubois and Dubois (2012) have designed a model for HR that fully incorporates environmental sustainability. They identify three contextual drivers which influence the social ecology of the organization. These are:

- insufficient natural resources;
- increasing pressure from stakeholder groups;
- radical transparency

The social ecology of the organization comprises the organizational environment itself including such things as leadership, culture, business strategy, work systems and processes, reporting mechanisms, and the whole set of more conventional HRM and HRD policy and implementation functions. However, it is L&D combined with effective communication that can really help staff appreciate new value orientations, new business practices, new ways of thinking, and new ways of designing work tasks or job roles. Creative technogical and social design thinking often forms an important part of the sustainable HRD process as was the case with General Electric's Ecoimagination initiative.

The demands on, and for, HRD will vary according to the degree a company integrates environmental sustainability into its business. Dubois and Dubois argue that HR need to incorporate certain internal and external social, financial, and natural environment elements in designing work and performance systems. HR managers will also need to explore alternative social design processes.

> Given the inherent technical and social complexity of sustainability challenges, this could include, for example, the use of social design charrettes, modeled after architectural and industrial design, to develop innovative and elegant social design solutions. Also, worth examining to build out the repertoire of design ideas for application to social systems are biomimicry and industrial ecology.
>
> (Dubois and Dubois 2012:819–820)

Sustainable HRM can therefore help companies to secure a sustained competitive advantage in retaining high quality staff as it necessarily delivers on the promises and work experiences communicated through its enhanced brand image. Additionally a range of opportunities emerge whereby new values can be crafted within the organization enabling a holistic worldview to emerge within and in relation to the firm's external environment and commitments (Figure 10.2).

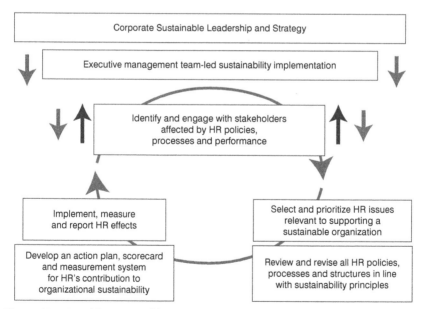

Figure 10.2 Possible sustainable organization roadmap showing HR contribution (source: adapted from Cohen, Taylor and Muller-Camen 2012:11)

Continuing professional development

> CPD [continuing professional development] is a process by which individuals take control of their own learning and development, by engaging in an on-going process of reflection and action (Megginson and Whitaker 2003:5)

Employees' need for CPD is probably greater now than ever before. There are few jobs for life and in a fast changing and uncertain world employability often rests with the individual being able to maintain and enhance his/her level of skills, knowledge, and experience. For those who see themselves as sustainability change agents, it is extremely important to keep up to date with new developments, ideas, policies, techniques, and opportunities. CPD is important to employers too and good HRM departments will facilitate and organize a wide range of learning and training opportunities which develop the individual personally and professionally.

HRM departments tend to focus on the needs and goals of the organization whereas the individual employee often wishes to orientate her future learning to this organization goal but will also want to plan her own personal career journey. An important starting point is often the development of an ERSI or 'extraordinarily realistic self-image' which is ultimately about ensuring the individual understands who and what she is. This can be achieved through a range of devices, self-assessment matrixes, or self-diagnostic psychological tests peddled by any number of CPD consultancy outfits and professional bodies. Interestingly, sustainability often features as an important element in the personal, political, and occupational identity of many people who in their personal and professional lives want to learn more about their place in the world as well as in the organization they work for.

Acquiring ecological self-knowledge

One way of embarking upon this process of acquiring ecological self-knowledge is to try to understand what you currently believe and know and then to work out what you need to do in the future, what changes you need to make within yourself and within your organization. In 1978 two American sociologists, William Catton and Riley Dunlap, designed what they called a New Ecological Paradigm (NEP) in contrast to the Dominant Social Paradigm (DSP) most people live by, adhere to, and reproduce in their everyday personal and professional lives. The DSP posits endless progress, economic growth, and abundance as pre-conditions of human development. Shallow ecology can be exemplified by environmental concerns motivated by anthropocentric interests, such as the fight against pollution and resource depletion, which is typically associated with sustainable development and is quite compatible with the DSP. Those committed to shallow ecology solutions are treating only the symptoms, and not the source of the symptoms, such as overpopulation and growth in consumption. DSP is opposed to the NEP, which highlights the disruption of ecosystems caused by modern industrial societies exceeding environmental limits. From this a test has been developed and refined over the years, and although like most psychological tests and value audits there are problems it does offer an interesting, valid and, useful snapshot of a person's ecological values...or lack of them (Dunlap et al. 2000).

Having done this, many people find that understanding sustainability requires a shift in perspective, some deep philosophical reflection, and perhaps considerable practical skills development whether in low carbon project management, conducting sustainability audits, supply chain management, stakeholder facilitation, or whatever. It is also important for individuals as well as organizations to see the big picture, to see how things are connected and how a vision for a sustainable and ecologically responsible business practice can develop.

For Ray Anderson, the former CEO of Interface, the carpet tile manufacturing and supply company, a pivotal moment was the reading of Paul Hawken's *The Ecology of Commerce* (Hawken 1993) which clearly stated to an intended business readership that business is both the direct cause of many environmental abuses but also holds the key to solving many problems derived from our unsustainability. From that moment on he vowed to change himself and his company, which he did, making Interface an exemplar of sustainable business practice. Indeed, for many sustainability educators, trainers and practitioners, being able to take a holistic approach and to apply the basic tenets of systems thinking is of paramount importance in initiating change management processes. Although systems thinking is significant in all areas, it is possibly in the area of architectural design, planning, and construction where such holistic thinking is most evident, for example, regarding design for biodiversity and ecological regeneration, low energy construction, biomimicry, eco-minimalism, materials durability, retrofitting, and whole life costing (see discussions in Chapter 11).

The need for environmental sustainability to characterize CPD in many professions is undoubtedly huge. In its first Sustainability Survey the UK-based organization National Building Specification (NBS) found that 73 per cent of its respondents had no sustainability related qualifications and only 47 per cent said they had confidence in their knowledge and skills in sustainable design. All professional institutions require their members to undertake a certain number of CPD hours per year. The Royal Institute of British Architects (RIBA) requires its members to complete 20 hours and have produced a core CPD curriculum of ten mandatory topics, one of which, 'climate: sustainable architecture', includes knowledge and skills-based learning outcomes.

UN Principles for Responsible Management Education

The UN Principles for Responsible Management Education (PRME) initiative was launched in 2008 with the intention to radically transform management education within higher education. At its core are six principles, broadly based on the philosophy of the 1948 UN Declaration of Human Rights and more recently the UNGC, which will hopefully inspire business schools to integrate social responsibility and sustainability in their curricula. The six principles are:

> **Principle 1 Purpose**: We will develop the capabilities of students to be future generators of sustainable value for business and society at large and to work for an inclusive and sustainable global economy.
>
> **Principle 2 Values**: We will incorporate into our academic activities and curricula the values of global social responsibility as portrayed in international initiatives such as the United Nations Global Compact.
>
> **Principle 3 Method**: We will create educational frameworks, materials, processes and environments that enable effective learning experiences for responsible leadership.
>
> **Principle 4 Research**: We will engage in conceptual and empirical research that advances our understanding about the role, dynamics, and impact of corporations in the creation of sustainable social, environmental and economic value.
>
> **Principle 5 Partnership**: We will interact with managers of business corporations to extend our knowledge of their challenges in meeting social and environmental responsibilities and to explore jointly effective approaches to meeting these challenges.
>
> **Principle 6 Dialogue**: We will facilitate and support dialog and debate among educators, students, business, government, consumers, media, civil society organisations and other interested groups and stakeholders on critical issues related to global social responsibility and sustainability.

Many business schools across the world are participating in PRME to demonstrate their proactive commitment to sustainability as well as, inevitably, to secure some competitive advantage in an increasingly competitive education market. This has become very important as the 'premium products' of a number of schools seems to be overly commodified and are perhaps losing their relevance in the face of obvious sustainability challenges. The major Master of Business Administration (MBA) accreditation bodies such as the Association to Advance Collegiate Schools of Business (AACSB) and the Association of MBAs (AMBA) now incorporate social responsibility and sustainability in their accreditation criteria and this, together with business schools' often close relationship to their corporate stakeholders, is likely to have a significant influence on both formal university education and more industrially situated HRD. A more critically focused, action orientated, transdisciplinary, and reflexive pedagogy is also required (Parkes and Blewitt 2011).

The aim overall aims of the UNGC and UN PRME are both ambitious and all encompassing, and are summarized succinctly in *Architects of a Better World* (UN Global Compact 2013:6):

> By aligning and scaling up corporate sustainability efforts, the Business Engagement Architecture will help business to contribute to global priorities – such as climate change, water, food, women's empowerment, children's rights, decent jobs and education – at unprecedented levels. With an emphasis on collaboration and co-investment, the Architecture illustrates the main building blocks necessary to enhance corporate sustainability as an effective contribution to sustainable development, creating value for both business and society.

PRME is important not least because it is from the world's business schools that the future business leaders will emerge.

Sustainability and leadership

Leadership for sustainability in business is not so much about heroic leaders at the top of the organization, although there are certainly examples of this, but more interestingly about people operating at different levels demonstrating genuine commitment in what they do. Cultivating authentic leadership is an important function of sustainable HRM and there has been growing interest in this in business, government, and in the academy.

Ray Anderson is frequently cited as having been a truly authentic leader but authentic leaders, even CEOs, sometimes have to be circumspect, sometimes have to curb their enthusiasm, mute their frustration with colleagues, and temper their own radical commitments. They will need to accept the pragmatics of small incremental but nonetheless positive changes over time in preference to massive and immediate change. These 'tempered radicals' invariably look to communicate with others, bring these others onside, and make a difference without getting fired (Meyerson 2001). They will challenge when and where opportune to do so but will bide their time on other occasions. They will seek to build alliances with colleagues within and outside the organization, so when it is possible to gently rock the boat, to engage in some low level disruptive self-expression or innovation, they can do so with some security and confidence. Tempered radicals are often leaders without formal power or authority but can nonetheless develop the ability to be taken seriously. To do so requires a considerable degree of emotional intelligence which involves the capacity to understand, empathize, work and be with others. However, being a tempered radical and a sustainability leader

---

Box 10.2 Authentic leadership

The main components of authentic leadership include:

- Positive psychological capital – confidence, optimism, hope and resiliency
- Positive moral perspective – moral capacities, efficacy, transparency courage and resiliency
- Leader self-awareness – being able to know and understand one's true talents, core values, beliefs, desires and sense of purpose
- Leader self-regulation – selfcontrol and the capacity to align values with intentions and actions
- Leadership processes and behaviours including the capacity to influence and contribute to the development of others including followers
- Follower self awareness/regulation – enabling followers to clarify their own values, identity, emotions and authentic behaviour
- Organization – the capacity for leaders to link leadership with perfomance and integrate both within the culture of the organization
- Veritable and sustained performance beyond expectations thus securing sustainable competitive advantage.

Source: Avolio and Gardner (2005)

---

is often a tough job albeit an important one but there are clear benefits to the individual and to the wider environment.

A recent report from the global consultancy Deloitte (2013) states that there is a causal connection between sustainability leadership and innovation – not a strong correlation but a *causal relationship*. This is because sustainability offers a different way of thinking and approaching situations encompassing systems theory, systems thinking, interconnectedness, inter-professional critical analyses, and cross disciplinary working. Sustainability imperatives will frequently introduce constraints such as reduced packaging, improving operating efficiency or enabling return, reuse and/or recycling, invariably requiring change and innovation and a move away from the business as usual model. In *A Journey of a Thousand Miles: The State of Sustainability Leadership 2011* produced by the Cambridge University Sustainable Leadership Programme seven key characteristics of sustainability leadership are identified. These are:

- systemic understanding;
- emotional intelligence;
- values orientation;

- compelling vision;
- inclusive style;
- innovative approach;
- long-term perspective.

There are, of course, many other ideas, theories, and speculations about what constitutes sustainability leadership but such leadership will certainly evolve as new leaders emerge and new issues and situations are addressed. Nicolas Ceasar, co-head of Sustainability Practice at Ashridge Business School, credits the following as extremely significant:

- mindfulness (staying aware of and paying close attention to the present moment);
- advocacy (arguing in favour of sustainability);
- holding discomfort (staying with the difficult stuff for long enough);
- femininity (displaying and using attributes of cooperation, understanding, pluralistic knowing and seeking alignment among collaborators).

While all these suggestions are undoubtedly helpful guides there can be no single prescription or best way of being or becoming a sustainability leader in business or anywhere else. Intelligence, creativity, and commitment are clearly important to sustainability for our world is ridden with risks and uncertainties as well as opportunities and potentialities. The ways in which these are dealt with will vary according to time, place, culture, company, and circumstance. A great deal will depend on being simultaneously pragmatic and principled but there is still a considerable amount of L&D to be undertaken by business and society. If the current model of business development and prominence given to unsustainable economic growth in policy and practice continues, fundamental and urgent shifts in consciousness and action, L&D are essential. A start has been made but a question remains as to how far we are all prepared to go. If we do go that necessary 'extra mile', as business consultants frequently say, we will need good sustainability leaders at every level and in every sphere. Indeed, we will all need to be leaders in some way.

Decent and sustainable work

If knowledge has traditionally been the business of education, it is quite clearly the business of business. Formal education and training is extremely important and today is often focused tightly on employability, flexible skill development, and the capacity to adapt and learn anew (see Chapter 4). Climate change is both an economic and an environmental imperative and is beginning to shape skills development, skills demand, and skills requirements. As discussed in Chapter 2, environmental technologies, bioscience, and green energy have been identified by government departments, labour organizations, and think tanks as necessary for sustainable development and economic regeneration.

A 2008 report by EEF/Deloitte noted that businesses have much to do if they are to realize the commercial opportunities being presented by an emerging low-carbon economy. Business must be creative in its thinking about and in its development of new products, services, and markets. IBM, for instance, offers an energy-management service to data centre clients who want to reduce energy costs and Xerox's Managed Print Services helps clients to optimize energy use and reduce printing costs. Manufacturers must not neglect the service opportunities associated with the low-carbon economy, particularly given the contribution that services can make to profitability and the general tendency for manufacturing, services, and knowledge to morph into one another.

The relatively new 3D printing technologies offer intriguing possibilities for creating a sustainable economy with a production process using less waste, print on demand or according to need processes, potentially more localized and operating at different scales, and enhanced possibilities for upcycling, although the downsides include questions over some life cycle impacts. New green work opportunities may at least partially re-humanize workforce development after decades of 'Fordist' work practices (see Chapter 3) for a green knowledge economy requires a considerable degree of participation and engagement, autonomy, trust, and cooperation and collaboration between work teams, whole professions, trades, academic disciplines, and various communities of practice. However, today much work is incredibly precarious, short term, relatively low paid, intensive, and without the security and welfare benefits that were for a while considered only just.

Clearly, the new (green) knowledge worker is not about to escape the pressures, stresses, and tensions of working in a highly competitive market society and neither is she likely to escape the relationship that binds working in a capitalist society with the ideology of consumerism, but something must give sooner or later. To a large extent, the essential creativity, innovation, and eco-productivity required in a greener and less exploitative economy will reside in the way work is organized, scheduled, experienced, or refused and how we get to grips with uncontrolled consumerism. Many sustainability advocates argue that consumerism frequently acts as a substitute for proper engagement with society and the natural environment. Consumerism is therefore not just about the overconsumption of material resources but the waste of human creativity and the degradation of work. Sustainable economic reform and green entrepreneurship, invention, and good design could liberate the creativity of individuals and societies. Despite all the entreaties to find meaning and value in work, meaning *per se* is something that should be valued for its own sake. Work contributes to the overall happiness of a person's life but it should not be a burden. As E.F. Schumacher wrote (1980:120), 'if we see work as nothing but an unpleasant necessity, it is no use talking about good work, unless we mean *less* work'.

Many sustainability practitioners have recognized that alienation at work and in society is in large part due to a lack of autonomy, an inability to exercise one's creative potential in a system that only sees value only in what can be realized in market terms. The French sociologist Andre Gorz suggested we need to create a time-based multi-activity society which must be based on those rich and autonomous qualities entrepreneurial green businesses need but which must also be far more than simply producing stuff and economic value. This leads us inevitably to the design and development of sustainable work systems whose holistic concern is the sustainable

---

Box 10.3 The International Labor Organization's Decent Work Agenda

Work is central to people's well-being. In addition to providing income, work can pave the way for broader social and economic advancement, strengthening individuals, their families and communities. Such progress, however, hinges on work that is decent. Decent work sums up the aspirations of people in their working lives.

The ILO has developed an agenda for the community of work. It provides support through integrated Decent Work Country Programmes developed in coordination with its constituents. Putting the Decent Work Agenda into practice is achieved through the implementation of the ILO's four strategic objectives, with gender equality as a crosscutting objective:

- **Creating jobs** – an economy that generates opportunities for investment, entrepreneurship, skills development, job creation and sustainable livelihoods.
- **Guaranteeing rights at work** – to obtain recognition and respect for the rights of workers. All workers, and in particular disadvantaged or poor workers, need representation, participation, and laws that work for their interests.
- **Extending social protection** – to promote both inclusion and productivity by ensuring that women and men enjoy working conditions that are safe, allow adequate free time and rest, take into account family and social values, provide for adequate compensation in case of lost or reduced income and permit access to adequate healthcare.
- **Promoting social dialogue** – involving strong and independent workers' and employers' organizations is central to increasing productivity, avoiding disputes at work, and building cohesive societies.

Source: ILO

development of economic, social, human, and ecological resources. A firm's operational and competitive objectives have to be realized but not at the expense of long-term environmental sustainability – 'only people and groups who operate sustainably are able to grasp, prioritize, and work toward ecological sustainability' (Docherty, Kira & Shani 2009:7). The development of one type of resource should not come at the expense of another, such as with the outsourcing of dangerous or lower paid work to other companies or countries where the environment, labour, and regulations are less important. Employees should be able to deal with the world's ecological and other demands through work-based learning and systems of worker co-determination. An effective capacity for inter-stakeholder collaboration, cooperation, communication, and understanding should be developed.

Green jobs in a green(ing) economy

A **green job** is any paid work for a company or organization that genuinely contributes to the development of a more sustainable society and a low carbon co-operative economy.

Green jobs can be seen in obviously green sectors of the economy, for example, solar energy, and in more mainstream firms that are going green. Green jobs include self-employment, consultancy, eco-entreprenueurship, teaching, engineering, horticulture, design, logistics, finance, indeed anything. Many green jobs are, and will be, based on existing skill sets. A person doesn't have to be an organic farmer to help create a more sustainable world but she may have to see her work as part of a total sustainable lifestyle package. It is difficult to contribute to a sustainable world if large parts of it are compartmentalized as being 'not relevant'. Green jobs, a green or greener economy, and a more socially just and sustainable society ultimately require systemic change at every level from the personal to the global. In the future green jobs will inevitably see the emergence of new occupations, new technologies, new market opportunities, and new occupational and organizational cultures.

For the International Labour Office and the European Centre for the Development of Vocational Training (Cedefop), the transition to a greener economy will affect skill needs in three ways (ILO, 2011):

1   The structural shifts in the economy to eco-efficiency and low carbon industrial processes will increase skill and employment demands within the non-fossil fuel energy industries and create demand for low carbon [project] management expertise in many others.

2   New green technologies will lead to the development of new occupational areas and demands for CPD for those changing or reorienting their existing careers.

3 In existing industrial sectors new skills and skill levels will be required as is already apparent in electric automobile maintenance and the design, building and maintenance of sustainable buildings as new techniques and materials replace conventional ones.

What will and is driving these changes include:

- physical changes in the environment;
- national and international policy and regulation;
- technological innovation;
- changes in markets and consumer demand.

The large-scale development of quality green jobs will require policy development, social dialogue, and economic action on local, national, regional, and global scales. Climate change and changes in consumer concerns are already making themselves felt as have been discussed previously in Chapters 2 and 9. Positive actions can overcome some of the problems and bottlenecks. The results of a Eurobarometer survey show increased demand for cleaner goods with 50 per cent of respondents in favour of taxing goods with a high environmental footprint and 83 per cent stating they consider environmental impacts before making a purchase. Thus, it is quite possible that a shift to a green economy could create up to 60 million new jobs by 2030 and changes in the agricultural, energy, and construction sectors could affect half the global workforce, that is 1.5 billion persons. In the EU alone nearly 15 million jobs exist in areas relating to biodiversity protection and ecological restoration. Brazil has recreated over 3 million new jobs in the green technology sector. As economies 'virtualize' and become 'smarter' new ICT jobs in software design, data centre management, and Internet security have been created. The NGO Global Action Plan (GAP) recently asked leading businesses including Sainsbury's, Bosch, and Siemens how they felt the green economy would influence work and employment. These companies suggested that a green economy could create whole new green careers including:

- green engineers;
- water footprinting managers;
- virtual health support workers;
- retail energy specialists;
- living roof/wall gardeners;
- green call-centre advisers;
- smart travel coordinators;
- traceability managers;
- clean car mechanics;

and, as the financial value of previously discarded materials including rare earth metals increases,

- landfill miners.

The creation of new jobs, together with the greening of existing jobs, could significantly reduce the currently high incidence of global unemployment and, to some extent, precarious work although the pay, conditions, and the skill levels of green jobs can be quite variable (Table 10.1). Certain existing jobs will disappear as they always have done but a progressive transition to a green economy will also require a move away from neo-liberalism to a more interventionist and developmentalist political economy to ensure such a transition does not cause social, economic, and political disruption. Area-based green economic development, focused around cities or city-regions, requires strategic private and public investment to stimulate the creation of green jobs and skills, new business models, businesses, and social and eco-entrepreneurship. This has occurred around Copenhagen, Denmark, which has been designated the Green Capital of Europe in 2014. All this involves considerable cooperation on R&D between universities and green businesses, the wide dissemination of new knowledge and innovation through business and other networks, the encouragement of business-to-business collaboration and knowledge transfer partnerships between business and higher education, cross sector linkages connecting local and global firms, facilitative governance structures maximizing the potential of triple helix partnerships (governments, business, and universities), and ongoing data gathering and evaluation.

Sustainable design

> **Sustainable design** is the process whereby physical objects such as buildings and chairs, services such as public transport, and organizational systems such as businesses and universities are created in accord with the integrated principles of social, economic, and ecological sustainability.

Moving from landfilling to recycling, applying C2C methodology and the circular economy principles (see Chapter 11), are ways of overcoming potential shortages, developing employment opportunities, and boosting local and national economies. They offer a host of new job and entrepreneurial opportunities. Designers come in various guises depending whether their interest is designing clothes, industrial products, computer software, genes, business strategies, buildings, sustainable lifestyles, or a new sustainable razor. Good design impacts upon all our lives and good sustainable design will embrace many stylistic and technical features and aesthetic considerations. It should also encompass in our age of disposability the lost properties of

Table 10.1 Green technologies and green jobs

Green technologies	Representative occupations in demand
Energy efficient building	Electricians, heating/air conditioning installers, carpenters, insulation workers, roofers, construction managers, roofers, building inspectors...
Smart grid	Computer software engineers, electrical engineers, electrical equipment assemblers, machinists, construction labourers, electrical power line installers and repairers...
Wind power	Environmental engineers, iron and steel workers, millwrights, sheet metal workers, construction equipment operators, industrial truck drivers, industrial production managers...
Solar power	Electrical engineers, electricians, industrial machinery mechanics, welders, metal fabricators, electrical equipment assemblers, construction equipment operators, labourers, construction managers...
Cellulosic biofuels	Chemical engineers, chemists, chemical equipment operators, chemical technicians, agricultural workers, farm product purchasers, agricultural and forestry supervisors, agricultural inspectors...

Source: Adapted from OECD (2012:24)

being durable, repairable and emotionally, even spiritually, satisfying. Good design goes beyond both utility and disposability, being in its fundamental conception deeply meaningful.

> **Ecotextiles** are fabrics which have a low, carbon, energy, and pollution impact.

For the ecotextiles consultant Kate Fletcher, the fashion industry, including designers, manufacturers, promoters, retailers and consumers, needs to be slowed down and good design can do this. Fast fashion is about greed whereas as 'slow fashion' is about quality and responsibility. She writes:

> Slow fashion is about choice, information, cultural diversity and identity. Yet, critically, it is also about balance. It requires a combination of rapid imaginative change and symbolic (fashion) expression as well as durability and long-term engaging, quality products. Slow fashion supports our psychological needs (to form identity, communicate and be creative through our clothes) as well as our physical needs (to cover and protect us from extremes of climate)...
>
> Slow fashion, with the shift from quantity to quality, takes the pressure off time. It allows suppliers to plan orders, predict the numbers of workers needed and invest in the longer term. It gives companies time to build mutually beneficial relationships. No longer will suppliers

have to employ temporary or subcontracted workers, or force workers to do excessive overtime to meet unpredictable orders with impossible deadlines. Instead, workers will have secure employment with regular hours and the opportunity for promotion.

(Fletcher 2007)

Sustainable business and sharing networks

Greening an existing business requires a different way of thinking and a different way of conducting commercial activities. There can be no business as usual in our world without compromising a firm's reputation and in the long-term harming the bottom line. Many new things will have to be done, a great deal of new and sometimes difficult learning will need to be undertaken and if we want our future to be sustainable, as well as prosperous, businesses need to combine competition with cooperation. An important aspect of this will involve collectively producing and sharing knowledge, and setting and agreeing to performance, ethical, and other standards. It will involve respecting both the limitations and opportunities afforded by smart technologies, and complex and sophisticated management information systems. The values, principles, and process of closed loop production and the circular economy are of primary significance in this regard.

Digital technologies have increased and enhanced information flows and to a considerable extent dematerialized large parts of the global economy. They have pointed the way, perhaps, to more environmentally friendly manufacturing processes. But these digital technologies are big consumers too – of energy, of rare earth metals, of time, and much more. The carbon footprint of ICT will soon overtake that of global aviation as more smartphones than people will inhabit the planet. We need to know what resources exist in our world. How much is left of what is finite and how we can ensure that those renewable resources, and the ecosystem services nature provides, are indeed renewed. Businesses need to be creative and innovative. Most importantly new networks need to be developed through which new knowledge, expertise, and emerging good practice can be shared.

Thus, the Green Business Network in the US, like others with similar titles in different countries and regions, help a growing numbers of businesses, investors, and consumers make connections and share good practice. The US Green Business Network certification publicly demonstrates a commitment that a company is environmentally responsible and committed to social change. Many of the texts available in the growing market in green or sustainable business handbooks, toolkits, and how-to manuals also offer valuable and easily accessible information.

The Environmental Sustainability Knowledge Transfer Network (ESKTN) was formed in September 2009 and aims to foster the more effective use of material and energy resources by UK businesses. The ESKTN supports the development and implementation of new innovative technologies and processes aiming to facilitate a transition to a low carbon, and resource and energy efficient economy. Knowledge transfers occur through connective relationships between businesses, universities, other research organizations, and government agencies. Similar networks exist internationally and ambitious projects in fashioning new cultural commons are not unknown. In January 2008 the Eco-Patent Commons was launched by IBM, Nokia, Pitney Bowes, and Sony in partnership with the WBCSD (see Chapter 5) with the aim of encouraging businesses to share knowledge innovation, protect the environment, and nurture future collaboration.

It works in a similar way to Creative Commons with donator patentees covenanting not to assert their patent rights so long as the patent is used for environmentally beneficial purposes. However, companies can terminate agreements, not support the patent donated and not actually pledge anything specific, which are probably the reasons why over hundreds of eco-friendly patents have been pledged by a variety of well-known firms from different industrial sectors, although it seems that four large firms have filed the majority of the patents. Many of these relate to environmental clean-up or clean manufacturing and are only marginally relevant to environmental protection or mitigating climate change impacts. Nonetheless, those patents which have been filed seem to be more valuable than many of those that have just been pledged. Businesses though are cautious about such sharing. As Hall and Helmers (2011) note, these patents:

> tend to be more derivative of previous technologies and somewhat narrower than other patents in their class, suggesting that they are not for very radical inventions. In fact, in our reading, patents in the commons protect relatively narrow technical solutions to specific problems rather than complex technologies. This also implies that they might be useful on their own and not require complementary patents not contained in the commons. Because they are usually distant from the firm's technology (patent) portfolio, one reason for pledging them may be that they are not very valuable to the firm holding them.

The idea of creating a global cultural and knowledge commons is a key element in moving towards sustainability but businesses are also keen to protect their own intellectual property and their actual, or anticipated, competitive advantage. A more radical and promising initiative is that of the Open Source Ecology Network (see Box 10.4 below).

Networks and sharing are therefore key ways by which businesses and other organizations generate and apply new knowledge, build capacity, and collaboratively address the many 'wicked', complex, and interconnected problems that beset us. To do this though requires the development of mindsets attuned to the needs, values, skills, strategies, and commitments to being a collaborative capacity builder. These commitments as Weber and Khademian (2008) suggest probably include:

> A commitment to governance that makes due recognition of the need for government regulation rather than accommodating laissez faire market freedoms
> A commitment to govern and operate within these rules but to do so in a cooperative and innovative manner
> A commitment to recognizing that change agents, coordinators or leaders need not necessarily always come from official or elite business or government circles
> A commitment to networks as mutual aid partnerships with the wider society
> A commitment to understanding that performance, capacity and accountability are inseparable
> A commitment and passion for genuine collaboration and meaningful co-operation

Networks differ in their size, the density of relations, degrees of cohesiveness, interconnectivity within subgroups and the extent to which they may be centralized. All these factors can influence the way the network operates and the effectiveness with which it tackles complex problems. It is no wonder that it isn't easy being green. So, when attempting to answer a question like 'what is a green business?', the answer is necessarily a complex one too. However, there are signs, indicators, books, training and development interventions, degree programmes, and certification schemes which help us formulate one.

Eco-entrepreneurship

An entrepreneur is a person who is able to identify an unsolved problem or an unmet want or need which they then attempt to satisfy commercially. A green or eco-entrepreneur is a person whose activities straddle both enterprise and sustainable development creating sustainable innovations that can achieve environmental and social goals in a holistic manner and be successful in the marketplace. Notable eco-entrepreneurs have included Anita Roddick, founder of the Body Shop, fashion designer Stella McCartney, green architect William McDonough and, formerly the youngest ever national president of the Sierra Club and author of *Strategy for Sustainability: A business manifesto*, Adam Werbach.

Like more conventional entrepreneurial activities, eco-entreprenural business ventures involve a degree of risk which can make outcomes unpredictable and failure a distinct possibility. In addition, given our

Box 10.4 The Open Source Ecology Network

Open Source Ecology (OSE) is a movement to create the open source economy. The movement consists of hundreds of entrepreneurs, producers, engineers, makers, and supporters around the world who share the open ethic.

The backbone of Open Source Ecology is open access to economically-significant information – product designs, techniques, and rapid learning materials for achieving this. Collaborative development, 24/7 around the globe, leads to best practice designs – accessible openly via the internet. Global collaboration in open product and process design leads to best practices being commonly available.

All wealth comes from nature – rocks, plants, sunlight, and water. Transparency of the connection between technology and nature means that people begin to respect nature. This happens when people begin to respect that their well-being comes from nature. This transparency is facilitated when economically productive activities happen as close to the community as possible – not out of sight, out of mind in remote locations.

The Global Village Construction Set (GVCS) is an open technological platform that allows for the easy fabrication of the 50 different *Industrial Machines* that it takes to build a small civilization with modern comforts. These include the 3D printer, 3D scanner, 50kw wind turbine, CNC torch/router table, laser cutter, nickel iron batteries, heat exchanger…The key features of GVCS are: open source, low cost, modular, user serviceable, DIY, closed loop manufacturing, high performance, heirloom design and flexible fabrication.

Source: Adapted from: http://opensourceecology.org/

imperfect world not all aspects of a green enterprise may be green, but on balance a green enterprise must have a positive impact. True eco-entrepreneurs intentionally, rather than accidentally, generate new products, services, techniques, and even organizations and in so doing attempt to pull the whole market towards respecting ecological limits. Thus, the idea is to create a market dynamic that realizes environmental progress, and the new business opportunities afforded by growing demand for renewable energy, hybrid cars, organic chocolate, and ecotourist holidays suggests how green enterprise has begun to influence the mainstream.

Ecological modernization, as previously referred to in Chapters 5 and 9, is clearly articulated in the changing business practices of many large corporations who have moved beyond basic regulatory compliance towards seeking to create market incentives through educating or otherwise inducing their clients, customers, and suppliers to accommodate sets of pro-sustainability values. Eco-entrepreneurs, of course, vary in what they do and how they present themselves. They have, not surprisingly, been categorized in a number of ways. Walley and Taylor (2002) have suggested the following ideal types:

- *Innovative opportunists* identify a green niche ripe for economic exploitation and are largely influenced by structural factors such as regulation
- *Visionary champions* try to transform the world and ground their business in environmentally sustainable values
- *Ethical mavericks* have a sustainability orientation that is often based on past experience and/or influences and are most frequently found in alternative-style businesses
- *Ad hoc enviropreneurs* are financially driven, often referred to as 'accidental green entrepreneurs'

Eco-entrepreneurs have important roles to play in creating a more sustainable world but they cannot do it without the existence of a supportive regulatory framework, financial and market opportunities, and a nurturing policy and educational environment. Eco-entrepreneurs cannot be created magically on the whim of policymakers or green pundits. Robert Isaak also makes a distinction between green business and green green business. He writes (Isaak 2002:90):

> Businesses that are not designed to be sustainable decrease our health, shorten our time on Earth and destroy the heritage we leave for our children, no matter where we are located globally. In contrast, green green businesses are models that can help show the way to increase productivity while reducing resource use in a manner that is harmonious with human health and the sustainability of non-human species as well. Green start-ups make it easier to 'fix' environmental components and processes from the outset. Green subsidiaries of larger firms can foster innovation and bring back the heightened motivation of social solidarity to businesses where it may be all too easy to slip into cynicism in an era of global economic crises.

Eco-entrepreneurs can operate on a for-profit or not-for-profit basis and many social entrepreneurs who invest their surplus in social causes or institutions often encompass green ideas and objectives.

Box 10.5 Ever thought of being a sustainable green wedding and event planner?

Event planning is a global industry worth approximately $500 billion. Event planners are responsible for designing and executing a variety of events (including weddings, celebrations, and conferences) on behalf of others.

An eco-friendly event planner needs to benefit from having a terrific network of contractors in his area who can provide eco-friendly services for proposed events, including cleaning companies, sustainable printers for cards and invitations, digital photographers, green dry cleaners, organic caterers, etc.

The broad scope of event planning means that business owners need to think carefully about all aspects of the experience ahead of time. If a potential eco event planner prides himself on ensuring sustainable behavior in all aspects of his life (home, office, transport, food, etc.), running a sustainable event-planning business may be just the thing.

Customers appreciate creative ideas that use best practices in sustainability. All the eco-friendly implements for any event are available, right down to eco-friendly confetti. Event planning requires a close relationship to customers, a high degree of organizational skills, and significant creativity in design and execution. A person must be detail-oriented enough to keep event details [in the] top of [his] mind and be able to estimate costs accurately, but be flexible enough to change plans at the last minute. A sustainable event planner will need to learn about sustainable practices in every aspect of the business.

Source: Adapted from Cooney (2010).

Case study

Unilever, Oxfam, and labour rights in Vietnam

Labour rights should be respected irrespective of where the business operates and organizations should acknowledge and redress iniquities or bad labour practices. Unilever recently cooperated with Oxfam in an investigation of its operations in Vietnam and its wider supply chain. The published report is an excellent example of corporate transparency and authentic commitment to respecting key labour rights and principles (Wilshaw et al. 2013:91):

> Oxfam concluded that Unilever's analysis shows that the best results come from factories with good conditions and empowered workers, however its business model does not fully reflect this. Based on the study, competitive advantage is still in practice pursued through downward pressure on labour costs, which pushes costs and risks onto workers.

In response to Oxfam's criticisms Paul Polman, CEO of Unilever responded (Wilshaw et al. 2013:95):

> Unilever's business model is one that is based on localized production which means that we must compete with other national as well as international business operations. This is why we generally set our wage levels to take account of the local competitive environment market by market. This being said, we aim to ensure that our overall compensation package is always above the minimum wage (where applicable), offers additional benefits (such as pensions, free or subsidized canteens, medical insurance, etc.), and provides training and skills development for all workers.

Sustainable business means sustainable, decent, and meaningful work.

Key terms

Enterprise, green jobs, knowledge, leadership, professional development, sharing and cooperation, skills, sustainable work.

Discussion questions

1   Identify the ways in which HRM can contribute to developing green business practices.
2   What role do business schools have in promoting a green economy and sustainable businesses?
3   In what ways is leadership important to achieving success as a sustainable business?
4   Is a green job necessarily a good job?
5   How can a competitive business also be a cooperative one?
6   How can eco-entrepreneurship be supported and developed?

End of chapter summary

Creating sustainable businesses is a people-centred complex of activities requiring the development, acquisition, and application of new knowledge, skills, and capabilities. To effect this, businesses need to be learning organizations which makes HR departments highly important parts of the enterprise. How new employees are recruited, selected, trained, and how learning is nurtured in partnership with business schools and external bodies such as professional associations are key elements in forming a green economy and creating decent green jobs. Leaders will be and are required at all levels and success will depend on good leadership but also the capacity to share, cooperate, and network. Perhaps the essence of a sustainable business is (eco)enterprise that must be key to all successful business operations. Consequently, money can be made from protecting and regenerating rather than destroying the environment. Many new technologies and technical skills, including those related to ICT, have the capacity to and are beginning to do this.

Further reading

CPSL (2011) *A Journey of a Thousand Miles: the state of sustainability leadership 2011*. Available at www.cpsl.cam.ac.uk

Docherty, P., Kira, M. Shani, A.B. Eds. (2009) *Creating Sustainable Work Systems*, 2nd ed. London: Routledge, pp. 1–21.

Dubois, C.L.Z. and Dubois, D.A. (2012) Strategic HRM as social design for environmental sustainability in organization. *Human Resource Management*, 51(6):799–826.

Isaak, R. (2002) The making of the ecopreneur. *Green Management International*, 38:81–91.

Walker, S. (2006) *Sustainable by Design*. London: Earthscan.

11 New strategic thinking

Structural and social solutions

Sustainability in general and sustainability in business is first and foremost a social process, and a process having to do with demographics, behaviours, and even human nature.

Addressing overpopulation

In Chapter 3 we noted that investment in family planning, contraception, education, and change in cultural perceptions needs to be considered a crucial opportunity for sustainability investment. A whole range of social and environmental problems, including poverty, could be if not solved but definitely helped by stabilizing population growth. If businesses fail to recognize overpopulation as a threat to sustainability and fail to invest in solving it, all other efforts at sustainable production, consumption, and indeed business development are likely to fail in the long term.

Addressing consumption

Considering the challenges outlined in relationship to consumption in Chapters 4 and 9, the following sections explore the possibility of how the things we produce and consume can be possibly made sustainable.

Consumer choice editing

As discussed in Chapter 4, individual consumer's sphere of influence can be too small to initiate significant change, and many consumers may be simply unwilling to consider sustainable options when offered many (cheap) choices of products. Many green consumption specialists have suggested that efforts to encourage sustainable living depend on structural changes that require political and corporate leadership. Consumer choice editing or restriction of unsustainable products can help eliminate unsustainable choices.

Sharing economy

Sharing economy, also called collaborative consumption, involves the new sharing that reduces waste, saves money and becomes more self-sufficient, all without buying more stuff.

> **Sharing economy** is a movement in which the consumer experience is rapidly evolving, with sharing becoming a more fulfilling experience than owning.

There is also a growing trend in websites like ifixit.com, which provide free product information and repair manuals, reducing some of the barriers to maintaining and repairing goods and electronics. Strangers can now leverage technology and access an exploding number of sites to share cars, rooms, items, and tasks. The sharing economy is said to connect people to their communities, save money, and be environmentally conscious. Examples of sharing include car sharing and computer-leasing companies. Yet, not everybody wants to share, and many items can simply not be shared. However, sharing and leasing have implications for how businesses can create value. Keeping a product in use for longer implies that direct sales of new products decrease, impacting ongoing profits that could otherwise be made.

These interventions into the manufacturing process can be seen as opportunities for new business. For example, instead of selling a product a retailer could rent it and create a new revenue stream focusing on maintenance. This could require capital outlay to set up a new business unit and trained staff to undertake the work (Tennant and Brennan 2015). This is a challenge to mainstream business operations and requires that new strategies be implemented.

Understanding sustainable consumption

Marketing psychologists, business economists, and even retailers have long discovered the opportunities offered by the knowledge of the human psyche in devising clever marketing strategies to entice consumers to their product. Sustainable businesses still have to come to terms with what certain social, cultural, and perhaps 'natural' human tendencies can be beneficial to their sustainable business. Defining the universals or certain features of our human behaviour may be difficult, as they are culturally variably expressed, yet the global spread of consumer culture under industrial conditions is indisputable. Examples of such human universals can be either harmful or hopeful. The use of technological innovation to improve production and medical technologies leads to both increased population growth and more extensive land use. The drive towards improving one's status through moving into the middle class through material possession leads to growth in consumption.

In adopting some of Kaplan's (2000) insights from the article 'Human nature and environmentally responsible behavior', and assuming that certain universal human propensities do exist, a number of suggestions for businesses wanting to promote sustainability (and still make profit!) can be made:

1   Be sensitive to going with the grain, to recognizing and working with the motivations and inclinations characteristic of us as humans and do not expect 'sustainable action' to spontaneously emerge.
2   Treat the human cognitive capacity as a resource.
3   Engage the powerful motivations for competence, being needed, making a difference, and forging a better life.
4   Rather than going against the grain of human nature by telling people to be good, to minimize damage, to economize, and to pick up their rubbish, solutions should be found in the human universals themselves.

If individual choices can be channelled in a way that would allow individuals to go with and not against the grain of human nature, some positive changes could be seen. Part of this human nature is also the diversity of individuals. While some segments of the population can learn to care about disadvantaged members of society or other species, others will be motivated by profit. Recognizing this has significant implications for business practice, as we shall further explain in the sections on the alternative frameworks of sustainability below.

Realizing impacts: direct and indirect

In Chapter 2 we mentioned that environmentally and socially significant behaviour can be defined by its impact.

> **Environmental impact** is the extent to which certain actions or behaviours change availability of certain resources or energy in the environment or alters certain structures and dynamics of ecosystems.

Social psychologist Paul Stern (2000) distinguished between at least two types of environmental impacts: direct and indirect. Some behaviour, such as clearing forest or disposing of household waste, directly causes environmental change. Other behaviour is indirectly significant, like storing your pension funds in a bank that makes unsustainable investments (of which most of us are not even aware of). Examining tax policies and ability to choose an investment bank that invests in renewable energy can have a greater impact than turning off your lights at home. The deeper causes of environmental problems lie within international development policies, commodity prices on world markets, and patterns of investment and consumption and not behaviours of individual consumers that are often unable (because the choices are simply not there or they cannot afford them) or too ill-informed or unwilling to be 'sustainable'.

As discussed in Chapter 9, realizing that indirect impact of policies supporting health and global consumption can have a detrimental effect on the long-term availability of resources for future generations, leads one to a more critical strategic thinking about addressing environmental problems.

Private and public action

Similarly, private and public sphere environmentalism can differ greatly in their impact. Consumer researchers and psychologists have focused mainly on behaviours in the private sphere: the purchase, use, and disposal of personal and household products that have environmental impact.

> **Private sphere environmentalism** refers to the purchase, use, and disposal of household products that have environmental impact.

However, private actions may stay 'invisible' to others or insignificant, given the relatively small impact of one individual in the world of 7 billion citizens. While your own decision to become a vegetarian might reduce a bit of environmental burden, participation in certain public actions, being a member of NGOs that promote vegetarianism or lobbies for animal-friendly policies at the government level can have a much more profound effect. However, the sense of guilt and impotence in solving huge environmental problems may be indeed be beyond the scope of individual human capacity to resolve.

> **Public sphere environmentalism** includes active kinds of environmental activism (petitioning, joining, or contributing to environmental organizations) and support of acceptance of public policies (willingness to pay higher taxes for environmental protection).

While private actions, such as attempts at responsible consumption, may contribute to some improvements, as the proponents of 'think globally, act locally' campaign would claim, public actions can have a much greater impact. While one can use public transport as a matter of personal choice, lobbying the government can have a much greater effect on the greater availability, dependability, affordability, and attractiveness of public transport to all segments of the population.

A similar observation can be made about social actions, like giving change to a homeless person on the street (private action), and being involved in organizations that attempt to address the underlying causes of urban poverty (public action). Certainly, 'walking your talk' is also important. Many companies have discovered that speaking about sustainability without effective action can lead to public scepticism, as in the case of climate change.

Business and NGO cooperation

Businesses working together with NGOs present another opportunity for both business and non-profit interests to mutually benefit. The danger for business is in appearing too soft for its stakeholders. Sometimes cooperating NGOs need to strike compromises between gaining funds and reasserting their mainstream position in society through cooperation. There is a danger of losing potential donors who think that such cooperation could compromise environment non-governmental organizations' (ENGOs') principles. However, the gains overweigh the risks. For example, banks can highlight their green investment marketing strategy by using an ENGO's logo.

Using WWF's panda logo on the climate credit card provided the Dutch bank Rabobank with symbolic gain. This gave the bank a competitive advantage over other banks and legitimization of its climate-related messages and providing the rationale for Rabobank to formally engage with WWF in partnership formation. On the other hand, WWF has gained extra credit with corporate leaders as a supporter of green investment (Van Huijstee and Glasbergen 2010).

Green investment

Many people would agree that money makes the world go round. It cannot be stressed enough how important green investment is. As consumers, the ability to choose where ones' pension funds are invested, supported by transparent investment policies of banks, could make a huge difference. Yet, before businesses and financial institutions invest in anything that appears green or sustainable, they need to realize the certain very salient paradoxes and bottlenecks outlined in this book, particularly in Chapter 9.

Tackling oil dependency and climate scepticism

Despite the flexibility mechanisms discussed in Chapter 2, emission reductions have not materialized, partially due to the fact that emission trading depends not only on its economic design but also on the politics surrounding this process (Pinske and Kolk 2009:109). The latest report from the UNEP reveals that in 2012 GHG emissions were 20 per cent higher than in 2000. If emissions are not cut they will reach 58 gigatons in 2020, which will raise global temperature much higher than the minimal target of 2 degrees, and significantly raise ocean levels (Figure 11.1).

In the case of coal, burning it gives off particles that harm health as well as produces CO_2. However, as discussed in Chapter 5, in rich countries the cost–benefit balance fails to tip the other way. While some rich countries and industries have claimed to find 'sustainable' energy solutions, such as shale gas in the US or biofuels in Europe, these have not addressed the challenges

Figure 11.1 The ocean (source: Engelbert Fellinger)

outlined in Chapter 9. In 2013 in Europe, which likes to see itself as a world leader on climate, increasing amounts of coal were used. As *The Economist* (2013c:52) wryly commented:

> EU energy policy is boosting usage of the most polluting fuel, increasing carbon emissions, damaging the creditworthiness of utilities and diverting investment into energy projects elsewhere. The EU's climate commissioner, Connie Hedegaard, likes to claim that in energy and emissions Europe is 'leading by example'. Oh-oh.

In order to find solutions to climate change, the role of powerful industrial lobbies that have a stake in oil dependency and promoting climate scepticism needs to be addressed by the public, governments, and by businesses. In order to ensure that the future of business – and indeed society – is secured, the solution lies in long-term investment in renewables.

Business and technological solutions

As we have noted in previous chapters, sustainability is not easy to achieve and many conventional sustainability approaches have simply failed to address both social and environmental problems. The WBCSD Vision 2050 report calls for a new agenda for business. With its best-case scenario for sustainability and pathways for reaching it, it is a 'platform for beginning the dialogue that must take place to navigate the challenging years to come'. However, not all business solutions outlined in the report prescribe – let along require – that businesses follow these pathways to sustainability beyond what is immediately required by the stakeholders – shareholders on the one hand, and to a lesser degree customers, NGOs, and pressure groups on the other hand.

The Dow Jones Sustainability Indices (DJSI) define the role of corporate sustainability leaders as achieving 'long-term shareholder value by gearing their strategies and management to harness the market's potential for sustainability products and services while at the same time successfully reducing and avoiding sustainability costs and risks'. This role, specified among other indicators as 'Meeting shareholders' demands for sound financial returns, long-term economic growth, open communication and transparent financial accounting' says very little about the challenges described in Chapters 2, 3, and 9.

It is largely through informed business investment that some of the greatest sustainability challenges can be confronted. Future corporate leaders may need to consider strategy that goes beyond basic accountability to the shareholder and promises of perpetual economic growth and ROIs in order to ensure that the most glaring social and environmental problems are addressed.

Besides growing population and unsustainable consumption, one of the biggest challenges of our time is returning to the closed loop system, in which nothing has to be wasted. This calls for intelligent innovation. Amory Lovins, of the Rocky Mountain Institute, a think tank that promotes energy efficiency, argues that a combination of thoughtful design and new technology can minimize or even eliminate the need for many modern amenities such as air conditioning through architecture and the use of natural landscapes.

In the following section we aim to introduce most promising – although not always conventional – approaches to production and consumption, and demonstrate how they differ from conventional views on sustainability. We shall also focus on the key principles of these alternative systems and delineate their implications and applications.

Business ecology and industrial ecology

The term 'business ecology' has been adopted by many companies and organizations and can refer to a number of different concepts. One of the central concepts is business ecosystem.

> **Business ecosystem** refers to the network of organizations – including suppliers, distributors, customers, competitors, government agencies, and so on – involved in the delivery of a specific product or service through both competition and cooperation.

Frosch and Gallopoulos (1989) introduced the concept of an 'industrial ecosystem'. This ecosystem analogy was based on observations of ecosystem functions and emphasized the optimization of energy and material flows within an industrial system, focusing on not just the minimization of waste but its complete elimination from the industrial cycle. This elimination (or rather full use) is made possible by the exchange of by-products between industrial actors, whereby the waste from one production process becomes an input to another.

In the framework of business ecology, business in the 'ecosystem' affects and is affected by the others, creating a constantly evolving relationship in which each business must be flexible and adaptable in order to survive, as in a biological ecosystem. Focusing on connections between operators within the 'industrial ecosystem', the industrial ecology approach aims at eliminating undesirable by-products. Similar to this is the concept of industrial ecology.

> **Industrial ecology** is the multidisciplinary field of research which combines aspects of engineering, economics, sociology, toxicology, and the natural sciences to study material and energy flows through industrial systems.

Industrial ecology adopts a systemic point of view, designing production processes in accordance with local ecological constraints, and attempting to shape them so they perform as close to living systems as possible. This framework is sometimes referred to as the 'science of sustainability', and its principles can also be applied in the services sector. From an industrial ecology perspective, any given efficiency measure has several types of environmental impacts. Since environment is often a free input, a price-based rebound effect is not expected, but other indirect effects, such as spillover of environmental behaviour, can occur.

Biomimicry

Inspired by Janine M. Benyus' (1997) book, *Biomimicry: Innovation Inspired by Nature*, biomimicry is defined as a 'new science that studies nature's models and then imitates or takes inspiration from these designs and processes to solve human problems'.

> **Biomimicry** or **biomimetics** is the imitation of the models, systems, and elements of nature for the purpose of solving complex human problems.

Biomimicry relies on three key principles. First, nature as model refers to the study and emulation of nature's forms, process, systems, and strategies to solve human problems. Second, nature as measure refers to the use of an ecological standard to judge the sustainability of technical innovations.

Third, nature as mentor uses an ecocentric stance in viewing and valuing nature for what we can learn from it, and how we can learn to appreciate nature's diversity – diversity that is utilized from a holistic perspective, as healthy ecosystems are complex communities of living things, each of which has developed a unique response to its surroundings, working in concert with other organisms to sustain the system as a whole.

C2C

In *Cradle to Cradle: Remaking the Way We Make Things* McDonough and Braungart (2002) support the framework that does not reach for sustainability as it is usually defined but seeks to create industrial systems that are essentially positive and waste free. Cradle to Cradle (alternatively C2C, or Cradle 2 Cradle) was dubbed by some the 'next industrial revolution'. McDonough and Braungart ask us to contemplate not just minimizing the damage the way eco-efficiency does (Chapter 9), but eliminating waste all together. Eco-efficiency is targeted at minimizing the damage by 'slowing the process of destruction' and 'making a bad design last longer'. By contrast, C2C proposes a positive framework of being 'all good'.

Key principles of C2C

As opposed to conventional eco-efficiency, the C2C framework stresses eco-effectiveness.

> **Eco-effectiveness** is an alternative design and production concept, advocating a positive agenda for the conception and production of goods and services by focusing on the development of products and industrial systems that maintain or enhance the quality and productivity of materials through subsequent life cycles.

Product design impacts the ease and success of all reuse methods, and strategies such as Design for Recycling (DfR) and Design for Disassembly and Design for Remanufacturing (DfREM) attempt to factor in these requirements at the design stage of the manufacturing process. These can include standardization of components, and designing products so that they can be upgraded (Tennant and Brennan 2014).

C2C certification schemes

C2C in business is applied through a combination of operational principles and certification schemes. The Cradle to Cradle Products Innovation Institute, a non-profit organization that administers the Cradle to Cradle Certified Product Standard; and the Cradle to Cradle Certified™ Products Program, a third party, multi-attribute eco-label administered by the Cradle to Cradle Products Innovation Institute.

We should note that the return to pre-industrial designs is not desired by most businesses (as there is little money to be made by asking people to return to their traditional dwellings and it does not sound 'progressive'). Thus, most C2C houses are based on innovative designs. Also, the founding fathers of the C2C system have been blamed for profiting from the lucrative certification system, monopolizing the market, and keeping authorship rights to their concepts preventing its wide usability. In his blog post,

Box 11.1 Three key principles of C2C

C2C identifies three key principles which should inform human design:

1   Waste equals food.
2   Use current solar income.
3   Celebrate diversity.

Waste equals food
Waste does not exist in nature because the processes of each organism contribute to the health of the whole ecosystem. A cherry tree's blossoms (Figure 11.2) fall to the ground and decompose into food for other living things. Bacteria and fungi feed on the organic waste of both the tree and the animals that eat its fruit, depositing nutrients in the soil in a form ready for the tree to use for growth. One organism's waste is food for another and nutrients flow indefinitely in cycles of birth, decay, and rebirth. In other words, waste equals food and it would help if we thought that way too. We understand the world in large part with the help of the verbal and visual metaphors we use and

Figure 11.2 Cherry tree (source: Engelbert Fellinger)

business, and education for that matter, uses military metaphors as a way of communicating and understanding what it does. Just consider how many times terms like strategies, targets, and logistics are used.

Understanding these regenerative systems allows engineers and designers to recognize that all materials can be designed as nutrients that flow through natural or designed metabolisms. Materials designed as biological nutrients, such as textiles and packaging made from natural fibres, can biodegrade safely and restore soil after use.

While nature's nutrient cycles comprise the biological metabolism, the technical metabolism is designed to mirror them. This is considered as a closed-loop system in which valuable, high-tech synthetics and mineral resources circulate in cycles of production, use, recovery, and remanufacture. Products can be fully dismantled so that their elements can be returned to biological or technical metabolisms. Ideally, every

continued ...

Box 11.1 continued

product can be designed from the outset so that after its lifetime is over, the product will then continue to live by becoming a nutrient within either a biological or technological cycle. Within this framework, designers and engineers can use scientific assessments to select safe materials and optimize products and services, creating closed-loop material flows that are inherently benign and sustaining.

However, in the case of business, a number of the waste methods require that reverse logistics is considered. If products are to be up-recycled, how are they taken back to the manufacturer or a third party? This requires collection, sorting and transportation, all of which can be costly. Tennant and Brennan (2014) note that if markets for secondary goods or materials are not mature, or refurbished goods are perceived as being of lower quality than new, this can impact the ability of businesses to generate revenue.

Use current solar income
Living things thrive on the energy of the sun. Trees and plants manufacture food from sunlight, an effective system that uses the Earth's unrivalled and continuous source of energy income. Despite recent precedent, human energy systems can be nearly as effective. C2C systems – from buildings to manufacturing processes – tap into current solar income using direct solar energy collection or passive solar processes, such as daylight, which makes effective use of natural light. Wind power-thermal flows fuelled by sunlight can also be tapped.

Celebrate diversity
Healthy ecosystems are complex communities of living things, each of which has developed a unique response to its surroundings that works in concert with other organisms to sustain the system. Each organism fits in its place and in each system the fittest thrive. Similarly to bionics and biomimicry, C2C takes nature's diversity as a prototype for many models for human designs, tailoring designs to maximize their positive effects in order to 'fit' within local natural systems and to enhance the local landscape where possible. McDonough and Braungart have successfully designed a number of urban areas and buildings taking into account local climate, materials, and both human and ecological needs.

In short, by modelling human designs on nature's operating system – generating materials that are 'food' for biological or industrial systems, tapping the energy of sun, celebrating diversity – C2C design creates a new paradigm for industry, one in which human activity generates a wide spectrum of ecological, social, and economic value and thus results in 'upcycling'.

Source: Compiled from various C2C websites.

Box 11.2 Applicability of C2C principles

- The framework is based on simple to understand ideas such as nutrient cycle;
- while critical of the current state of production (or industrial capitalism), the framework is essentially positive and does not put stress on negative effects, but rather solutions;
- the framework uses practical easy-to-explain design and product ideas to complement its theoretical or ethical underpinnings;
- practical and technological applications are well suited for designers, market and distribute product developers, and business executives.

Source: Compiled from various C2C websites.

McIntire-Strasburg (2008) hopes that C2C design will flourish if its owners decide to open source C2C, or if other business professionals shift to other similar certification systems. The compromise between a building that is both profitable to its makers and yet has a possibility to be widely used in the region (thus, affordable to all) is one of the greatest challenges of the application of C2C (Figure 11.3).

Circular economy

In their 1976 research report to the European Commission in Brussels, 'The Potential for Substituting Manpower for Energy', Walter Stahel and Genevieve Reday sketched the vision of the circular economy and its impact on job creation, economic competitiveness, resource savings, and waste prevention. These authors put forward the argument for a 'self-replenishing economy', based on a 'spiral loop system' through product-life extension activities that cycle materials: reuse, repair, reconditioning, and recycling. The term circular economy encompasses more than the production and consumption of goods and services, and includes a shift towards renewable energy and the role of diversity as a characteristic of resilient and productive systems. The idea of a circular economy synthesized a number existing strands of work and specifically enabled the analysis and communication of its broad economic potential.

The functional economy emphasizes turning products into services ('product service shift', or PSS), arguing that selling the use or function of the product rather than the product itself would enable the efficient cycling of materials and simultaneously give incentives for innovation (Scott 2011). Importantly, Stahel (1984) argued that product life-extension activities should lead to an increase in job creation as labour is required to keep

PROGRAM CATEGORY	BASIC	BRONZE	SILVER	GOLD	PLATINUM
MATERIAL HEALTH			✓		
MATERIAL REUTILIZATION			✓		
RENEWABLE ENERGY & CARBON MANAGMENT				✓	
WATER STEWARDSHIP			✓		
SOCIAL FAIRNESS					✓
OVERALL CERTIFICATION LEVEL			✓		

Figure 11.3 Cradle to Cradle product scorecard (source: adapted from Cradle to Cradle Products Innovation Institute http://www.c2ccertified.org permission of Will Duggan)

products in use through each use-phase. The circular economy should be "restorative by intention", where environmental impact is decoupled from economic growth. To be restorative implies that businesses have a positive environmental impact (Hawken 1993).

The Ellen MacArthur Foundation

The application of the circular economy at an economic level has risen to prominence since the 2012 World Economic Forum (WEF) with the launch of the Towards a Circular Economy Report by the Ellen MacArthur Foundation. The report emphasized factors such as increased design for reuse, new, or enhanced recovery models and access over ownership models that promote greater circularity as well as a lucrative business opportunity.

The Ellen MacArthur Foundation, founded in 2009 by Dame Ellen MacArthur, is a registered charity with the aim of giving the concept of the circular economy a wide exposure and appeal. The Ellen MacArthur Foundation works in education, business innovation and analysis and provides businesses, educators, and policymakers with a number of useful case studies and practical resources to inspire and enable the transition to a circular economy.

The circular economy reports developed by the Foundation, with analysis by McKinsey & Company, established a clear framework and economic case for a transition to the circular economy. The reports highlighted a combined annual trillion dollar opportunity globally in net material cost savings for companies making the transition to the circular economy. The Foundation has created the Circular Economy 100 programme, a global platform bringing together leading companies, and enabling them to benefit from subsequent first mover advantages (http://www.ellenmacarthurfoundation. org/business/ce100).

The Blue Economy

Initiated by former Ecover CEO and Belgian businessman Gunter Pauli, the Blue Economy is an open source movement bringing together concrete case studies, initially compiled in the Club of Rome (see Introduction). Pauli founded the open source Zero Emission Research & Initiatives network (ZERI) in 1994. There are parallels between the Blue Economy and C2C in that waste is not per se an issue, but the concern should be with what is done with it. ZERI's main guiding principle is '...everything is to be reused by generating additional value', with a target of zero emissions (Pauli 2011:15). As the official manifesto states, 'the waste of one product becomes the input to create a new cash flow'. The concept of the Blue Economy is better understood either as an economic model or an innovative business model that permits social and technological organizations to respond to basic human needs.

> The **Blue Economy** stands for a different way of designing business by using the resources available in cascading systems, where the waste of one product becomes the input to create a new cash flow.

ZERI, a global network of creative professionals that embraces innovative business models, is promoting 'innovative business models' that are 'capable of bringing competitive products and services to the market responding to basic needs while building social capital and enhance mindful living in harmony with nature's evolutionary path' (http://www.theblueeconomy. org/).

Based on twenty-one founding principles, the Blue Economy insists on solutions being determined by their local environment and ecological characteristics. These principles are quite similar to the C2C and circular economy models discussed above.

In Table 11.1 you will find an overview of hopeful sustainability frameworks that go beyond conventional canons and carry the promise of transforming the economy and society without harm to environment.

These are the promises for the future. It will be you, the reader, who will help to make a transition to the sustainable society possible.

Box 11.3 The principles of the Blue Economy®

- Solutions are first and foremost based on physics. Deciding factors are pressure and temperature as found on site.
- Substitute something with nothing – question any resource regarding its necessity for production.
- Natural systems cascade nutrients, matter, and energy – waste does not exist. Any by-product is the source for a new product.
- Nature evolved from few species to a rich biodiversity. Wealth means diversity. Industrial standardization is the contrary.
- Nature provides room for entrepreneurs who do more with less. Nature is contrary to monopolization.
- Gravity is the main source of energy; solar energy is the second renewable fuel.
- Water is the primary solvent (no complex, chemical, toxic catalysts).
- In nature the constant is change. Innovations take place in every moment.
- Nature only works with what is locally available. Sustainable business evolves with respect not only for local resources, but also for culture and tradition.
- Nature responds to basic needs and then evolves from sufficiency to abundance. The present economic model relies on scarcity as a basis for production and consumption.
- Natural systems are non-linear.
- In nature everything is biodegradable – it is just a matter of time.
- In natural systems everything is connected and evolving towards symbiosis.
- In nature water, air, and soil are the commons, free and abundant.
- In nature one process generates multiple benefits.
- Natural systems share risks. Any risk is a motivator for innovations.
- Nature is efficient. So sustainable business maximizes use of available material and energy, which reduces the unit price for the consumer.
- Nature searches for the optimum for all involucrated elements.
- In nature negatives are converted into positives. Problems are opportunities.
- Nature searches for economies of scope. One natural innovation carries various benefits for all.
- Respond to basic needs with what you have, introducing innovations inspired by nature, generating multiple benefits, including jobs and social capital, offering more with less.

Source: Compiled from different Blue economy sites, particularly http://www.blueeconomyconsulting.com/blue-economy; and http://www.theblueeconomy.org/

Table 11.1 Overview of frameworks

Thinkers	Concepts/Frameworks	Level of application	Seminal work by year
Robert Ayres and Allen Kneese	Industrial metabolism – understanding material and energy flows at the national level and within urban areas	Industrial system	Ayres and Kneese (1969)
Barry Commoner	Ecological principles used to structure national economy	National	Commoner (1971)
Walter Stahel	Circular or loop economy through product life-extension.	Product design	Stahel (1984)
Robert Frosch and Nicholas Gallopoulos	Industrial ecosystem	Industrial system	Frosch and Gallopoulos (1989)
Paul Hawken	Circular economy, restorative economy	Community	Hawken (1993)
John T. Lyle	Regenerative design	National, industrial	Lyle (1996)
Thomas Graedel	Earth system ecology – biological systems and industrial systems influence each other, therefore they should be studied from a synthesized perspective	Industrial system	Graedel (1996)
Janine Benyus	Biomimicry design framework based on looking at form, function, and processes in natural systems	Product design	Benyus (1997)
Gunter Pauli	Coined the term 'upcycling'. Developed the concept of the Blue Economy in a report for the Club of Rome	Enterprise development	Pauli (1998, 2010)
Michael Braungart and William McDonough	C2C design framework. Introduced concepts of technical and biological nutrients and argued there is a distinction between eco-efficiency and eco-effectiveness	Product design	McDonough and Braungart (2002)

Source: Adapted from Tennant and Brennan (2014).

Case study

Incorporating C2C Design into Herman Miller Products

Herman Miller Inc. is a manufacturer of office furniture. In the 1990s the company started to collaborate with C2C architect William McDonagh, resulting in a new product assessment tool known as 'the Design for the Environment' (DfE). Herman Miller quickly applied this tool to the design and manufacture of the Mirra Chair, which led to a number of important changes including the selection of new material used for the chair's spine, the elimination of all polyvinyl chloride (PVC) components, and a design facilitating recycling and disassembly using everyday tools. The new materials invariably had a green chemistry composition because most plastics are produced from virgin polymers. Many of the other new components were metallic because metals already have a quite sophisticated recycling infrastructure. Thus by using the DfE assessment tool, ecological considerations were directly factored into the design process to create a remarkable and certified C2C product.

In addition, Herman Miller's Green House operations, housed in a LEED pioneer building in West Michigan, uses 100 per cent renewable energy achieved through renewable energy credits and a power purchase agreement. Herman Miller's new Aeron office chair is GREENGUARD certified meaning it is a low emitting product. The powder coat paint finish on its metallic parts produce tiny amounts of volatile organic compounds (VOCs). The chair is also 94 per cent recyclable and is composed of 54 per cent recycled materials. Its steel components contain around 35 per cent recycled content and are 100 per cent recyclable. Both the Mirra and Aeron chairs are manufactured to ISO 14001 standards and carry a 12 year, 24 hour warranty.

But this is not the end, for C2C methodology requires and inspires continual quality improvement and development, at all levels within the supply chain, and seeks not just to minimize but to eliminate negative impacts.

Question

Check the current situation on Herman Miller. Do you think its product could serve as the best practice example of sustainable product? What could be better?

Key terms

Biomimicry, the Blue Economy, business ecosystem, circular economy, collaborative consumption, consumer choice editing, Cradle to Cradle (C2C), downcycling, eco-effectiveness, environmental impact, industrial ecology, sharing economy, sustainable consumption.

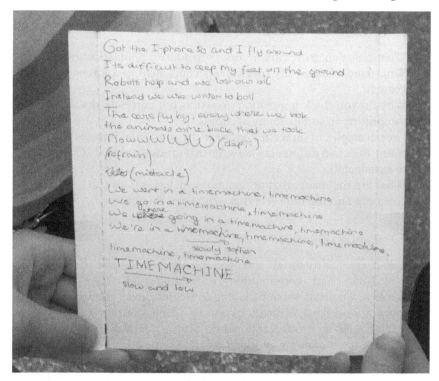

Figure 11.4 Song about the future (source: photo Helen Kopnina, composed by Eve Oostendorp (13), Ananda Pradhan (12), and Eden Fellinger (7).

Lyrics:

Got the I-phone so and I fly around
Its difficult to ceep my feet on the ground
Robots help and we lost own air
Instead we use water to boil
The cars fly by, every where we look
the animals come back that we took
NowwwwWW (clap!)
(refrain)
We went in a time machine, time machine
We go in a time machine, time machine
We where going in a time machine, time machine,
We're in a time machine, time machine, time machine
Slowly soften
time machine, time machine
TIME MACHINE
Slow and low

Discussion questions

1   What policy measures are necessary to address population growth?
2   What kind of company investments could help to address population growth?
3   Why do you think population growth is not currently discussed as the top priority in sustainability agendas?
4   Give examples of direct and indirect environmental impacts.
5   Name the main differences between eco-efficiency and C2C approaches to sustainability.
6   What are the main areas of common concern within C2C, the circular economy, and the Blue economy schools of thought?

End of chapter summary

In this chapter, structural and social solutions to the challenges of overpopulation and consumption were addressed. New forms and mechanisms of consumption, including consumer choice editing and sharing economy, are outlined. Strategic action is outlined in terms of direct and indirect as well as private and public actions. Tackling oil dependency and climate scepticism are outlined as necessary ways forward. Concrete business solutions are proposed through a number of frameworks that are significantly different from the conventional ones. Business ecology and industrial ecology are highlighted, and C2C, the circular economy, and the Blue Economy are emphasized.

Further reading

Benyus, J.M. (1997) *Biomimicry: Innovation Inspired by Nature*. New York: Harper Collins Publishers.

Braungart, M. (2013) *Waste to Energy*. http://catalystreview.net/2010/02/cradle-to-cradle-transitioning-from-waste-incineration-to-beneficial-materials/

Pauli, G. (2011) *From Deep Ecology to The Blue Economy: A Review of the Main Concepts Related to Environmental, Social and Ethical Business That Contributed to the Creation of the Blue Economy*. ZERI. http://www.zeri.org/ZERI/Home_files/From%20Deep%20Ecology%20to%20the%20Blue%20Economy%202011.pdf

Glossary

Absolute poverty   Absolute poverty measures poverty in relation to the amount of money necessary to meet basic needs such as food, clothing, and shelter.

Agenda 21   A key set of plans aimed at achieving global sustainable development in the twenty-first century. This document was adopted by United Nations Conference on Environment and Development (UNCED) as a programme of action on sustainable development for all sectors of government and society in each country.

Anthropocene   Anthropocene is an informal geologic term that serves to mark the evidence and extent of human activities that have had a significant global impact on the ecosystems. The term describes the influence of human behaviour on the Earth's atmosphere in recent centuries as so significant as to constitute a new geological epoch.

Anthropocentrism   Human-centredness, the position that humans are more important and superior to other species or the assessment of reality through an exclusively human perspective. Anthropocentrism is a major concept in environmental ethics and is often seen as the cause of problems created by human interaction with the environment.

Belgrade Charter   The Belgrade Charter was launched in 1975 by the United Nations Environment Program (UNEP) and United Nations Educational, Scientific and Cultural Organization (UNESCO) calling for the use of environmental education to develop 'a new global ethic'.

Biofuels   A biofuel contains energy produced from geologically recent carbon fixation which occurs in living organisms such as plants and microalgae. These fuels are made by a process of biomass conversion.

Biomimicry   Biomimicry or biomimetics is the imitation of the models, systems, and elements of nature for the purpose of solving complex human problems.

Biospheric egalitarianism   Biospheric egalitarianism, otherwise known as ecological justice, concerns the rights of other species independently of human interest.

Blue Economy The Blue Economy stands for a different way of designing business by using the resources available in cascading systems, where the waste of one product becomes the input to create a new cash flow.

Brand A term, quality, or symbol connoting trust and distinction of a product, service, or company in comparison with others.

Brand value Often used by marketing to refer to the financial value of the brand.

Building Research Establishment Environmental Assessment Methodology Green building certification scheme that sets the standard for best practice in sustainable building design, construction, and operation.

Business ecosystem Business ecosystem refers to the network of organizations – including suppliers, distributors, customers, competitors, government agencies and so on – involved in the delivery of a specific product or service through both competition and cooperation.

Carbon Disclosure Project A not-for-profit organization that collects information on the GHG emissions of the world's 500 large companies.

Circular economy The circular economy refers to an industrial economy that is restorative by intention; aims to rely on renewable energy; minimizes, tracks, and hopefully eliminates the use of toxic chemicals; and eradicates waste through careful design. The concept of the circular economy is grounded in the study of non-linear, particularly living, systems.

Civil society A contested term that usually refers to all people, their activities, and their relationships that are not part of the process of government operations. It may also be used to cover all processes other than government and economic activity.

Clean Development Mechanism Emission credits for financing approved climate-friendly projects in developing countries.

Commodification of nature Commodification of nature refers to an area of research within critical environmental studies concerned with the ways in which natural entities and processes are made exchangeable through economic valuation.

Competitive advantage The term given to a firm when it creates a means of securing some form of superiority, such as profitability or market share, over its competitors through offering its customers greater value.

Conspicuous consumption Conspicuous consumption denotes the deliberate accumulation of goods and services intended as a means of displaying the buyer's superior socio-economic status.

Consumer choice editing Consumer choice editing denies consumers the chance to buy non-sustainable goods. And by eliminating consumer choice, retailers can draw attention to a range of environmental and social issues that customers may not have previously considered.

Conference of the Parties Conference of the Parties (COP) is an association of all the countries that are Parties to the United Nations Framework

Convention on Climate Change (UNFCCC). COP and the UNFCCC have been meeting annually to assess progress in dealing with climate change. The COP is the 'supreme body' of the Convention, its highest decision-making authority.

Cradle to Cradle The Cradle to Cradle framework considers not just minimizing the damage, but proposes how contemporary waste and depletion of resources can be completely avoided by adhering to the 'waste=food' principle.

Deep ecology Deep ecology is a position in environmental ethics that recognizes that humans are interconnected with other species and that nature has intrinsic value, meaning that other species also have a right to live independent of human interests.

Demographic transition The process by which a country moves from high birth and high death rates to low birth and low death rates with population growth in the interim.

Dependency theory Developed countries continue to exploit developing countries through development aid, foreign debt, and disadvantageous trade, making poor countries dependent on handouts.

Downcycling Downcycling is the process of converting waste materials or useless products into new materials or products of lesser quality and reduced functionality.

Earth Charter The Earth Charter is a declaration of fundamental ethical principles for building a just, sustainable, and peaceful global society. The Earth Charter project began as a United Nations initiative, but was carried forward and completed by a global civil society initiative, the Earth Charter Commission, an independent international entity.

Earth Summit The Earth Summit in Rio de Janeiro held in 1992 has established 'Framework conventions' on climate change and biodiversity, identifying basic aims, principles, norms, institutions, and procedures for action.

Ecocentrism A term used in environmental ethics to denote a nature-centred, as opposed to human-centred, system of values. An ecocentric or a biocentric approach recognizes the intrinsic value of non-human species – that is, it values nature for its own sake.

Eco-labelling Eco-labelling is a voluntary approach to environmental certification practiced around the world.

Ecological justice While environmental justice in an anthropocentric approach is concerned with equal distribution of natural resources as well as environmental risks and benefits among humans, ecological justice refers to justice between all living species (see also biospheric egalitarianism).

Ecological modernization This theory presupposes that while the initial stages of industrial development involve environmentally damaging and socially unfair practices, the later stages of industrial development actually lead to improved environmental and human conditions.

Environmental justice Environmental justice refers to inequitable distribution of environmental burdens to vulnerable groups such as ethnic minorities or the economically disadvantaged populations; or to the developed and developing countries' unequal exposure to environmental risks and benefits; or to intergenerational justice between present and future generations; or to ecological justice.

Environmental impact Environmental impact defines the extent to which certain actions or behaviours change the availability of certain resources or energy from the environment or alters certain structures and dynamics of ecosystems.

Environmental Kuznets Curve According to the Environmental Kuznets Curve (EKC) hypothesis, it is believed that during early industrialization, economies use material resources more intensively, until a threshold is reached after which structural changes in the economy lead to progressively less-intensive materials use and thus high income levels and economic growth will lead to environmental improvement.

Environmental Management System Environmental Management System (EMS) is a tool for managing the impacts of an organization's environmental impacts by providing a clearly structured approach to planning and implementing environment actions.

Ethical consumerism Ethical consumerism, also called responsible consumption, ethical purchasing, moral purchasing, ethical shopping, or green consumerism, is a type of consumer behaviour that is based on choices of certain products or services associated with socially and environmentally responsible products.

Ethical investment The application of ethical principles to determine or filter potential investment opportunities in named securities.

Fairtrade Fairtrade is an alternative approach to conventional trade and is based on a partnership between producers and consumers.

Fordism Fordism is a manufacturing philosophy that aims to achieve higher productivity by standardizing the output, using conveyor assembly lines, and breaking the work into small deskilled tasks. Fordism came to signify mass production of affordable consumer goods

Fracking The hydraulic fracturing of underground areas to extract shale gas.

Global Council on Business Conduct The Council's mission statement states: 'The Conference Board is dedicated to equipping the world's leading corporations with the practical knowledge they need to improve their performance and better serve society.'

Governance The act, process, power, or manner of governing.

Green economy The green economy refers to a sustainable economy and society with zero carbon emissions, the application of the triple bottom line at both corporate and macroeconomic (global) levels. A green economy therefore operates within the ecological carrying capacity of the planet with energy primarily derived from renewable resources.

Greenhouse effect The greenhouse effect is a process by which thermal radiation from a planetary surface is absorbed by the atmosphere and is re-radiated in all directions. Since part of this re-radiation is back towards the surface, it results in an elevation of the average surface temperature or global warming.

Green Revolution Refers to a series of research, development, and technological initiatives occurring that increased agriculture production worldwide, particularly in the developing world, beginning most markedly in the late 1950s in Mexico.

Green 10 A group of environmental non-governmental organizations (NGOs) active at the European Union (EU) level.

Human resource development A theory and practice aimed at developing and enhancing the value and capacities of a firm's employees – sometimes referred to as human resources or human capital.

Human resource management The process of managing an organization's workforce

Human rights Rights inherent to being human, for example the right to life, first codified by the United Nations Declaration on Human Rights of 1948.

Industrial ecology Industrial ecology is the study of material and energy flows through industrial systems.

Joint Implementation One of the market mechanisms intended to combat climate change: industrialized states share the credit for emission reductions achieved in specific joint projects.

Knowledge management The process of creating, developing, sharing, and applying organizational data, information, and knowledge.

Kyoto Protocol Signed in Japan in 1997 to establish legally binding commitments by industrialized states to limit their GHG emissions.

Life Cycle Analysis (Assessment) A tool for the systematic measurement, analysis, and assessment of a product or service from source or conception to completion or disposal.

Limits to Growth Limits to Growth is a 1972 book about the computer modelling of exponential economic growth and increase in human population with finite resource supplies. Based on the evidence of the correlation between the escalating rates of economic growth and environmental degradation, international governments were called upon to address global trends in growing population and consumption.

Major Group One of a list of nine categories of NGOs specified in Agenda 21.

The Natural Step The Natural Step (TNS) is a globally recognized network of offices and individual associates that share the same brand, principles, and training in strategic sustainable development. TNS is based on four scientific principles. Reworded in sustainability principles they provide explicit guidance for any organization interested in moving towards sustainability.

Neo-colonialism   Neo-colonialism refers to unequal economic and political power between former colonial powers and former colonies, and the continuous influence of developed over developing countries.

Neo-liberalism   Neo-liberalism is a modern politico-economic theory favouring free trade, privatization, minimal government intervention in business, and reduced public expenditure on social services.

Network   Network refers to a coalition of NGOs or individual people, at the minimum sharing information and at the maximum devising a common political strategy. Use of the term implies the relationships are loose and informal.

Post-colonialism   Post-colonialism signifies the shift in power and trade relations, characterized by international development programmes and labour migration. Post-colonialism examines the manner in which emerging societies grapple with the challenges of self-determination and how they incorporate or reject Western norms and conventions, such as legal or political systems.

Post-Fordism   Characterized by transition from industry to services to 'experience economy'; spreading of consumer economy; the globalization of financial markets; and increases in global trade and exploitation of natural resources.

Post-materialist values hypothesis   The (disputed) belief that while wealthier societies can 'afford' to care about the environment, the developing countries or poor people worry about meeting their basic needs.

Rebound effect   Rebound effect refers to the consumer response to the introduction of new eco-efficient technologies or products which tend to offset the beneficial effects by perpetuating or actually increasing consumption of these products. The rebound effect is generally expressed as a ratio of the lost benefit compared to the expected environmental benefit when holding consumption constant

Relative poverty   Relative poverty defines poverty in relation to the economic status of other members of the society: people are poor if they fall below prevailing standards of living in a given societal context.

Risk society   Society preoccupied with future and safety, generating notions of risk – external and manufactured; systematic way of dealing with hazards and insecurities introduced by modernization.

Shallow ecology   Shallow ecology encompasses concerns that connect the environment to human interests, in the sense that the natural environment is only seen as useful in as far as it provides resources that can be used to satisfy human needs.

Sharing economy   Sharing economy or collaborative consumption is a movement in which the consumer experience is rapidly evolving, with sharing becoming a more fulfilling experience than owning.

Social movement   A large number of people who challenge established social norms and express themselves through a variety of forms of mass social and/or political action.

Society for Business Ethics An international organization providing a forum for research, teaching, or the practical application of ethical principles and concepts to the management of businesses.

Stakeholder An organization, group, community, or person who has an interest in the activities of another organization.

Supply chain The often complex network created by different companies and/or organizations producing, handling and/or distributing a specific product or service.,

Sustainable development The Brundtland Report famously termed sustainable development as 'development that meets the needs of the present without compromising the ability of future generations to meet their own needs' (WCED 1987).

Sustainable development goals In June 2012, governments agreed at Rio+20 (or Earth Summit 2012) to launch a UN led process to create a set of universal sustainable development goals (SDGs).

Stern Review The Stern Review on the Economics of Climate Change is a report released in October 2006 by economist Nicholas Stern. The report discusses the effect of global warming on the world economy. To date, it is significant as the largest and most widely known and discussed report of its kind.

The Economics of Ecosystems and Biodiversity A global initiative focused on drawing attention to the economic benefits of biodiversity including the growing cost of biodiversity loss and ecosystem degradation, it presents an approach that captures the values of nature in monetary terms.

Tragedy of the commons The tragedy of the commons is defined as free access and unrestricted demand for a finite resource that ultimately reduces it. The benefits of exploitation accrue to individuals, while the costs of the exploitation are borne by all those to whom the resource is available. This, in turn, causes demand for the resource to increase.

Transnational Any relationship across country boundaries, in which at least one of the actors is not a government. Most commonly applied to companies, but only when they go beyond trade, to own or control branches, subsidiaries, or affiliates in more than one country.

United Nations Framework Convention on Climate Change The United Nations Framework Convention on Climate Change (UNFCCC) is an environmental treaty with the goal of preventing 'dangerous' anthropogenic (i.e. human-induced) interference of the climate system.

Bibliography

Publications

Ainger, K. (2002) Earth Summit for sale, *New Internationalist*, 347:20–22.

Amnesty International (2013) *Bad Information: oil spill investigations in the Niger Delta.* http://www.amnesty.org/en/library/asset/AFR44/028/2013/en/b0a9e2c9-9a4a-4e77-8f8c-8af41cb53102/afr440282013en.pdf

Anderson, R.C. (1998) *Mid-Course Correction*, Atlanta, GA: Peregrinzilla Press.

Avolio, B.J. and Gardner, W.L. (2005) Authentic leadership development: Getting to the root of positive forms of leadership. *The Leadership Quarterly*, 16(3):315–338.

Ayres, R. U. and Kneese, A. V. (1969) Production, consumption, and externalities. *The American Economic Review*, 59, 282–97.

Bartlett, A. (1994) Reflections on sustainability, population growth, and the environment. *Population & Environment* 16 (1):5–35.

Bartlett, A. (1998) *The New Flat Earth Society.* http://www.albartlett.org/articles/art1998jan.html

Barrett, N. (2014) *Inside Sodexo's First Integrated Report.* GreenBiz.com, 21 January. http://www.greenbiz.com/blog/2014/01/21/inside-sodexos-first-integrated-report

Baxter, B. (2005) *A Theory of Ecological Justice.* New York: Routledge.

BBMG, Globescan and SustainAbility (2013) *Rethinking Consumption: consumers and the future of sustainability.* http://www.globescan.com/component/edocman/?view=document&id=46&Itemid=591

Beavan, C. (2009) *No Impact Man: The Adventures of a Guilty Liberal Who Attempts to Save the Planet, and the Discoveries He Makes About Himself and Our Way of Life in the Process.* New York: Farrar, Strauss and Giraux.

Beck, U. (1992) *Risk Society.* London: Sage.

Begley, E. Jr. (2008) *Living Like Ed: One Man's Guide to Living an Environmentally Friendly Life.* Clarkson Potter Publishers.

Benyus, J.M. (1997) *Biomimicry: Innovation Inspired by Nature.* New York: Harper Collins Publishers.

Berns, M., Townend, A., Khayat, Z., Balagopal, B., Reeves, M., Hopkins, M.S. and Kruschwitz, N. (2009) Sustainability and competitive advantage. *MIT Sloan Management Review*, 51(1):19–26.

Berry, R.H. and Yeung, F. (2013) Are investors willing to sacrifice cash for morality? *Journal of Business Ethics*, 117:477–492.

Bhagat, R. (2013) *Beyond Checkbook Philanthropy. The Hindu Business Line.* http://www.thehindubusinessline.com/opinion/columns/rasheeda-bhagat/beyond-chequebook-philanthropy/article5477817.ece

Blowfield, M. (2013) *Business and Sustainability*. Oxford: Oxford University Press.

Blewitt, J. 2013. EfS: Contesting the market model of higher education. In *The Sustainable University: Progress and Prospects*. S. Sterling, L. Maxey and Heather Luna eds. New York: Routledge, pp. 51–70.

Bodley, J. (2008) *Victims of Progress*. 5th edition. Lanham, MD: Altamira Press.

Bonnett, M. (2007) Environmental education and the issue of nature. *Journal of Curriculum Studies* 39(6):707–721.

Bonnett, M. (2013) Sustainable development, environmental education, and the significance of being in place. *Curriculum Journal*, 24(2):250–271.

Boots (2008) Animal Testing Policy. Available at: http://www.boots-uk.com/App_Portals/BootsUK/Media/PDFs/CSR%202010/Animal-Testing-Policy-Statement-Jan08nosig2.pdf

Braungart, M. (2013) *Waste to Energy*. http://catalystreview.net/2010/02/cradle-to-cradle-transitioning-from-waste-incineration-to-beneficial-materials/

Brechin, S. R. and Kempton, W. (1997) Beyond postmaterialist values: National versus individual explanations of global environmentalism. *Social Science Quarterly*, 78:121–137.

Brown, P. (2002) Preface to special issue on environmental health. *The Annals of the American Academy*, 584(1):7–12.

Campbell, M. (2012) Why the Silence on Population? In *Life on the Brink: Environmentalists Confront Overpopulation*, Philip Cafaro and Eileen Crist, eds. Athens, GA: University of Georgia Press, pp. 41–56.

Carson, R. (1962) *Silent Spring*. Boston, MA: Houghton Mifflin.

Carter, N. (2007) *The Politics of the Environment: Ideas, Activism, Policy*. New York: Cambridge University Press.

Casagrande, D. and Peters, C. (2013) Eco-Myopia Meets the Longue Durée: An Information Ecology of the Increasingly Arid Southwestern USA. In *Environmental Anthropology: Future Directions*. H. Kopnina and E. Shoreman-Ouimet, eds. New York and Oxford: Routledge, pp. 97–144.

Castells, M. (2001) Information Technology and Global Capitalism. In *On the Edge. Living with Global Capitalism*, W. Hutton and A. Giddens, eds. London: Vintage.

Catton, W. (2012) Destructive Momentum: Could an Enlightened Environmental Movement Overcome it? In *Life on the Brink: Environmentalists Confront Overpopulation*, P. Cafaro and E. Crist, eds. Athens, GA: University of Georgia Press, pp. 16–29.

Catton, W. and Dunlap, R. (1978) Environmental Sociology: A New Paradigm. *The American Sociologist*, 13: 41–49.

Chanana, R. and Luther, T. (2013) *Women of Pure Wonder*. New Delhi: Roli Book.

Circular Economy Reports (various dates) http://www.ellenmacarthurfoundation.org/business/reports

Cohen, E., Taylor, S. and Muller-Camen, M. (2012) *HRM's Role in Corporate Social and Environmental Sustainability*. http://www.shrm.org/about/foundation/products/documents/4-12%20csr%20report%20final%20for%20web.pdf

Cohn, R. (2012) *Interview. Putting a Price on the Real Value of Nature*. 5 January. http://e360.yale.edu/feature/putting_a_price_on_the_real_value_of_nature/2481/

Commoner, B. (1971) *The Closing Circle: Confronting the Environmental Crisis,* New York: Knopf.

Cooney, S. (2010) *Ecopreneurship Opportunity: green wedding and event planner. TriplePundit.* 24 September. http://www.triplepundit.com/2010/09/ecopreneurship-opportunity-green-wedding-and-event-planner/

Crane, A. and Matten, D. (2010) *Business Ethics: Managing Corporate Citizenship and Sustainability in an Age of Globalization.* Oxford: Oxford University Press.

Crist, E. (2012) Abundant Earth and the Population Question. In *Life on the Brink: Environmentalists Confront Overpopulation,* P. Cafaro and E. Crist, eds. Athens, GA: University of Georgia Press, pp. 141–151.

Crist, E. (2013) Ecocide and the extinction of animal minds. In *Ignoring Nature No More: The Case for Compassionate Conservation,* Marc Bekoff, ed. Chicgo, IL: Chicago University Press, pp. 45-53.

Daly, H. (1991) *Steady State Economics.* Washington, DC: Island Press.

Dauvergne, P. and Lister, J. (2012) Big brand sustainability: Governance prospects and environmental limits. *Global Environmental Change,* 22(1):36–45.

Davidson, K. (2009) Ethical concerns at the bottom of the pyramid: Where CSR meets BOP. *Journal of International Business Ethics,* 2(1):22–32.

Death, C. (2011) Summit theatre: Exemplary governmentality and environmental diplomacy in Johannesburg and Copenhagen, *Environmental Politics,* 20(1):1–19.

Deloitte (2013) *Sustainability Driven Innovation: harnessing sustainability's ability to spark innovation.* http://www.deloitte.com/assets/Dcom-UnitedStates/Local%20Assets/Documents/IMOs/Corporate%20Responsibility%20and%20Sustainability/us_DS_Sustainability_Driven_Innovation_102513.pdf

Docherty, P., Kira, M. and Shani, A.B. (2009) What the World Needs Now is Sustainable Work Systems. In P. Docherty, M. Kira and A.B. Shani, eds. *Creating Sustainable Work Systems,* second ed. London and New York: Routledge, pp. 1–21.

Dubois, C.L.Z. and Dubois, D.A. (2012) Strategic HRM as social design for environmental sustainability in organization. *Human Resource Management,* 51(6):799–826.

Dunlap, R. and Mertig, A. (1997) Global environmental concern: An anomaly for post-materialism. *Social Science Quarterly,* 78:24–29.

Dunlap, R. E. and York, R. (2008) The globalization of environmental concern and the limits of the postmaterialist values explanation: Evidence from four multinational surveys. *The Sociological Quarterly,* 49:529–563.

Dunlap, R.E., Van Liere, K.D., Mertig, A.G. and Jones, R.E. (2000) measuring endorsement of the new ecological paradigm: A revised NEP scale. *Journal of Social Issues,* 56(3):425–442.

Easterly, W. (2006) *The White Man's Burden: Why the West's Efforts to Aid the Rest Have Done So Much Ill and So Little Good.* New York: The Penguin Group, Inc.

Eccles, R.G., Ioannou, I. and Serafeim, G. (2013) *The Impact of Corporate Sustainability on Organizational Processes and Performance.* Harvard Business School, Working Paper 12-035. http://www.hbs.edu/faculty/Publication%20Files/12-035_a3c1f5d8-452d-4b48-9a49-812424424cc2.pdf

The Economist (2005) The Biggest Contract. 26 May. http://www.economist.com/node/4008642

The Economist (2009) Getting Warmer. Special Report on Climate Change. 3 December. http://www.economist.com/node/14994872

The Economist (2012) Climate change: Theatre of the absurd. 1 December, p. 62.

The Economist (2013a) China, India and climate change: Take the lead. 2 February, p. 68.

The Economist (2013b) Air conditioning: No sweat. 5 January, p. 41–42.

The Economist (2013c) Europe's dirty secret: The unwelcome renaissance. 5 January, p. 51–52.

The Economist (2013d) The future of energy: Batteries included? 2 February, pp. 63–64.

Ehrlich, P. R. (1968). *The Population Bomb*. New York: Ballantine Books.

Ekins, P. (1991) The sustainable consumer society: A contradiction in terms? *International Environmental Affairs* 3:243–257.

Elliott, J. (2013) *An Introduction to Sustainable Development*. New York: Routledge.

Ernst and Young. (2013) *Six Growing Trends in Corporate Sustainability 2013*. An EY survey in cooperation with GreenBiz Group. http://www.ey.com/Publication/vwLUAssets/Six_growing_trends_in_corporate_sustainability_2013/$FILE/Six_growing_trends_in_corporate_sustainability_2013.pdf

European Commission (2012) *Action Plan: European Company Law and Corporate Governance: A Modern Legal Framework for More Engaged Shareholders and Sustainable Companies*. Brussels: EU. Available at: http://www.ecgi.org/tcgd/2012/documents/121212_company-law-corporate-governance-action-plan_en.pdf

European Commission (2013) *Attitudes of Europeans Towards Building the Single Market for Green Products*. Brussels: EU. Available at: http://ec.europa.eu/public_opinion/flash/fl_367_sum_en.pdf

Ferwerda, W. (2012) *Nature Resilience: Organising Ecological Restoration by Partners in Business for The Next Generation*. Rotterdam School of Management/IUCN. https://portals.iucn.org/library/efiles/edocs/2012-068.pdf

Fletcher, K. (2007) *Slow Fashion. The Ecologist*, 1 June. http://www.theecologist.org/green_green_living/clothing/269245/slow_fashion.html

Forum for the Future (2011) *The Creative Industries Sustainability Beacon Project: Final Report*. http://www.forumforthefuture.org/sites/default/files/project/downloads/creativeindustriessustainabilitybeaconproject.pdf

Foster, J.B. (2012) The planetary rift and the new human exemptionalism: A political-economic critique of ecological modernization theory. *Organization and Environment*, 25(3):211–237.

Foster, R.J. (2008) *Coca-Globalization*. London: Palgrave Macmillan.

Frosch, R.A. and Gallopoulos, N.E. (1989) Strategies for manufacturing. *Scientific American*, 261:144–152.

Frynas, J.G. (2009) Corporate social responsibility in the oil and gas sector. *Journal of World Energy Law & Business*, 2(3):178–195.

Gao, S.S. and Zhang, J.J. (2006) Stakeholder engagement, social auditing and corporate sustainability. *Business Process Management Journal*, 12(6):722–740.

Giddens, A. (1990) *The Consequences of Modernity*, Cambridge: Polity Press.

Giddens, A. (2009) *Global Politics and Climate Change*. Cambridge: Polity Press.

Ginsberg, J.M. and Bloom, P.N. (2004) Choosing the right green marketing strategy. *MIT Sloan Management Review*, 46(1):79–84.

Godin S. (2009) *define: Brand*. Blog post, 13 December. http://sethgodin.typepad.com/seths_blog/2009/12/define-brand.html

Goldacre, B. (2012) *Bad Pharma: How Drugs Companies Mislead Doctors and Harm Patients*. London: Fourth Estate.

Goleman, D. (2002) *The New Leaders*. London: Little, Brown.

Goodman, M.K. (2004) Reading Fairtrade: Political ecological imaginary and the moral economy of Fairtrade foods. *Political Geography*, 23:891–915.

Grant, J. (2008) *The Green Marketing Manifesto*. London: John Wiley & Sons.

Graedel, T. E. 1996. On the concept of industrial ecology. *Annual Review of Energy and the Environment*, 21, 69–98.

Greening, L.A., Greene, D.L. and Difiglio, C. (2000) Energy efficiency and consumption—The rebound effect—A survey. *Energy Policy*, 28:389–401.

Hahn, R. (2009) The ethical rationale of business for the poor – Integrating the concepts bottom of the pyramid, sustainable development, and corporate citizenship. *Journal of Business Ethics*, 84:313–324.

Hale, T., Held, D. and Young, K. (2013) *Gridlock: Why Global Cooperation Is Failing When We Need It Most*. Cambridge: Polity Press.

Hall, B.H. and Helmers, C. (2011) *Can the Patent Commons Help Eco-technology Diffusion?* United Nations University, 13 October. http://unu.edu/publications/articles/can-patent-commons-help-diffusion-of-green-technologies.html

Hall, C. and Day, J. (2009) Revisiting the limits to growth after peak oil. *American Scientist*, 97:230–238.

Hanson, D. and Middleton, S. (2000) The challenges of eco-leadership. *Greener Management International*, 29:95–107.

Harvey, D. (1990) *The Condition of Postmodernity: An Enquiry into the Origins of Cultural Change*. Cambridge, MA: Blackwell.

Hawken, P. (1993) *The Ecology of Commerce: A Declaration of Sustainability*. New York: Harper Collins Publishers.

Held, D. (2004) *A Globalizing World?: Culture, Economics, Politics*. New York: Routledge.

Hobson, K. (2002) Competing discourses of sustainable consumption: Does the 'rationalization of lifestyles' make sense? *Environmental Politics*, 11(2):95–120.

ILO (2010) *Global Wage Report 2010–11*. Geneva: ILO. Available at: http://www.ilo.org/wcmsp5/groups/public/@dgreports/@dcomm/@publ/documents/publication/wcms_145265.pdf

ILO (2011) *Skills for Green Jobs: a global view*. Geneva, ILO. http://www.ilo.org/wcmsp5/groups/public/---dgreports/---dcomm/---publ/documents/publication/wcms_159585.pdf

ILO (2012) *Global Employment Trends 2012: preventing a deeper jobs crisis*. Geneva: International Labor Office. http://www.ilo.org/wcmsp5/groups/public/---dgreports/---dcomm/---publ/documents/publication/wcms_171571.pdf

Inglehart, R. (1977) *The Silent Revolution: Changing Values and Political Styles among Western Publics*. Princeton, NJ: Princeton University Press.

Interbrand (2013) *Best Global Brands 2013*. http://www.interbrand.com/Libraries/Branding_Studies/Best_Global_Brands_2013.sflb.ashx

International Union for the Conservation of Nature (IUCN) (2013) *Why is Biodiversity in Crisis?* http://www.iucn.org/iyb/about/biodiversity_crisis/

IPCC (2014) *Fifth Assessment Report* http://www.ipcc.ch/

Isaak, R. (2002) The making of the ecopreneur. *Green Management International*, 38:81–91

Isenhour, C. (2010) On conflicted Swedish consumers, the effort to stop shopping and neo-liberal environmental governance. *Journal of Consumer Behavior*, 9:454–469.

Islamic Bank of Britain (2013) Islamic Bank of Britain completes first Scottish business finance deal. 13 December Press release. Available at: http://www.islamic-bank/com/useful-info-tools/about-us/latest-news/jan-dec-2013/islamic-bank-of-britain-completes-first-scottish-business-finance-deal/

Johansson, P. (2010) Debt relief, investment and growth. *World Development*, 38(9):1204–1216.

Kaplan, R. (2013) Walmart Launches Sustainability Hub. *Walmart Blog*, 09 January. http://blog.walmart.com/walmart-launches-sustainability-hub

Kaplan, S. (2000) Human nature and environmentally responsible behavior. *Journal of Social Issues* 56(3):491–508.

Kho, J. (2012) Will Walmart meet its sustainability goals? *GreenBiz.com*, 08 March. http://www.greenbiz.com/blog/2012/03/07/will-walmart-meet-its-sustainability-goals

Klein, N. (2000) *No Logo*. London: Flamingo.

Kollmuss, A. and Agyeman, J. (2002) Mind the gap: Why do people act environmentally and what are the barriers to pro-environmental behavior? *Environmental Education Research*, 8:239–260.

Kopnina, H. (2012) Education for Sustainable Development (ESD): The turn away from 'environment' in environmental education? *Environmental Education Research*, 18 (5):699–717.

Kopnina, H. (2013) Schooling the World: Exploring the critical course on sustainable development through an anthropological lens. *International Journal of Educational Research*, 62:220–228.

Kopnina, H. (2014a) Christmas tale of (un)sustainability: Reflecting on consumption and environmental awareness on the streets of Amsterdam. *Sustainable Cities and Society*, 10:65–71.

Kopnina, H. (2014b) Environmental justice and biospheric egalitarianism: reflecting on a normative-philosophical view of human-nature relationship. *Earth Perspectives*. 1–8.

Kuenkel, P., Gerlach, S. and Frieg, V. (2011) *Working with Stakeholder Dialogues*. Stoughton, WI: Books on Demand.

Liddick, D.R. (2006) *Eco-Terrorism: Radical Environmental and Animal Liberation Movements*. Westport, CT: Praeger Publishers.

Lidskog, R. and Elander, I. (2009) Addressing climate change democratically: Multi-level governance, transnational networks and governmental structures. *Sustainable Development*, 18(1):32–41.

Linton, J.D., Klassen, R. and Jayaraman, V. (2007) Sustainable supply chains: An introduction. *Journal of Operations Management*, 25:1075–1082.

Lyle, J. T. (1996) *Regenerative Design for Sustainable Development*, New York: Wiley.

Makower, J. (2013) *State of Green Business 2013*. Oakland, CA: GreenBiz Group.

Malthus, T. (1826) *An Essay on the Principle Of Population* 6th edition. London: John Murray.

Mattoo, A. and Subramanian, A. (2013) *Greenprint: A New Approach to Cooperation on Climate Change. Centre for Global Development*. Washington, DC: Brookings Institution Press.

McDonough, W. and Braungart, M. (2002) *Cradle to Cradle: Remaking the Way We Make Things*. New York: North Point Press.

McIntire-Strasburg, J. (2008) *Robbing the Cradle to Cradle? William McDonough a saint... and a sinner.* Blog post. http://sustainablog.org/2008/11/robbing-the-cradle-to-cradle-william-mcdonough-a-saint-and-a-sinner/

Meadows, D.H., Meadows, D.L., Randers, J. and Behrens, W.W. (1972) *Limits to Growth: A Report for the Club of Rome's Project on the Predicament of Mankind.* New York: Universe Books.

Megginson, D. and Whitaker, V. (2003) *Continuing Professional Development.* London: CIPD.

Meyerson, D.A. (2001) Radical Change: the quiet way. *Harvard Business Review,* October, 92–100.

Milne, M.J. and Gray, R. (2013) W(h)ither ecology? The triple bottom line, the Global Reporting Initiative, and corporate sustainability reporting. *Journal of Business Ethics,* 118:13–29.

Mitchell, S. (2013) *Walmart's Assault on the Climate.* ILSR. http://www.ilsr.org/wp-content/uploads/2013/10/ILSR-_Report_WalmartClimateChange.pdf

Mol, A.P.J. (2002) Ecological modernization and the global economy. *Global Environmental Politics,* 2:92–115.

Mol, A.P.J. and Sonnenfeld, D.A. Eds. (2000) *Ecological Modernisation around the World: Perspectives and Critical Debates.* London and Portland, OR: Routledge.

Naess, A. (1973) The shallow and the deep: Long-range ecology movement. A summary. *Inquiry,* 16:95–99.

Næss, P. (2011) Unsustainable growth, unsustainable capitalism. *Journal of Critical Realism,* 5(2):197–227.

Nattrass, B. and Altomare, M. (2001) *The Natural Step for Business.* Gabriola Island, Canada: New Society Publishers.

Natural Capital Coalition (2012) TEEB for Business Coalition Prospectus. Available at: http://www.naturalcapitalcoalition.org/js/plugins/filemanager/files/TEEB-for-Business-Coalition.pdf

Neff, J. (2011) *Unilever Struggles to Quantify Carbon Footprint of Digital Advertising. Advertising Age.* 12 December. http://adage.com/article/news/unilever-quantify-carbon-footprint-digital-ads/231480/

Nemetz, P.N. (2013) *Business and the Sustainability Challenge: An Integrated Perspective.* New York: Routledge.

Nonaka, I. and Toyami, R. (2003) The knowledge-creating theory revisited: Knowledge creation as a synthesizing process. *Knowledge Management Research & Practice,* 1:2–10.

Noth, K. (2008) Farm Subsidies are the Real Culprit. *Bloomberg Businessweek,* 13 May. http://www.businessweek.com/stories/2008-05-13/farm-subsidies-are-the-real-culpritbusinessweek-business-news-stock-market-and-financial-advice

Novo Nordisk (2012) *The Blueprint for Change Program.* http://www.novonordisk.com/images/Sustainability/PDFs/Blueprint%20for%20change%20-%20US.pdf

OECD (2004) *OECD Principles of Corporate Governance.* Paris. http://www.oecd.org/corporate/ca/corporategovernanceprinciples/31557724.pdf

OECD (2012) *ICT Skills and Employment: New Competences and Jobs for a Greener and Smarter Economy.* OECD Digital Economy Papers, No. 198, OECD Publishing. http://www.oecd-ilibrary.org/science-and-technology/ict-skills-and-employment_5k994f3prlr5-en

Ometto, A.R., Hauschild, M.Z. and Roma, W.N.L. (2009) Lifecycle assessment of fuel ethanol from sugarcane in Brazil. *International Journal of Life Cycle Assessment*, 14:236–247.

Parkes, C. and Blewitt, J. (2011) 'Ignorance was bliss, now I'm not ignorant and that is far more difficult' – Transdisciplinary learning and reflexivity in responsible management education. *Journal of Global Responsibility*, 2(2):206–221.

Pauli, G. (1998) *Upsizing: The Road to Zero Emissions: More Jobs, More Income and No Pollution*, Greenleaf Publishing.

Pauli, G. (2010) *The Blue Economy: 10 Years, 100 Innovations and 100 Million Jobs* A Report to the Club of Rome, Taos, NM: Paradigm Publications.

Pauli, G. (2011) *From Deep Ecology to The Blue Economy: A Review of the Main Concepts Related to Environmental, Social and Ethical Business That Contributed to the Creation of the Blue Economy.* ZERI

Pearce, F. (2008) *Confessions of an Eco-Sinner: Tracking Down the Sources of my Stuff.* Boston, MA: Beacon Press.

Pearse, G. (2012) *Greenwash: Big Brands and Carbon Scams.* Collingwood, Australia: Black Inc.

Phalan, B. (2013) *Biofuel Crops: food security must come first.* http://www.theguardian.com/environment/2013/aug/29/biofuel-crops-food-security-prices-europe

Pierce, M. ed (2011) *A Journey of a Thousand Miles: The State of Sustainability Leadership.* .Cambridge: Cambridge University Press.

Pinske, J. and Kolk, A. (2009) *International Business and Global Climate Change.* New York: Routledge.

Porter, M.E and Kramer, M.R. (2006) Strategy and society: The link between competitive advantage and corporate social responsibility. *Harvard Business Review*, 84(12):78–91.

Potsdam Institute for Climate Impact Research (2012). https://www.pik-potsdam.de/

Prokesch, S. (2010) The sustainable supply chain. *Harvard Business Review*, 88(10):70–72.

PWC (2011) *Tomorrow's Corporate Reporting: A Critical System at Risk.* London: Tomorrow's Company.

Robinson, J. (2003) Future subjunctive: Backcasting as social learning. *Futures*, 35(8):839–856.

Rees, W. (2010). What's blocking sustainability? Human nature, cognition, and denial. *Sustainability: Science, Practice, & Policy* 6(2):13-25.

Sachs, J. (2012) *Winning the Story Wars.* Harvard, MA: Harvard Business Review Press.

Sacks, J. (2008) *Common Wealth; Economics for a Crowded Planet.* London: Penguin.

Schmidheiny, S. (1992) *Changing Course: A Global Business Perspective on Development And The Environment.* http://www.wbcsd.org/pages/edocument/edocumentdetails.aspx?id=72

Schumacher, E.F. (1980) *Good Work.* London: Abacus.

Scott, J.T. (2011) New Standards for Long-Term Business Survival. In *Sustainable Business Performance*. W.R. Stahel, ed. London: Palgrave.

Senge, P. (2006) *The Fifth Discipline.* New York: Random House.

Shiva, V. (2000) *Stolen Harvest: The Hijacking of the Global Food Supply.* Cambridge, MA: South end Press.

Singer, M. and Evans, J.M. (2013) Water Wary: Understandings and Concerns about Water and Health among the Rural Poor of Louisiana. In *Environmental*

Anthropology: Future Directions. H. Kopnina and E. Shoreman-Ouimet, eds. New York: Routledge, pp. 172–188.

Stahel, W.R. (1984) The Product-Life Factor. In *An Inquiry into the Nature of Sustainable Societies, the Role of the Private Sector*. Susan Grinton Orr, ed. Houston, Texas: HARC.

Stahel, W. R. and Reday-Mulvey, G. (1981) *Jobs for Tomorrow: The Potential for Substituting Manpower for Energy*. Vantage Press.

Stern, D.I. (2004) The rise and fall of the Environmental Kuznets Curve. *World Development*, 32(8): 1419–1439.

Stern, P. (2000) Toward a coherent theory of environmentally significant behavior. *Journal of Social Issues*, 56(3):407–424.

Stern Review on the Economics of Climate Change (2006) http://mudancasclimaticas. cptec.inpe.br/~rmclima/pdfs/destaques/sternreview_report_complete.pdf

Stone, C. D. (1972) Should trees have standing: Toward legal rights for natural objects. *Southern California Law Review* 45: 450–87.

Strang, V. (2013) Notes for plenary debate. World Anthropology Congress. ASA-IUAES conference, Manchester, 5–10 August 2013. Motion: 'Justice for people must come before justice for the environment'. http://www.youtube.com/watch?v=oldnYTYMx-k

Sunstein, C.R. (2005) *Laws of Fear: Beyond the Precautionary Principle*. Cambridge: Cambridge University Press.

SustainAbility (2011) *Signed, Sealed... Delivered? Behind Certifications and Beyond Labels*. London: SustainAbility

TEEB (2010) *The Economics of Ecosystems and Biodiversity Report for Business – executive summary*. http://www.teebweb.org/publication/teeb-for-business-executive-summary/

Tennant, M. and Brennan, G. (2015) Business and Production Solutions: Closing the Loop. In *Sustainability: Key Issues*. H. Kopnina and E. Shoreman-Ouimet, eds. New York: Routledge.

Tercek, M. and Adams, J. (2013) *Nature's Fortune: How Business and Society Thrive by Investing in Nature*. New York: Basic Books.

Tett, G. (2014) Climate change and the V-word. *Financial Times*, 24 January. http://www.ft.com/cms/s/2/cbae70bc-83c2-11e3-86c9-00144feab7de.html

The Telegraph (2013) Rio Tinto threatens to exit Madagascar after CEO is trapped by protesters, 11 January. http://www.telegraph.co.uk/finance/newsbysector/industry/mining/9797182/Rio-Tinto-threatens-to-exit-Madagascar-after-CEO-is-trapped-by-protesters.html

Turner, G. (2010) *A Comparison of the Limits of Growth with Thirty Years of Reality*. CSIRO Working Paper Series. http://www.csiro.au/files/files/plje.pdf

UN (n.d.) *Principles of Responsible Management Education* available at: http://www.unprme.org/the-6-principles/

UN Global Compact (2011) *Guiding Principles on Business and Human Rights* New York: United Nations. Available at: http://www.ohchr.org/Documents/Publications/GuidingPrinciplesBusinessHR_EN.pdf

UN Global Compact (2013) *Architects of a Better World*. http://www.unglobalcompact.org/docs/about_the_gc/LeadersSummit2013Report.pdf

UNEP (2007) *Life Cycle Management: a business guide to sustainability*. Paris, UNEP. http://www.unep.org/pdf/dtie/DTI0889PA.pdf

UNEP (2013) *Millennium Ecosystem Assessment. Current state & trends assessment.* http://www.unep.org/maweb/en/Condition.aspx

UNESCO (2012) *Shaping the Education of Tomorrow. 2012 Full-length Report on the UN Decade of Education for Sustainable Development.* Paris: DESD Monitoring & Evaluation – 2012.

Unilever (2012) Unilever Sustainable Living: Waste & Packaging Online Report 2012. http://unilever.com/images/Waste___packaging_PDF_generator_tcm_13-320109.pdf

Unmuessig, B. (2013) *Nature, Inc.?* http://www.project-syndicate.org/commentary/the-limits-of-market-based-environmental-protection-by-barbara-unmuessig

Van Huijstee, M. and Glasbergen, P. (2010) NGOs moving business: An analysis of contrasting strategies. *Business Society,* 49(4):591–618.

Walley, E.E. and Taylor, D. (2002) Opportunists, champions, mavericks ... ? A typology of green entrepreneurs. *Greener Management International,* 38:31–43.

WCED (1987) *Brundtland Report. Our Common Future.* World Commission on Environment and Development. Oxford: Oxford University Press.

Weber, E.P. and Khademian, A.M. (2008) Wicked problems, knowledge challenges, and collaborative capacity builders in network settings. *Public Administration Review,* March/April:334–349.

Welford, R. (1998) Life Cycle Assessment. In *Corporate Environmental Management 1.* Welford, R. ed. London: Earthscan, pp. 138–147.

Werbach, A. (2009) *Strategy for Sustainability: A Business Manifesto.* Harvard, MA: Harvard Business School Press

Wijkman, A. and Rockström, J. (2012) *Bankrupting Nature: Denying Our Planetary Boundaries.* New York: Routledge.

Wilk, R. (2004) Questionable Assumptions about Sustainable Consumption. In *The Ecological Economics of Consumption.* Lucia Reisch and Inge Røpke, eds. Cheltenham: Edward Elgar, pp. 17–31.

Wilk, R.W. (2009) Consuming Ourselves to Death. In *Anthropology and Climate Change: From Encounters to Actions.* S. Crate, ed. Durham, NC: Duke University Press, pp. 265–267.

Wilshaw, R., Unger, L., Chi, D.Q. and Thuy, P.T. (2013) *Labour Rights in Unilever's Supply Chain: From Compliance towards Good Practice.* Oxford: Oxfam. http://www.oxfam.org/sites/www.oxfam.org/files/rr-unilever-supply-chain-labor-rights-vietnam-310113-en.pdf

WIPO (2013) *World Intellectual Property Report: brands – reputation and image in the global marketplace.* Geneva, WIPO. http://www.wipo.int/export/sites/www/freepublications/en/intproperty/944/wipo_pub_944_2013.pdf

World Bank (2013) *Poverty Overview.* http://www.worldbank.org/en/topic/poverty/overview

World Economic Forum (2012) *More with Less: scaling sustainable consumption and resource efficiency.* http://www.weforum.org/reports/more-less-scaling-sustainable-consumption-and-resource-efficiency

Zavestoski, S. (2010) Environmental Health Organizing in a Globalizing World: The Emergence of a Global Anti-Toxics Movement and its Political, Legal and Economic Challenges. In Kopnina, H. and Keune, H. (eds) *Health and Environment: Social Science Perspectives.* New York: Nova Science Publishers, Inc.

Žižek, Slavoj (2010) *First as Tragedy, Then as Farce*: http://www.youtube.com/watch?v=cvakA-DF6Hc

Online resources

Agenda 21 http://www.un.org/esa/dsd/agenda21/

Apple http://www.apple.com/environment/

The Blue Economy: http://www.theblueeconomy.org/

Census: https://www.census.gov/population/projections/

Conservation International http://www.conservation.org/partners/pages/default.aspx

Convention on Biological Diversity Outlook (CBD) http://www.cbd.int/gbo3/

Copenhagen: European Green Capital: http://ec.europa.eu/environment/europeangreencapital/winning-cities/2014-copenhagen/

Cradle to Cradle Certified CM http://www.mbdc.com/cradle-to-cradle/cradle-to-cradle-certified-program/

Cradle to Cradle Products Innovation Institute http://www.c2ccertified.org/

Dow Jones Sustainability Indices: http://www.sustainability-indices.com/sustainability-assessment/corporate-sustainability.jsp

Earth Charter Initiative: http://www.earthcharterinaction.org/content/pages/Read-the-Charter.html

EEA http://www.eea.europa.eu/

European Environment Agency: http://www.eea.europa.eu/about-us/address.html

Ellen MacArthur Foundation: http://www.ellenmacarthurfoundation.org/

Ethical consumer: http://www.ethicalconsumer.org/

Fairphone: http://www.fairphone.com/

Fairtrade: http://www.fairtrade.net

Global Compact http://www.unglobalcompact.org/

Green Business Network (US): http://www.greenbusinessnetwork.org.uk/about/about-the-green-business-network

Green 10: http://www.eeb.org/activities/transparency/g-10-position-220206.pdf

GRI G4 Sustainability Reporting Guidelines: https://www.globalreporting.org/reporting/g4/Pages/default.aspx\

Herman Miller Inc: http://www.hermanmiller.com/

International Institute for Applied Systems Analysis http://www.iiasa.ac.at/web/home/research/researchPrograms/WorldPopulation/

International Integrated Reporting Committee: http://www.theiirc.org/

International Labour Organization http://www.ilo.org/global/about-the-ilo/decent-work-agenda/lang--en/index.htm

International Organization for Standardization (ISO): http://www.iso.org/iso/home.html

International Sustainable Development Foundation: http://www.isdf.org/

International Union for the Conservation of Nature (IUCN) http://www.iucn.org/iyb/about/biodiversity_crisis/

ISO (IWA 9:2011): http://www.iso.org/iso/home/store/catalogue_tc/catalogue_detail.htm?csnumber=55328

Kyoto Protocol: http://unfccc.int/kyoto_protocol/items/2830.php

OECD Extended Producer Responsibility (EPR) Fact Sheet http://www.oecd.org/env/waste/factsheetextendedproducerresponsibility.htm

Patagonia http://www.patagonia.com/eu/enGB/patagonia.go?assetid=70722

SC Johnson Green Choices: http://www.scjohnson.com/en/green-choices/overview.aspx

Society for Business Ethics: http://www.societyforbusinessethics.org/

Sodexo CSR: http://www.sodexo.com/en/corporate-responsibility/corporate-responsibility-home.aspx

Sustainable Development Solutions Network (SDSN): http://unsdsn.org/thematicgroups/tg12/

Sustainable Development 2015: http://www.sustainabledevelopment2015.org/index.php/uncsd-official-docs/sdgs-an-introduction

Tata Steel: http://www.tatasteel.com

UNDP: http://www.undp.org/content/undp/en/home.html

UNEP: http://www.unep.org/

UNEP: Life Cycle Management: http://www.unep.org/resourceefficiency/Home/tabid/55480/Default.aspx

UNESCO. Poverty http://www.unesco.org/new/en/social-and-human-sciences/themes/international-migration/glossary/poverty/

UNFPA http://www.unfpa.org/rh/planning.htm

Universal Declaration of Human Rights: http://www.un.org/en/documents/udhr/

Virgin Sustainability Report 2012 http://www.virgin-atlantic.com/corporate/images/Sustainability_Report_2012.pdf

World Business Council for Sustainable Development (WBCSD): http://www.wbcsd.org/

World Business Council on Sustainable Development, Vision 2050: http://www.wbcsd.org/vision2050.aspx

World Business Council: http://www.wbcsd.org

World Health Organization (WHO): http://www.who.int/en/

Zero Emissions Research Institute (ZERI): http://www.zeri.org/

Videos

The Meatrix: http://www.themeatrix.com/

Schooling the World Documentary: http://schoolingtheworld.org/film

Žižek, Slavoj (2010) *First as Tragedy, Then as Farce* (2010): http://www.youtube.com/watch?v=cvakA-DF6Hc

The Story of Stuff: http://storyofstuff.org/movies/

Index